60 SECOND MEMOS

BRANDON TOROPOV

PRENTICE HALL
Paramus, NJ 07652

Library of Congress Cataloging-in-Publication Data

Toropov, Brandon
  60-second memos / by Brandon Toropov
    p. cm.
  Includes index.
  ISBN 0-13-472630-8. —ISBN 0-13-472648-0 (pbk.)
  1. Memorandums—Handbooks, manuals, etc. I. Title.
HF5726.T59 1997
651.7'55—dc21
                                                     97-18027
                                                     CIP

This book is not intended as a source of legal advice. Persons in need of advice on employment, hiring, or other issues should seek the services of a qualified professional.

Printed in the United States of America

10 9 8 7 6 5 4 3 2 1   10 9 8 7 6 5 4 3 2 1

ISBN 0-13-472630-8 (c)   **ISBN 0-13-472648-0 (pbk)**

ATTENTION: CORPORATIONS AND SCHOOLS

Prentice Hall books are available at quantity discounts with bulk purchase for educational, business, or sales promotional use. For information, please write to: Prentice Hall Career & Personal Development Special Sales, 240 Frisch Court, Paramus, New Jersey 07652. Please supply: title of book, ISBN, quantity, how the book will be used, date needed.

 PRENTICE HALL
Career & Personal Development
Paramus, NJ 07652
A Simon & Schuster Company

On the World Wide Web at http://www.phdirect.com

Prentice Hall International (UK) Limited, *London*
Prentice Hall of Australia Pty. Limited, *Sydney*
Prentice Hall Canada, Inc., *Toronto*
Prentice Hall Hispanoamericana, S.A., *Mexico*
Prentice Hall of India Private Limited, *New Delhi*
Prentice Hall of Japan, Inc., *Tokyo*
Simon & Schuster Asia Pte. Ltd., *Singapore*
Editora Prentice Hall do Brasil, Ltda., *Rio de Janeiro*

Introduction

"I have no idea what to write!"

"I don't feel like putting together a memo!"

"Sure, there's a problem . . . but who has the time to tackle it on paper?"

Do these sentiments sound familiar? Don't worry. This book will help you write the messages that are tough to write . . . and tougher still to schedule the *time* to write.

Using Written Communication to Manage the Day Better

These days, time is a more precious commodity than ever. Fortunately, if you've got access to this book and a good word processor, you can use your time to the very best advantage. When you're under the gun, and you have to compose a memo you don't feel like writing, take advantage of this tool.

60-Second Memos offers hundreds of adaptable models for compelling written messages in all kinds of challenging business situations. Each of the hundreds of topics covered features two approaches you can take, typically a concise version of the memo you need to develop and a somewhat more detailed one you can use to amplify your message. Use either, or a combination of the two, to get your message across.

You may decide to customize a particular memo so that it fully incorporates the specifics of your situation. Each of the memo topics covered in *60-Second Memos* helps you do this quickly and painlessly by highlighting key suggestions and identifying the common mistakes you'll want to avoid when dealing with the topic in question.

Whether your memo has to help you deliver an important message to a problem employee, pass along unpopular news about budget limitations, or reinforce messages on important policies and procedures, this book will help you get the message out swiftly, appropriately, and with a minimal amount of wheel-spinning.

Got a Minute?

For each situation, my aim has been to provide you with models you can use more or less as is to develop, in short order, a memo that does what you need it to. In most cases, you can use the models in this book to develop a short note that's ready to send out—via hard copy, e-mail or other means—in about a minute. At the very least, in that period of time, you'll be able to set up a basic outline of what needs to be said.

60-Second Memos helps you get even tough memos out of the way whenever you need to . . . so you can focus on the rest of your day.

When to Send a Standard Written Memo

You should use one of the memos that appear in this book as a model for a traditional "hard-copy" written memo when . . .

- You want to attach new emphasis to a specific course of action that must be undertaken in the very near future, or you aim to highlight the necessity of paying attention to a problem that has been on the "to-do" list for too long. The beauty of "hard copy" is that people actually have to do something with the piece of paper you send them: file it, act on it, or, if they're feeling brave—or possessed of a clean conscience— throw it away.

- You want to provide a relatively detailed list of guidelines and procedures for your reader to consult over the long term. Another advantage of "hard copy" is that it can be posted prominently and referred to indefinitely.

- You want to establish a paper trail. Formal complaints, reports, or warnings may require that you develop—and perhaps receive signatures acknowledging receipt of—individual pieces of paper. Other situations benefiting from paper records may include instances in which you have to demonstrate progress toward a particular goal, or compliance with established regulations or guidelines. If the messages you send and the responses you receive are going to need to be consulted later, you may decide that an ongoing paper archive, with copies retained on your end, makes the most sense.

- The issues you want the other person to focus on are too detailed to address in an e-mail message. (See below.)

When to Send an E-Mail Message

The memo models in this book can also be adapted to e-mail correspondence, most of which will probably take the form of late-breaking updates or general advisories. You'll generally find that the briefer of the two sample messages for a given situation probably represents the best outline for you to consider in drafting e-mail correspondence.

You should always select your topic line or first sentence of opening text with an eye to winning interest. This habit is especially important to cultivate when you're creating electronic correspondence. "Burying" the most important part of your e-message—by withholding key instructions or information until the end of the memo—may lead to big problems. Why? Well, these days, e-mail traffic can be overwhelming. As a result, many e-mail users only peruse the first screenful of data before deciding whether or not to scroll all the way to the end. If you don't get to the point immediately and wrap up in short order, you may not convince your reader to read to the end of the message!

Consider adapting the memos in this book to electronic-message format when . . .

- You're providing information on a new and important set of circumstances likely to be helpful to the recipient's decision-making process. (Complaints of "information overload" are rampant in our computer-happy working world, but cut-to-the-chase electronic messages are often the very best way to keep important players informed about recent events. These messages certainly consume less time than convening a meeting and following up individually, as one inevitably must, with people who couldn't attend.)

- You want to reinforce a previously delivered message in a dramatic way. (*Occasional* use of tactful electronic messages to emphasize important points can help you turn "intended" follow-up into actual follow-up among subordinates. What's more, the recipient of your message can't hedge on the commitment you're outlining . . . at least not immediately, and not without going to the trouble of composing and sending a message in response.)

- You're communicating with off-site team members on routine, concisely stated matters that don't have by-the-end-of-day urgency. (If you've got a time-sensitive message for a team member who's not immediately accessible, your best bet may be to use the model memos in this book to formulate a dramatic fax message. Faxes usually denote urgency—and they have a way of rising to the top of the pile—but they shouldn't be appealed to for everyday matters.)

How the Book is Structured

This book is divided into fifteen chapters and an Appendix. Its focus is on helping you address even the most sensitive or challenging situations quickly and easily . . . on paper.

Chapter One: Reassignments, Internal Vacancies, and Job Descriptions, lets you match the right person to the right spot, pass along unwelcome news tactfully, and make a few words count for a lot when you must address the most sensitive individual human resource matters.

Chapter Two: Staff Reductions, Cutbacks, and Resource Allocation Issues, lets you make the most of precious commodities like time, cash, and attention. This chapter helps your organization make the most of the resources at its disposal without coming across as insensitive.

Chapter Three: Personnel and Human Resource Issues, lets you establish and implement important measures without causing a fuss or ruffling feathers. It also shows you how to use memos to execute policies in tough situations involving drug and alcohol abuse, smoking, and employees with an unacceptable attitude or who stop performing at acceptable levels.

Chapter Four: Accommodations for Disabled Employees, Diversity Training, Sexual Harassment Policies, and other Potential Problem Areas, shows you how to handle these sensitive issues safely, appropriately, and diplomatically. It also lets you know how to approach your superior on paper when there's a real problem on the horizon.

Chapter Five: Dealing with Non-Customer Outsiders such as Vendors, Consultants, and Members of the Media, shows you how to handle outsiders in ways that don't cause bad press, division, or discord. In addition, it gives you tools for making the best of the occasional bad situations that arise involving outsiders.

Chapter Six: Vacation Scheduling, Benefits Policies, Overtime, and Leave, lets you outline potentially confusing policies clearly and directly, and keep people focused on productive activity . . . rather than time-consuming searches for loopholes and exceptions.

Chapter Seven: Union-Related Topics, shows you how to outline appropriate guidelines, develop key correspondence, and encourage positive outcomes for everyone, even in situations that can all too easily become polarized.

Chapter Eight: Sales Department Performance, shows you how to support and encourage the members of your sales team . . . and get them back on the winning track when they hit a plateau (or perhaps even a valley).

Chapter Nine: Effective Customer Service, shows you how to reinforce (or introduce) a customer-based focus in your organization. This chapter helps you address common problem areas quickly . . . or prevent them altogether.

Chapter Ten: Quality Control, shows you how to use simple messages to get your people excited about quality . . . and shows what to write when it's time for everyone to stop and take a good, long look at what's going out to your customers.

Chapter Eleven: Internal Efficiency, lets you overcome obstacles to peak efficiency by sending messages that spotlight constructive alternate approaches. This chapter will help you replace habits that waste time, effort, and energy.

Chapter Twelve: Implementing New Policies and Initiatives, helps you avoid the most common negative reactions from team members who must adapt to new circumstances and objectives.

Chapter Thirteen: Workplace Safety, shows you how to reduce risks for everyone by sending messages that will keep team members focused on safety.

Chapter Fourteen: Internal Scheduling, Management Information Gathering, Training, and Other Operational Issues, lets you handle a wide range of day-to-day operational questions—and helps you prevent little problems from becoming big ones.

Chapter Fifteen: Of Particular Interest to Managers Supervising Off-Site Workers, lets you coordinate a team mentality among employees who don't make regular appearances at the office. It also helps you refocus or reassign those who are having trouble contributing as home workers.

The Appendix: A Guide to Style, will help you improve your writing style and keep your memos enthusiastic, direct, and effective. It will also show you the most common pitfalls associated with writing business memos.

Keep It Handy!

60-Second Memos will help you:

- Improve your written communication skills,
- Spend less time in unnecessary face-to-face meetings,
- Focus on essential tasks quickly and effectively, and
- Cut your to-do list down to size.

Keep it next to your computer at all times!

—BT

Contents

Chapter 3:
Personnel and Human Resource Issues   65

Chapter 4:
Accommodations for Disabled Employees, Diversity Training, Sexual Harassment Policies, and Other Potential Problem Areas 111

Chapter 5:
Dealing with Non-Customer Outsiders such as Vendors, Consultants, and Members of the Media 127

Role of Consultant • Government Regulatory Agency Investigating • Notice: Expect Unfavorable Media Attention; Guidelines for Response • Notice to Expect Unfavorable Media Attention • Obtaining Authorization before Releasing Statements to Media • Outlining Official Company Response for Media and Others • Problem with Product Defect: Guidelines on Working with Media Consultant • Problem with Product Defect: Guidelines on Working with Regulatory Agency • Problems with Vendor: Do Not Assign Purchase Orders • Problems with New Vendor: Business May be Severed • Reporter to Visit Premises for Feature Story • Reporting Changes Suggested by Consultant • Responding to Request for Information from Government Regulatory Agency • Specific Reporter Likely to Call Staff Members—Do Not Cooperate • Upcoming Meeting with Important Vendor; Problems to Be Reviewed • Upcoming Radio/Television Broadcast on Company Likely to Affect Company Morale • Vendor Expects Unrealistic Payment Terms; Guidelines for Counterproposal • Vendor Has Placed Our Organization on Credit Hold; Guidelines for Resolution • Vendor Short-Shipped Us; Hold Payment Until Resolved

Chapter 6:
Vacation Scheduling, Benefits Policies, Overtime, and Leave   149

Announcing Flex-time Policy • Approving Overtime Pay • Correcting Error in Pay • Deadline for Submitting Required Benefit Application Forms • Dealing with Excessive Accumulated Leave • Denying Overtime • Denying Request for Change in Work Schedule • Denying Request for Change in Work Venue • Denying Request for Leave • Denying Request for Vacation Time • Employee Is Still on Probation and Is Ineligible for Benefits Package • Family-Leave Policy • Filling Out Leave Forms • Guidelines: Overtime • Policy for Vehicles Leased by Company • Referring Employee with Benefits Inquiry to Personnel • Requesting Leave

Chapter 7:
Union-Related Topics   165

Confidentiality Concerning Current Offer from Union • General Memo: Change in Operations During Strike or Work Stoppage • Impending Strike Action or Work Stoppage • Meeting with Union Representative; Strategies for Avoiding Strike or Work Stoppage • Request for Input on Evaluating

Chapter 8:
Sales Department Performance   179

Chapter 10:
Quality Control   263

Addressing Concerns of Marketing Department with Regard to Quality Problems • Addressing Concerns of Marketing Department with Regard to Revised Production Schedule • Client Requires New Specifications • Dealing with Unacceptable Quality-Control Procedures on the Part of a Long-standing Vendor • Denial of Request for Waiver from Specifications • Design Flaw in Prototype • Encouraging All Employees to Develop Familiarity with Product • Encouraging Customer Service Department to Relay Complaints Quickly to Quality Control People • Encouraging Operations Department to Be on Lookout for Quality Problems Before Shipment • Encouraging Subordinates to "Stop the Line" • Encouraging Subordinates to Pass Along Ideas for Better Quality Control • Explaining Employee Error to Superior • Explanation of New Quality Standards to Front-line Customer Service People • External Packaging and Related Items: Proofreading Checklist • General Memo: Quality Problems on Recent Project • Handling Persistent Quality-Control Problems in a Single Department • Importance of Consulting Checklists Before Passing Work On • Managers: Importance of Spot-Checking Checklist Compliance • Multiple Review of Product Prototypes is Essential • Planning Random Quality Tests Throughout the Production Process • Possible Product Defect: Plans for Action • Proposing New Specifications • Recommending a Product Recall • Refusing to Move Forward with Project Until Key Questions are Resolved • Requesting Additional Funds to Address Recent Quality Concerns • Requesting Extension of Deadline to Address Recent Quality Concerns • Requesting Help in Eliciting Consumer Feedback • Requiring Overtime from Employees to Address Recent Quality Concerns • Requesting Private Meeting to Address Quality Concerns • Spot-Checking for Quality in Problem Department

Chapter 11:
Internal Efficiency   291

Abuse of Company Charge and Expense Accounts: Strategies for Review by Accounting Department • Announcing the New E-Mail Network • Attendance Problems: Company Meetings • Breaks that Run Beyond Allotted Time • Car Pooling Problems: Tardiness • Change of Service Agreements on Company Computers • Company Dress: Casual Day Guidelines • Company Dress: General Guidelines • Computer and Copier

Chapter 12:
Implementing New Policies and Initiatives   *329*

Chapter 15:
Of Particular Interest to Managers Supervising Off-Site Workers   399

Appendix A:
A Brief Guide to Style and Usage   409

Index   417

Reassignments, Internal Vacancies, and Job Descriptions

Changes in personnel, in job descriptions, and in the internal structure of a department can affect both working relationships and morale. Employees must be kept informed when these changes are in process, and they must also be made aware of appropriate opportunities open to them as a result of those changes.

In this chapter, you will learn ways to pass along personnel news, good and bad, likely to affect individual employees. These will include memos that:

- Announce job openings, new personnel, employee departures, and changes in department or individual job situations.

- Inform employees of company policies, procedures, and guidelines in handling such issues as discrimination, internal or external hires, the filing of paperwork, etc.

- Notify team members of important actions taken or about to be taken, such as upcoming performance reviews or the discharge of an employee; recommendations and inquiries affecting new hires, position changes, raises, and terminations; and responses to individual requests and inquiries.

Additional Duties to Subordinate's Job Description

To:

From:

Date:

Regarding: New duties

I spoke with Roberta yesterday about your strengths as a reader and text reviewer . . . and about some upcoming projects in the department.

Beginning August 1, you'll be working at least one day a week in the proofreading area for the magazine people. I've incorporated this work in your revised job description (now in your mailbox). Could you take a look at your current workload for the next three months and advise me on any revised completion dates we should consider? If you want to discuss any aspect of this new assignment with me, please let me know.

Alternate Version:

Roberta has asked me to put you in charge of some of the proofreading work arising in the magazine area. This assignment will take advantage of your thoroughness, detail orientation, and grammatical skills. I don't believe it will have a major impact on your work in other areas. The magazine people estimate that there will be four to five articles for you to proofread per week—approximately one day out of five.

The new duties, reflected in your revised job description, begin August 1. Let's talk soon about how other projects on your schedule will be affected by this change.

DEVELOPING A CUSTOMIZED MEMO? REMEMBER TO . . .

- Highlight your appreciation of the person's unique skills—and, if possible, make it clear that those skills are guiding or supporting your decision.

- Focus on *how* the changes will affect the subordinate's workflow, not *whether* the change will take place.

- If necessary and appropriate, refer to any "other duties as required" language that already appears in the person's job description.

Announcing an Appointment to a New Position

To:

From:

Date:

Regarding: David Barnes

On January 1, David Barnes becomes our new Graphic Design Specialist. He'll be overseeing our internal cover design efforts, and will still attend the weekly graphics staff meetings. David will be reporting to me as he undertakes this new assignment.

Let's all wish him the best!

Alternate Version:

David Barnes has an exciting new set of responsibilities.

Effective January 1, David, who now serves as Graphics Coordinator, will be moving into the color production area. David will be heading up our internal cover design efforts, and will work under the title Graphic Design Specialist.

This is a lateral move; David will still attend the weekly meetings of the graphics staff, and will still report to me. Let's all wish David the best as he begins to develop an exciting in-house project!

DEVELOPING A CUSTOMIZED MEMO? REMEMBER TO . . .

- Specify the key duties of the new job.
- Outline any appropriate organizational changes.

Announcing a Change in Job Title

To:

From:

Date:

Regarding: Change in Job Title

I'm pleased to report that, effective immediately, your formal title will be "Coordinator of Information Services," a formulation that more accurately describes the wide-ranging nature of the duties you are now performing.

Thanks so much for all the hard work you've put in on the challenging new assignments that have crossed your desk recently.

Alternate Version:

As you probably remember, your job description was altered significantly during your last salary review. Before January 1, you were not responsible for developing the raw data for reports, providing estimates for the first draft of the departmental expense forecasts, or training new personnel in important new computer procedures. For the last three months, you have been. Although your salary was revised to reflect these changes, your formal job title—"Assistant to the Vice President for Research and Development"—was not.

The new title, just approved, is "Coordinator of Information Services."

Thanks for all your efforts, and keep up the good work!

DEVELOPING A CUSTOMIZED MEMO? REMEMBER TO . . .

- Explain the reasons that are guiding your decision—and, if possible, make it clear that the team member's sterling contributions have made the formal change possible.
- Express appropriate thanks for the person's contributions thus far.

Announcing Job-Sharing Policy

To:

From:

Date:

Regarding: Job-sharing policy

That overloaded home and work routine may be about to get a whole lot easier . . . with very little effort on your part.

Even if you have not yet found a partner with whom to share your position, you may be able to take advantage of ABC's job-sharing program. For further information on the program, please feel free to give me a call at extension 8763.

Alternate Version:

Spread the word! ABC Corporation now has a job-sharing program.

Many currently filled positions, as well as any number of posted job openings, are eligible for supervisor-approved redesign in order to incorporate a two-person work team rather than a single full-time employee. Flexible hours and pro-rated benefits are just some of the advantages of the job-sharing approach.

If you are interested in pursuing a different work schedule in partnership with someone else in the organization, or if you'd like to enter your name in our pool of job-sharing candidates, please contact me at extension 8763. *You do not need to have found a job partner to take advantage of the job-sharing program.*

Developing a Customized Memo? Remember to . . .

- Highlight any job-matching services the program may offer.
- Emphasize the program's convenience and accessibility.
- Provide clear contact information.

Announcing Job-Swapping Policy

To:

From:

Date:

Regarding: Job-Swapping Policy

ABC Corporation has now established a job-swapping program that will allow employees to apply for transfers to other departments or divisions . . . without having to wait for a formal opening.

Approval from *both* sets of employee supervisors is required. The people in Human Resources estimate that coordinating a successful transfer will require between thirty and sixty days. This is an exciting new resource for ABC employees, one that I'm sure many will want to review closely. Carol Haining is coordinating the project. You may reach her at extension 411.

Alternate Version:

Have you checked out the ABC job-swapping system? If your supervisor agrees to the swap you propose, you may be able to take advantage of this program.

Check with Carol Haining in the Human Resources department (extension 5411) for details on how to use the computer database to check for other ABC employees who may wish to exchange jobs with you in order to enhance skills, arrange for an easier commute, or relocate to another part of the country.

DEVELOPING A CUSTOMIZED MEMO? REMEMBER TO . . .

- Detail any relevant requirements for participation.
- Provide clear contact information.
- Outline the main benefits of the program.

Announcing a Promotion

To:

From:

Date:

Regarding: Brian Bell

Brian Bell, whose tenure with ABC extends back to 19XX, is being promoted to the position of Director of Customer Service. He will begin his duties effective January 1.

Let's all wish Brian the best as he begins his challenging and exciting new job.

Alternate Version:

Effective January 1, Brian Bell will be our new Director of Customer Service. Congratulations, Brian!

Brian has been here for six years; he started out as a front-line phone representative, and served most recently as our coordinator of premium fulfillment. He will be moving to the office directly across from the conference room.

Here's wishing Brian all the best as he takes on his new responsibilities.

DEVELOPING A CUSTOMIZED MEMO? REMEMBER TO . . .

- Mention the person's name (first or first and last) at least twice.
- Issue unmistakable congratulations for having been named to the new position.
- Encourage others to wish the person well.

Announcing a Retirement

To:

From:

Date:

Regarding: Robin Shore's retirement

Best of luck, Robin!

Robin Shore is retiring after twenty years at ABC Corporation. Her enthusiasm, precision, and dedication have been invaluable assets to ABC for two decades. We all join in wishing her and her husband Frank the very best.

Alternate Version:

After more than twenty years of service to ABC Corporation, Robin Shore is retiring this week.

Robin joined our firm in (year) as a telemarketing representative, and eventually found her niche in the Human Resources department, of which she has been the director for the past six years. She has been one of the most exuberant and exciting forces in our organization. She will be missed by everyone at ABC Systems.

Let's all wish Robin the very best as she and her husband Frank begin the next phase of their lives in the sunny state of Arizona, where they plan to move later this year!

DEVELOPING A CUSTOMIZED MEMO? REMEMBER TO . . .

- Mention the person's name (first or first and last) at least twice.
- Issue unmistakable congratulations.
- Avoid any mention of past controversies or setbacks.

Changing an Assignment

To:

From:

Date:

Regarding: The Peters assignment

Sorry for the mixup, but . . . would you please get the Peters materials back to me as soon as possible? I assigned it to you by mistake . . . and someone in the New York office may already be working on it. If we do decide to go ahead with this project through our office, we will probably need to incorporate some new specifications.

I'd appreciate it if you could get these materials back to me as soon as possible. Many thanks.

Alternate Version:

Hold everything!

There's a very good chance that the work I gave you to do on the Peters assignment may have already been completed. My mistake!

Would you please return the printouts and copy samples I gave you so that I can check the status of this project with the people in the New York production office? I'll let you know of the status on this proposal once I've finished talking everything over with the appropriate people. If we do end up going ahead with this assignment, we may need to discuss some new specifications.

DEVELOPING A CUSTOMIZED MEMO? REMEMBER TO . . .

- Apologize for the confusion *once.*
- Explain the current status of the project.
- Lay out exactly what you want the person to do next.

Department to Be Expanded

To:

From:

Date:

Regarding: Expansion of the department

The Accounting and Disbursement departments are joining forces!

All accounting work for the Northeast Division will now be conducted through one department. This will result in considerable increases in efficiency, and should reduce a good deal of overlap between our two work areas.

New space and equipment is being arranged right now; when I have details on the hows, wheres, and whens of the new quarters, I will pass them along.

Alternate Version:

Thanks to the new reorganization campaign, our department will be undergoing an expansion later this month. There will no longer be two accounting units. The eleven people who presently work in the magazine accounting section will be reassigned: Nine (Mel Tyler, Ellen Bianco, Howard Hamilton, Juanita Hart, Ben Powers, Stephen Lowenstein, Larry White, and Pamela Chu) will be coming to work in our area, while three (Andrew Cote, Meghan Tragert, and Laura Cote) will be moving into non-accounting functions in other parts of the organization.

I do not yet know who will be working where, but I will let you know as soon as I do. This is an exciting and demanding time, one that will require a certain flexibility from everyone as we adjust to the new situation. Please do your best to make the newcomers feel welcome over the next month or so.

DEVELOPING A CUSTOMIZED MEMO? REMEMBER TO . . .

- Detail, where appropriate, exactly what each new person will be doing. (You may wish to skip this step, however, if you expect that ego problems on the part of the people named may arise. Consider in-person meetings instead in such a situation.)
- Anticipate and address questions that are unresolved but high on your readers' priority list (such as workspace assignments). Make it clear that you are on the case.

Details of Upcoming Job Description Change

To:

From:

Date:

Regarding: Change in formal job description

As we discussed earlier in the year, your job description is being changed to reflect your current responsibilities. A copy of the new description will be forwarded to you by the end of this week. I look forward to discussing it with you.

Alternate Version:

In January, we discussed the possibility of altering your job description to include more work on interior page design and less on indexing and data entry work. I have just gotten approval for this change, and have been asked to develop a revised written job description for you.

This new job description should be ready in one week. I look forward to going over it with you soon!

DEVELOPING A CUSTOMIZED MEMO? REMEMBER TO . . .

- If at all possible, base your memo on past discussions and shared conclusions.
- Specify appropriate timelines.

Extension of Temporary Assignment

To:

From:

Date:

Regarding: Temporary assignment

Sometimes the jobs get bigger than we'd anticipated.

Can you stay on in your current capacity as a temporary worker until September 1? The Connors project has extended beyond the anticipated completion date, and I'm very happy with your contributions thus far.

If you're willing to stay on for the next two months, please see Deborah Harris as soon as you can. Thanks again for all your hard work.

Alternate Version:

Just such a situation is facing ABC Corporation right now. We would like to extend your temporary assignment until September 1 of this year. Your work on the Connors project has been very strong. Our project deadline has been extended by the client, and we'd like you to keep making contributions.

If you would like to accept our offer of an extension, please see Deborah Harris in the Human Resources office as soon as possible.

Thanks for all your help thus far!

DEVELOPING A CUSTOMIZED MEMO? REMEMBER TO . . .

- Make it clear that the position under discussion is temporary, rather than full-time.
- Express appreciation for the worker's contributions thus far.

File Written Copy of Changes in Job Description

To:

From:

Date:

Regarding: Your copy of the new job description

Here's the revised job description we discussed. You'll find the new language concerning text development is much closer to your actual day-to-day duties.

Please hold on to this photocopy, which is submitted for your records. The original is on file with the people in Human Resources.

Alternate Version:

Here it is! The changes in responsibility we discussed recently have been incorporated in the enclosed revised job description. Please keep this copy on file for your reference; a duplicate has been sent along to Human Resources.

If you have any questions regarding this new job description, please don't hesitate to contact me.

DEVELOPING A CUSTOMIZED MEMO? REMEMBER TO . . .

- Specify which part of the job description has been revised.

- Make it clear that the copy you are passing along is for the employee's personal records.
- If you are sending an e-mail message, let the person know that the new job description should be printed out and stored as "hard copy."

Filing Appropriate Paperwork with Human Resources after Filling a Vacancy

To:

From:

Date:

Regarding: Post-hire paperwork

When is a hire not a hire? When the hiring manager fails to submit the various "payroll entry" forms!

The same goes for all manner of internal personnel maneuvers. If you don't fill out the forms, they don't show up for the payroll service! Please make life easier for everyone and promptly submit all the forms necessary when you hire someone, authorize a transfer, or change someone's rate of pay. If you have questions about what needs to be submitted, please see Allan or me.

Alternate Version:

The people in Human Resources have asked me to remind everyone that a hire is not complete until the paperwork has been put through. This means not only getting your new person to supply appropriate identification as required by law, but also taking the time to complete the necessary internal forms that will allow our payroll service to process the new hire's checks. Any manager who has hired someone *must* check in with Allan to fill out a "payroll entry" form. The same procedure applies to employees who are given departmental transfers and/or changes in rates of pay.

Thanks for making things easier on everyone by working with Allan to get new hires up and running as smoothly as possible.

- Keep the message short and sweet: "Get the forms package from the people in Human Resources." (Long lists of forms, deadlines, and requirements may cause your readers' eyes to glaze over.)

- Provide at least one specific contact person for your readers to search out when they have questions.

Guidelines: Avoiding Discrimination in Hiring

To:

From:

Date:

Regarding: Interview protocol

Just a reminder for hiring managers: Inappropriate questions about an applicant's religious practices, physical disabilities, sexual preferences, or ethnic background should not be asked during employment interviews.

ABC Corporation is an equal opportunity employer. A detailed summary of proper and improper interviewing techniques is available through the Human Resources office. Please review it before you conduct any interview.

Thanks for your cooperation!

Alternate Version:

ABC Systems is an equal opportunity employer. Please bear in mind the following when interviewing candidates for temporary or permanent positions here:

- Questions that are abusive or harassing, or that lead a candidate to believe that sexual favors are required for employment or advancement, will not be tolerated.

- Questions about the candidate's race, religion, marital status, future parenting plans, sexual preferences, or physical disabilities are inappropriate and illegal. Don't ask them.

- Questions about how the candidate would perform the tasks associated with the job in question *are* appropriate (and important!)-so do ask them. Asking a candidate to outline any religious beliefs she holds that might lead to a "poor fit" with ABC is totally inappropriate. On the other hand, asking her whether she is available to work on weekends, since Saturday and Sunday work is an intrinsic part of our work here, is entirely proper.

Questions? Please see me!

DEVELOPING A CUSTOMIZED MEMO? REMEMBER TO . . .

- State clearly and unambiguously that your organization is an equal opportunity employer.
- Let your readers know how to get more information on appropriate interviewing techniques.
- Keep a copy of the memo for your own files. Also forward one to your legal department, if you have one. You may need to appeal to it if there is trouble at some point.

Introducing a New Team Member

To:

From:

Date:

Regarding: Our newest team member

Welcome aboard!

After four years as marketing director at Bell Turbine, Ellen McLaughlin is signing on here as Vice President of Marketing. She'll be attending the Friday board meetings starting this week.

Here's wishing her all the best as she tackles her new responsibilities.

Alternate Version:

Effective December 1, Ellen McLaughlin will be joining our team as Vice President of Marketing.

Ellen has a long and impressive record of achievement with Bell Turbine Group, where she headed up the Marketing department for four years. She will be attending the Friday afternoon executive board meetings beginning this week.

Stop by her new office (to the right of the reception area) and introduce yourself!

Developing a Customized Memo? Remember to . . .

- Keep the tone upbeat and optimistic.
- Briefly mention the new staff member's past work history.
- Mention any formal organizational changes, especially those that affect the new person's colleagues.

Introducing a Team Member Who Once Worked for a Competing Firm

To:

From:

Date:

Regarding: Paul Roberts

As you may know, ABC Corporation has been looking long and hard for just the right person to fill the position of Senior Creative Consultant. During his time at OtCo over the past five years, Paul has had many opportunities to distinguish himself as one of the most innovative minds in the industry. While at OtCo, he oversaw several award-winning campaigns. I am sure that his joining our team will benefit us all.

Please join me in offering Paul and his family a warm and hearty welcome to the ABC organization.

Alternate Version:

As you may have heard, Paul Roberts has signed on with ABC Corporation. Today is his first official day on the job.

I'm sure everyone here joins me in welcoming Paul to the team—and in heaving a sigh of relief that his next big project will be one that benefits our organization, not one of our competitors! Our new Senior Creative Consultant's office is located on the third floor, across from the Finance department. Please stop by today and introduce yourself to the newest member of the ABC family.

Developing a Customized Memo? Remember to . . .

- Mention the new team member's name at least twice.
- Encourage others in the organization to stop by and introduce themselves.

Necessity of Filling Long-Vacant Position

To:

From:

Date:

Regarding: Accounting manager position

Mitch left us three months ago, and you're still trying to fill in for him. You've done a fine job on an interim basis, but I'm concerned about the toll the unfilled vacancy is taking on you. I'd like to talk about ways we can accelerate the search. Can you take half an hour or so and put together a list of at least three new recruitment options we can consider?

Alternate Version:

When Mitch left as accounting manager, we agreed that you would step in and fulfill his duties on an interim basis until you could find a suitable new candidate. It's been three months now, and we still don't have someone we can feel good about for this position.

I'm glad you're willing to fill in, but I'd like to discuss this issue with you by the close of business Wednesday. Please stop by my office on Wednesday afternoon so we can review some new recruiting options.

Developing a Customized Memo? Remember to . . .

- Express your thanks for the person's work.

- Specify a date and time at which new options for finding the right person for the job will be discussed.

Notice of Department-Wide Review of Job Descriptions

To:

From:

Date:

Regarding: Job descriptions

I need you to look at the formal written job descriptions for everyone in your department, not including yourself. (Lost someone's copy? A new one is available from Sharon Martin in Human Resources.) I want to get a *one-page* memo from you for each person in your department on ways you think the job description could be changed or revised for increased efficiency. You may also include suggestions on revisions that will bring the job description more closely into line with the actual day-to-day demands of the person's job.

Please keep the summaries to a single page—and get them to me by 5:00 on Thursday, July 11.

Alternate Version:

In keeping with the acquisition of our company by SyVision Corporation, we're undertaking a top-to-bottom review of all job descriptions. Can you summarize what each person in your department does, and how you feel he or she could do it better, in a single-page memo per person? (There's no need to write a memo about yourself.) If you need another copy of someone's job description, please contact Sharon Martin.

This is *not* a prelude to a downsizing campaign. It is, instead, an effort on the part of our new partners to find out exactly what has worked—and hasn't worked—in the past. The objective is to help us do our jobs better.

Remember—no more than one page! Thanks in advance. I need to have the suggested changes on my desk no later than 5:00 on Thursday, July 11.

- Allay fears that the task you're asking for help on is the first step in a workforce reduction campaign (if you can honestly do so).
- Let your readers know whom to contact if they need help tracking down job descriptions.

Notification that Subordinate Is Discharged Due to Falsification of Resume

To:

From:

Date:

Regarding: Termination

ABC Corporation has a clear policy on fraudulently presented credentials. Your interview statements and resume led me to believe you were a graduate of Yale University, an assertion the University categorically denies.

As a result, you are hereby terminated as an employee of ABC Corporation. Please see Marion Henderson in the Human Resources department immediately. She will bring you up to date on your final pay arrangements and other aspects of your exit procedure.

Alternate Version:

This letter will serve as your official notice of termination.

Upon review of the resume you submitted to us as part of the interview process, I have determined that it is misleading throughout, and demonstrably false in several places. Specifically, I have determined that you are not a graduate of Yale University, as you claimed, both in the very first line of your resume and during the face-to-face interview process we concluded last month.

I would like you to clean out your desk and remove all of your personal belongings from this facility by the close of business today. Please see Marion Henderson in Human Resources for more information on your exit procedure.

Developing a Customized Memo? Remember to . . .

- Give the reader a clear "next step" to follow.
- Make it absolutely clear that your decision is final.
- If at all possible, deliver the memo during an in-person meeting.
- Check with your company attorney ahead of time. Follow all appropriate legal and organizational guidelines when conducting this or any termination.

Notification that Subordinate Is Discharged Due to Falsification of References

To:

From:

Date:

Regarding: Termination

This letter will serve as your official notice of termination.

A number of the written references you supplied during the interview process were not composed by the former employers you cited. I know this because I have spoken to representatives of both of the companies you identified, who have informed me that the people whose names appear on these letters have never been employed by them.

I would like you to clean out your desk and remove all of your personal belongings from this facility by the close of business today. Please see Marion Henderson in Human Resources for more information on your exit procedure.

Alternate Version:

When you interviewed for a position at ABC Corporation, you supplied me with six written references. Recent verification efforts have made it clear to me that four of those references were fabricated, and attributed to persons who never worked at the organizations you identified.

As a result, you are hereby terminated as an employee of ABC Corporation. Please clear out your work area and see Marion Henderson in the Human

Resources department immediately. She will bring you up to date on your final pay arrangements and other aspects of your exit procedure.

Developing a Customized Memo? Remember to . . .

- Give the reader a clear "next step" to follow.
- Make it absolutely clear that your decision is final.
- If at all possible, deliver the memo during an in-person meeting.
- Check with your company attorney ahead of time. Follow all appropriate legal and organizational guidelines when conducting this or any termination.

Notification that Subordinate is to Be Discharged Due to Poor Performance During Probationary Period

To:

From:

Date:

Regarding: Discharge from position

As you may remember, your full-time employment was conditional upon your attaining certain performance goals over a ninety-day period. It is clear to me that your entry speed on our computer system is not adequate to the demands of the position, which are specified at forty entries per hour in your probation guidelines.

Your services will no longer be required at ABC Corporation. I regret that this partnership did not work out for us. Please clean out your work area and see Marion Henderson in Human Resources for more information on your exit procedure.

Alternate Version:

Although the news can't be welcome for you to hear—it's certainly not pleasant for me to pass along—I have to tell you that your performance during our mutually agreed ninety-day probationary period has not been satisfactory.

We had agreed that you would gain a working knowledge of our firm's computer system and perform at a forty-entry-per-hour level while processing field reports. I have been monitoring your progress closely over the past month, and it is clear to me that the system is not second nature to you yet. The highest rate I have been able to verify in your work is six entries per hour. There have also been attendance and tardiness problems.

As a result, today will be your last day here at ABC Corporation. I regret that this partnership did not work out for us. Please remove all personal items from your work area and see Marion Henderson in Human Resources for more information on your exit procedure.

DEVELOPING A CUSTOMIZED MEMO? REMEMBER TO . . .

- Give the reader a clear "next step" to follow.
- Make it absolutely clear that your decision is final.
- If at all possible, deliver the memo during an in-person meeting.
- Check with your company attorney ahead of time. Follow all appropriate legal and organizational guidelines when conducting this or any termination.

Observe Recruiting Guidelines on Internal Hires

To:

From:

Date:

Regarding: Recruiting guidelines on internal hires

Nobody likes unpleasant surprises.

Even if you're hiring someone who has previously worked for ABC as a contract or part-time worker, you *must* follow the procedures laid out in the hiring manual developed by Human Resources when it comes to verifying resume materials and personal references. Otherwise the company could be exposed to unnecessary legal risk.

Questions? Please see me or Anne Halliday.

Alternate Version:

Just a reminder for hiring managers—reference checks and resume verification are *always* mandatory for applicants with whom you have not worked before—even when the potential hire is a person who has worked for ABC in the past as a contract or part-time worker.

These procedures are in place for the company's protection, and for yours. Even a long-standing exaggeration or deception about an applicant's background can come back to haunt us. Reference checks and resume verification are especially helpful if you are relying on an applicant's (unverified) technical expertise in a new area.

Please see me if you have any questions about this policy.

DEVELOPING A CUSTOMIZED MEMO? REMEMBER TO . . .

- Make it clear that there are potentially serious problems for the manager (and the company) if the guidelines aren't followed.
- Let the reader know whom to contact if there are questions.

Opening in Department

To:

From:

Date:

Regarding: Opening for Editorial Assistant

Growth in the ThriftySet series of local bargain guides has led to an opening for an Editorial Assistant.

This person will be responsible for developing new information for our upcoming Washington and Dallas books, and for verifying data in new editions of existing books in the series. Some travel is required. See the attached job description for a detailed summary of the job's requirements, the likely background of the successful applicant, and the salary range the position offers.

To arrange an interview for this position, please contact me directly.

Alternate Version:

If you . . .

. . . like to travel,

. . . have strong writing and fact-checking skills,

. . . and are eager to find the very best bargain . . .

you may want to consider applying for the position of Editorial Assistant in the Mr. Thrifty book division. If you'd like to see a job description and/or make a formal application for the job, please drop by my office.

DEVELOPING A CUSTOMIZED MEMO? REMEMBER TO . . .

- Identify the most important requirements of the position.
- Let the reader know how to submit a formal application, including whom to contact.

Position Eliminated; Recruiting Efforts to Cease

To:

From:

Date:

Regarding: Elimination of position

Due to budgetary restrictions, we will not be filling the position left open by Margaret Cheney's departure. We will continue for the foreseeable future with four Account Executives, rather than five.

Any telephone inquiries about this position should be forwarded to Melissa Daniels in my office, who will inform applicants of the best ways to learn about other openings at ABC.

Alternate Version:

I received word from Mr. Collins today that the Account Executive position left open when Margaret Cheney left the firm will not be filled. This position is being eliminated from our current fiscal year budget.

Before Mr. Collins reached this decision, a brief advertisement was placed in the weekend papers describing the opening and encouraging applicants to forward resumes to my attention. Would you please develop a boilerplate letter for mail inquiries, and leave word with Sharon at the reception desk that we are not accepting any more phone queries for this position?

Thanks!

DEVELOPING A CUSTOMIZED MEMO? REMEMBER TO . . .

- Make it perfectly clear that the position is not going to be filled by a new person at any time in the foreseeable future. If there's no daylight, don't lead people to believe there is any.
- Set up procedures for dealing with applicants who may believe the position is still open.

Post All Job Openings

To:

From:

Date:

Regarding: Posting of job openings

Help us keep our commitments!

Current, legally enforceable guidelines arising out of our agreement with the union *require* that we post all job openings and interview qualified internal candidates. So . . .

Please don't forget to post your job openings!

Alternate Version:

Remember our recent union agreement!

Any and all positions for which we consider applicants *must* be posted on the job board located in the employee lounge area. This is not an optional matter, but a legally enforceable requirement resulting from our recent union negotiations.

If you have any questions concerning this requirement, please feel free to contact me. Thanks!

> DEVELOPING A CUSTOMIZED MEMO? REMEMBER TO . . .
>
> • Explain why the openings must be posted.
> • Keep the tone polite, upbeat, and professional.

Query of Subordinate: Would You Consider a Lateral Change in Position?

To:

From:

Date:

Regarding: Possible lateral move

An opening has come up for a Graphic Designer position; I'm posting the job description today.

It occurred to me that this position might be up your alley, given your comments at our lunch last week. The pay would be the same as your current job, but if you were hired for this job you'd have a good deal more exposure to the types of layout and photo projects we discussed.

Are you interested in arranging an interview? Please let me know. I'll be scheduling other candidates beginning this week.

Alternate Version:

Would you be interested in applying for the Graphic Designer position that has just opened up?

The details of the job opening are posted in the employee lounge. I'll be interviewing a number of candidates; maybe you should be one of them. If you think this position makes sense for you, why not swing by my office so we can discuss it?

- Make it clear that your letter does not constitute a formal job offer. (You can do this by, for instance, referring to the other candidates you must interview.)
- Suggest that the person review the formal job description.
- Point the person toward someone who can supply more information about the position.

Recommending a Hire

To:

From:

Date:

Regarding: Bertha Dawson's candidacy

You asked me to review all the applicants for the Graphic Designer opening, and I've done so. The clear leader, as far as I'm concerned, is Bertha Dawson. She has four years of experience in the field, top-notch samples, a realistic, upbeat attitude about the work involved, and a superior set of references—which I called to confirm.

My recommendation is that we offer her the position immediately.

Alternate Version:

You asked for input on our most pressing personnel issue. Here's my feeling on the Graphic Designer position: I think we should offer it to Bertha Dawson as soon as possible.

Bertha made an excellent in-person presentation, has a knockout portfolio that impressed everyone who looked it over, and supplied very enthusiastic references. If it were up to me, I'd offer her the job today.

Developing a Customized Memo? Remember to . . .

- Supply at least three specific reasons supporting your recommendation.
- Frame your memo in terms of a recommendation, not a final decision.

- Mention that you or someone else has personally checked references. (If no one has, don't make a positive recommendation to hire!)

Recommending a Raise

To:

From:

Date:

Regarding: Milton Vessey

I had a great meeting with Milton the other day. He reminded me of how well the LPLR mailing went—it resulted in a brand new market for us—and of the training work he's done, which isn't part of his job description. Finally, he pointed out how subpar performers (like Wendy) have a way of improving their work habits when they spend time with Milton. It's all true.

He asked for a 15% raise. My instinct, given his superior performance, is to grant a 10% raise. How would you approach this?

Alternate Version:

Milton made a compelling case for himself a few days ago in my office.

He's personally designed and overseen a successful national mailing that resulted in a huge new market for ABC, he's trained three associates in our graphic design system, and he's got a way of turning subpar performers who work next door to him into key contributors. (Witness the sudden disappearance of Wendy's tardiness problem once she started working next to Milton.)

Based on these factors, I'm inclined to grant him a raise of 10%—compared to the 15% he requested. What do you think?

DEVELOPING A CUSTOMIZED MEMO? REMEMBER TO . . .

- Keep the word "raise" out of the headline or first sentence of the memo. (Your reader may tune out instantly.)

- Quantify the specific reasons you believe this person deserves an increase in pay. Focus, as much as possible, on bottom-line issues and on problems solved.
- Be willing to reconsider submitting your written request for a raise if you cannot point to specific accomplishments.

Recommending Dismissal

To:

From:

Date:

Regarding: Ellen Phelps

I think we've reached a crossroads in our relationship with Ellen.

Her productivity—or lack of it—continues to be a serious problem. She is abusive and insulting to fellow employees. And she seems incapable of showing up for work on time.

My recommendation: We terminate her this week. I will conduct the meeting if you feel that this course of action is the best one to pursue.

How do you feel about this?

Alternate Version:

Things have gone from bad to worse with Ellen. Today marked the fourteenth straight day she showed up late for work. When she finally does make it in, she's likely to be abusive of her coworkers. Her productivity, in terms of entries per hour on the system, is easily the lowest in the department.

I recommend that we cut our losses and terminate Ellen this week. I will conduct the meeting myself if you agree that this is the way to go.

What do you think?

Developing a Customized Memo? Remember to . . .

- Be absolutely certain that only the person whom you intend to read the message will receive it. If you have any questions about the security of your message system, you should strongly consider delivering this message in person, rather than on paper.

- Volunteer to conduct the meeting yourself. (It probably won't be much fun, but you'll avoid the common problem of waiting too long to fire an employee who has no business working for your company.)
- Consult your Human Resources department or appropriate legal counsel for advice on conducting the termination meeting, if one is scheduled.

Rejecting Application for Internal Opening

To:

From:

Date:

Regarding: Application for Internal Opening

I've had the chance to review your application for the position of Purchasing Specialist. Although your background and experiences offer many signs of strong fit with the company and point toward a record of solid contribution, I ended up concluding that the position required someone with more familiarity with the current computer system.

Please know that I was impressed with the potential you've shown over the past year in your current position. I hope you'll continue your career growth here at ABC, and that you'll feel free to contact me about future opportunities.

Alternate Version:

I'm sorry to pass along the news that you were not selected for the position of Purchasing Specialist.

I reviewed your resume and your file closely and I found that your work for ABC over the past year has been exemplary. I also felt that you showed poise and enthusiasm during your interview. However, after careful consideration, I've concluded that your present level of experience does not match the needs of the position as it is currently structured. I think you have a lot to offer ABC, and I encourage you to continue to look for opportunities to advance within the company. Please feel free to contact me if you would like information on other assignments that would help lead you into the purchasing field.

Developing a Customized Memo? Remember to . . .

- Get the bad news out of the way in the first paragraph.
- Praise the person's initiative and offer support for future growth within your organization.

Rejecting Internal Application for Position Due to Lack of Experience/Seniority

To:

From:

Date:

Regarding: Application for Internal Opening

Thank you for your application for the position of transportation coordinator. I'm sorry to tell you that you were not selected for the position.

Upon reviewing your file I found that your work for ABC has been exemplary. However, I feel that it would best serve the needs of the company to go with someone with more experience in the areas of 'Just-in-Time' inventory support. You'll recall that the job description for this position noted a requirement of two years in this area.

I sincerely hope that you will continue to apply for other positions within the organization. Feel free to contact me at anytime if you would like to discuss career enhancement opportunities.

Alternate Version:

Thank you for applying for the position of Transportation Coordinator.

Although I was impressed with the eagerness and enthusiasm you displayed both in person and in your written application for the job, I have confirmed with Nancy that the job description for this position requires a minimum of three years of experience in a fulfillment and cargo transportation setting.

Perhaps there will be another opening in the department for you to consider applying for in the near future. In the meantime, may I ask that you keep in touch with me from time to time about your ideas and career goals as they relate to this department?

Thanks again for your time and effort.

DEVELOPING A CUSTOMIZED MEMO? REMEMBER TO . . .

- Get the bad news out of the way in the first paragraph.
- Cite, if you can, specific requirements of the job description that support your decision.
- Praise the person's initiative and offer support for future growth within your organization.

Rejecting Request for a Raise (Schedule Issues)

To:

From:

Date:

Regarding: Request for Raise

I received your request for a raise today, and I wanted to let you know right away that I cannot formally accept it for consideration until the end of the fourth quarter.

I'm glad to see that you have taken the initiative to show the quality of your work. However, it is ABC's policy to review all salaries in January, and it would be unfair to make a single exception to this rule. May I suggest that between now and December you continue to gather examples of the fine work you have been doing for the firm, with an emphasis on how it has served to achieve the department's goals? Perhaps you could include a list of any courses, seminars, community activities, and other factors that might prove useful in evaluating your performance.

I look forward to seeing your file in December.

Alternate Version:

It was good to meet with you yesterday. You gave me a great deal to think about.

As I suspected, a quick check with Nancy has confirmed that there is no way for me to consider a raise outside of ABC's formal salary-review structure. This takes place in the early part of January each year. It might be nice if I could change the policy, but I can't. There is a bright side, however.

You've made an excellent start on charting your performance and preparing your self-review, and I certainly appreciate your initiative in doing so. Please hold on to the materials you've prepared and update them appropriately so we that can discuss everything in detail come January.

Thanks again for taking the time to talk with me about what you hope to accomplish here.

Developing a Customized Memo? Remember to . . .

- Avoid any evaluation of performance issues.
- Encourage the employee to continue to accumulate data that demonstrates key contributions to the organization.

Rejecting Request for a Raise (Performance Issues)

To:

From:

Date:

Regarding: Request for Raise

Thanks for your memo. It gave me a great deal to think about.

Although I'm not in a position to offer you a salary increase now, I would like to suggest that we meet on a weekly basis to work toward the goals we discussed in our recent meeting. If there has been significant progress toward these goals by April 1, I will strongly consider asking for a retroactive salary increase. But I need to work with you to make that happen.

What do you say? Shall we schedule our meeting for 8:30 each Wednesday morning?

Alternate Version:

I received your written response to our recent salary review meeting and have reviewed it carefully. It's clear that you've put a lot of time and effort into looking closely at the way you approach your work here at ABC, and I think that's a great starting point for the future.

I look forward to our next formal quarterly meeting. If there have been significant steps forward in the areas we discussed, I will strongly consider making a recommendation for a retroactive salary increase at that time. The decision regarding your current salary level, however, is going to have to remain the same.

It's never easy determining yearly pay levels. Personnel reviews are probably one of the hardest parts of any manager's job. I want you to know, though, that I've given this decision a good deal of thought. I certainly hope we can move together toward achieving the goals we discussed at our last meeting. What do you think of my suggestion that we get together on a weekly basis?

Developing a Customized Memo? Remember To . . .

- Make it clear that the current rate of pay will not be raised at present.
- Thank the employee for his or her input, and make it clear that you value it and take it seriously.
- Offer clear steps that will help the employee make progress toward improving performance and winning consideration for a higher rate of pay.

Rejecting Request for Change in Job Description

To:

From:

Date:

Regarding: Request for Change in Job Description

At my weekly meeting with Ruth this week I discussed your request for a change in your job description. We both came to the conclusion that the time is not right for a reorganization along the lines you suggested to me.

If you feel that there is a problem with your current workload and would like to discuss this matter further, please stop by my office so we can talk about it. We'll look into ways we can work together to make the system work for you.

Alternate Version:

I understand your frustration about your current workload. Everyone's been stretched pretty thin lately. It's been a busy time.

If you feel there are difficulties in handling your workload within the existing system, then let's get together for an hour or so over lunch to discuss the matter in detail. I'm sure if we look at all the angles we can resolve the obstacles together. A formal change in your job description isn't the answer—but a close look at where the work is coming from and how it's being scheduled just might be.

Please let me know what would be a good time to get together.

DEVELOPING A CUSTOMIZED MEMO? REMEMBER TO . . .

- Make it clear that the current job description will not be altered.
- Suggest that the employee meet with someone face-to-face to review the current challenges of the job.

Requesting Feedback on Development of Job Description

To:

From:

Date:

Regarding: Duties of the New Position

As you may have already heard, we've finally gotten approval to create a new position: Product Scale-up Specialist.

This is good news, but the decision won't be finalized until I put together a formal job description. I know everyone probably has some idea about the duties this new person should hold. May I ask you to put them down on paper and forward them to me this week?

Thanks for helping us track down the right person for this important job!

Alternate Version:

At long last, a budget line for the much-discussed new position, Product Scale-up Specialist, has been approved!

This new position will affect everyone in the department. I would appreciate any feedback you can give me as to how we can structure the position to help us make things run more smoothly. If you have ideas you think I should hear before I put together the formal job description, please leave them in my box this week.

I look forward to hearing from you.

DEVELOPING A CUSTOMIZED MEMO? REMEMBER TO . . .

- Open with the good news—more help is on the way in the department.
- Make it clear that the input of current team members is essential to the personnel process.

Requesting Additional Material for the Evaluation of an Application for Internal Opening

To:

From:

Date:

Regarding: Request for Additional Information in Application

I was glad to see your application for the new opening in the engineering department.

After giving your application a quick review I found that there are a few items I will require from you to make a proper evaluation of your credentials for the position.

1. A photocopy of your Certified Industrial Process Engineer certificate.
2. A copy of one of your recent exposure monitoring studies.
3. Names, dates, and credits earned for any professional development courses you've taken in the past two years.

Please forward this material to me by the end of this week.

Alternate Version:

I received your application for the new position in the engineering department, but I can't pass it along until I receive the following from you:

1. A photocopy of your Certified Industrial Process Engineer certificate.
2. A copy of one of your recent exposure monitoring studies.
3. Names, dates, and credits earned for any professional development courses you've taken in the past two years.

If you get these materials to me by the end of the week, I'll be able to include your completed application in the batch of "internal hire requests" Carol will review before considering outside resumes.

Thanks!

DEVELOPING A CUSTOMIZED MEMO? REMEMBER TO . . .

- Leave no doubt whatsoever about what you need to process the application.
- Strongly consider using a numbered or bulleted list.
- Specify when you need the material.

Scheduling Exit Interview

To:

From:

Date:

Regarding: Before you leave, let's talk

I realize that you will soon be leaving the company for a new position at The Other Company. I would like to set up an appointment to meet with you one last time.

Your contributions to the company over the past five years are much appreciated. I'd like to discuss your thoughts on the job you're leaving, what the next person who holds it should know about, and the challenges you see on the horizon. Five years is a long time, and you've been here to see just how much your job as Director of Customer Service—and ABC Corp. as a whole—has grown and changed in that time.

Let's get together as soon as your schedule will allow. Best of luck in your future employment. We're going to miss you.

Alternate Version:

I want our next Director of Customer Service to benefit from the experience you've accumulated over the past five years.

With that goal in mind, I'd like to ask for twenty to thirty minutes of your time on Tuesday or Wednesday to discuss what you've learned here at ABC during your tenure, what you would look for in the person who will take over your job, and the kinds of challenges you foresee for that person. I know you're awfully busy now closing things out, but I think it's important that we get together to discuss your insights.

Please let me know what a good time to meet would be. And congratulations once again on your new position.

DEVELOPING A CUSTOMIZED MEMO? REMEMBER TO . . .

- Acknowledge the employee's experience and contributions.
- Congratulate the person on entering the next phase of his or her career.

Chapter 2

Staff Reductions, Cutbacks, and Resource Allocation Issues

One of the hardest things any employer has to do is to make cuts. Whether this involves terminating employees, freezing salaries, making changes in benefits or compensation packages, or reducing budgets, cutbacks put the employer in the unenviable position of being "the bad guy."

This chapter will offer suggestions for easing the pain of announcing reductions, restrictions, and reorganizations. In addition to describing the best ways to make such potentially stressful announcements, this part of the book will show you how to balance the negative with the positive, and let you respond accurately and sensitively to employee concerns.

Addressing Issues Related to Downsizing Measures

To:

From:

Date:

Regarding: Company reorganization campaign

No matter what you may hear, there has been no decision to implement further staff cuts.

Please remember that company policy requires at least four months' notice to affected parties before any position is eliminated.

Irresponsible speculation about impending staff cuts won't help us focus on keeping customers satisfied or bring us any closer to the goal of emerging as a market leader in the widget industry. If you want a full review of the positive signs we're seeing as a result of the recent reorganization campaign, please stop by Human Resources for a copy of the quarterly report. Thanks to you, ABC Corporation is turning the corner—and we're doing it because we're all pulling together!

Alternate Version:

ABC Corporation is committed to the goal of emerging as a global market leader in the widget industry.

As you know, competitive pressures in the industry are extremely intense. Some recent changes in overall organizational structure and staffing levels have received a good deal of publicity. What has not been as widely discussed is the fact that these changes have significantly improved our competitive position, and have made ABC Corporation a better, stabler, and more productive place to work.

You may encounter rumors about future staff cutbacks. Please remember that any further phaseout of positions must, by company policy, be preceded by at least four months' advance notice to the employees involved.

Thanks for helping ABC Corporation turn the corner—and post its best quarterly results in six years!

- Offer readers signs of continuity and stability. (If you can, cite internal safeguards that give workers advance notice of layoffs.)
- Focus on recent positive events within the organization.
- Thank employees for their contributions and good efforts.

Announcing Outplacement Programs for Dismissed Workers

To:

From:

Date:

Regarding: Outplacement programs now in effect

As the Board of Directors promised, ABC Corporation outplacement assistance programs have been put into place to benefit those affected by the recent company reorganization moves.

Please take a moment to review the programs available, all of which are outlined in the attached circular. ABC is working with the BBW Group, one of the region's most prestigious outplacement firms. Their wealth of outplacement experience can help to point you toward the next stage of your career growth.

If you have any further questions, or would like to offer a suggestion about making the programs described in the circular work better, feel free to contact me at extension 2283.

Alternate Version:

ABC Corporation has, as promised, secured the help of one of the region's most outstanding outplacement firms to help those affected by the recent reorganization campaign. The BBW Group has signed on to help you move to the next stage in your career.

Please review the enclosed circular closely. It offers a summary of the resume workshop, interview preparation, one-on-one counseling, and referral network resources available to you.

If you have any questions about the particulars of the program we're offering with the BBW Group, please don't hesitate to contact me at extension 2283.

DEVELOPING A CUSTOMIZED MEMO? REMEMBER TO . . .

- Focus on the positive by using phrases like "career growth" and "next phase" rather than "job search" or "termination."
- Supply the name of an in-house person for readers to contact.

Announcing Budget Cutbacks and Their Immediate Effects

To: Senior Managers

From:

Date:

Regarding: Budget changes

ABC Corporation's new budget guidelines require all of us to work toward the goal of minimizing expenses when and wherever possible. I've taken some initial steps to make the new numbers work, steps you should know about and explain to your people one-on-one.

Effective immediately: 1) All capital improvement projects not yet funded will be frozen pending review by the Executive Council. 2) All department expenditures over $75 must be approved by the department head. 3) All travel plans must be approved by the appropriate department head; the newly installed video teleconferencing facilities should be used whenever possible.

These changes may take some getting used to, but I'm confident that they will help make ABC Corporation a stronger competitor. If you want to discuss other opportunities for us to reduce waste and eliminate duplication of effort or unnecessary expense, please feel free to contact me directly.

Alternate Version:

During my recent meeting with the president, a number of new expenditure guidelines were finalized. These changes, made in accordance with our ongoing cost-cutting campaign, are effective immediately.

1. All capital improvement projects not yet funded will be frozen pending review from the president's office.

2. All department expenditures over $75 must be approved by the department head.

3. All travel plans must be approved by the appropriate department head; the newly installed video teleconferencing facilities should be used whenever possible.

I realize these steps mark a significant departure from our past practices, but given the current competitive climate ABC Corp. faces, they are essential.

Please feel free to contact me if you have any questions about the new policies, or if you would like to share your own ideas on the best ways for us to reduce expenditures companywide.

DEVELOPING A CUSTOMIZED MEMO? REMEMBER TO . . .

- Offer brief summaries of the key changes.
- Make it clear which changes are effective immediately. (Your memo will be easier to grasp if you stick to a few initiatives that are *all* effective immediately.)
- Supply your reader with a contact person who can handle questions about the new procedures.

Announcing the Cancellation of the Company Child Care Reimbursement Program

To:

From:

Date:

Regarding: Phaseout of the child care reimbursement program

Effective January 1st, the ABC Corp. will no longer be able to reimburse its employees for child care costs.

This difficult decision was made only after long and careful thought. If competitive pressures within the industry had left my office any other option than canceling this program, I would certainly have avoided this step.

Parents take note: a new ABC program may help you in your efforts to secure quality, affordable childcare. ABC employees may arrange for child care expenses to be deducted from their pay on a before-tax basis and set aside in a reserved account.

Please contact Human Resources for details about this program.

Alternate Version:

Competitive pressures within the widget industry have forced me to take a long, hard look at our company's expenditures. After doing so, I've concluded that there is no alternative but to phase out our child-care expense reimbursement program, effective January 1.

I realize that this extremely difficult decision will not be welcome news for those ABC employees who are parents of small children. I would like to point out, though, that we are simultaneously implementing a new program that allows childcare costs to be deducted from employee paychecks on a pretax basis. Please see Debbie in Human Resources for all the details.

Although the phaseout of the reimbursement program is certainly unfortunate, I'm convinced it is a necessary step in our efforts to put our company on a more sound financial footing, and that, in turn, increases employment security for us all.

DEVELOPING A CUSTOMIZED MEMO? REMEMBER TO . . .

- Make it clear that financial constraints leave you no option other than canceling the program, and that the decision is a difficult one.
- Outline an alternate program—or even an unrelated government program—that may help cushion the blow for working parents.

Announcing Change in Employee Bonus Plan

To:

From:

Date:

Regarding: Change in annual bonus plan

Effective immediately, there will be a change in the computation of the annual bonus payout. Since its inception, the bonus program has stressed departmental, rather than companywide, performance. This policy no longer reflects the outlook of ABC Corporation.

A new bonus program, one that places a greater emphasis on interdepartmental teamwork, has been developed by the Benefits Working Group and will take the place of the yearly bonus plan described in your employee handbook. This new bonus program will reflect overall company financial performance, and has the potential for higher payouts at all levels. (See the summary in your mailbox.) If you have any questions about the new bonus plan, please don't hesitate to contact Doris in Human Resources.

Alternate Version:

This is the last year that employee bonuses will be calculated on a department-by-department basis. A newer, more team-oriented bonus plan will be in effect come January 1. Beginning with the next fiscal year, employee bonuses will be determined by the financial performance of the company as a whole.

I've attached a summary of the main features of the new plan. I think it's very exciting, and I hope you will, too. Hats off to the Benefits Working Group who spent many hours developing this innovative program. If you have questions, please feel free to contact Doris in Human Resources for more information.

DEVELOPING A CUSTOMIZED MEMO? REMEMBER TO . . .

- Explain why the new program is replacing the old one.
- Supply your readers with the name of a contact person who will handle questions about the new program.

Announcing Departure of Department Manager

To:

From:

Date:

Regarding: Larry Brown

Larry Brown has informed me that he will be leaving ABC Corporation to pursue other career opportunities, effective May 1st. During his time here

Larry has contributed much to ABC Corp., most recently serving as Accounting Manager during a critical period in the firm's development. I'm sure I speak for everyone when I wish Larry and his family all the best in their future plans.

Alternate Version:

Effective on the first of next month, Larry Brown will be leaving our company to pursue other opportunities. In his absence, Harrison Barber will be handling Accounting Manager duties on an interim basis while ABC conducts a search for a replacement.

Larry deserves our best wishes as he continues his career in a new setting, and he goes with our thanks for his past service to ABC Corp.

DEVELOPING A CUSTOMIZED MEMO? REMEMBER TO . . .

- Keep the tone businesslike and neutral (especially if there were problems leading up to the departure).
- Focus on the future, not on past problems.

Announcing Scaled-Back Benefits Package

To:

From:

Date:

Regarding: A change in our benefits package

Maria Viejo and I have been taking a critical look at ABC's full-time employee benefits package. We've been forced to make some tough choices, given the constraints within which the company must now operate.

Our recommendations were to eliminate the company dental plan and increase the employee contribution to the corporate health plan from 5% to 45%. These recommendations were accepted by the President and the Board of Directors. They felt, as we did, that this change represented the best approach to the situation, and was certainly preferable to eliminating company support for the medical plan altogether.

The new benefits package is effective June 15th. This decision was, as you know, some time in coming, and it certainly was not an easy one for anyone. We hope you will understand how we came to settle on it as the best path available.

Alternate Version:

After a long, arduous, and difficult review of the available options, ABC Corp. has modified its benefit package for full-time employees. Effective June 15th, the dental package will no longer be offered; also, the portion of the basic health plan supported by the company will be changed to 55%.

These changes come about only after a lengthy period of evaluation that was emotionally and professionally demanding for everyone involved. Although the end result is not what any of us would have offered as a first choice, the new arrangement does leave important benefits intact, and it allows the company to operate within unalterable financial constraints during a critical phase in its development.

Thanks in advance for your understanding of what has been a very demanding decision-making process.

DEVELOPING A CUSTOMIZED MEMO? REMEMBER TO . . .

- Present the new arrangement as the best available alternative, and acknowledge openly that your decision has been dictated by financial constraints that no one enjoys.
- Ask for support and understanding for a difficult, but necessary, decision.

Announcing Scaled-Back Temporary Help Resources

To:

From:

Date:

Regarding: Temporary help

Temporary help assignments must now be approved by the Senior Vice President of your department.

A word of caution: We have significantly less funding to work with in this area this fiscal year than in years past. Please help us operate as efficiently as we possibly can—reserve your requests for temporary help approvals for projects that simply cannot be fulfilled via on-site personnel.

Thanks in advance for helping us use our resources as intelligently as possible.

Alternate Version:

Effective immediately, ABC Company will fulfill temporary help requests only after approval from the Senior Vice President of the requesting department. Overall authorization levels of temporary workers exceeded budgets by 17% in the past quarter; given the current cash restraints and the reduced budget levels for the category this quarter, managers will no longer issue temporary worker authorizations on their own.

Thanks for your cooperation on this change in procedure.

DEVELOPING A CUSTOMIZED MEMO? REMEMBER TO . . .

- Make it clear that resources in the area in question are lower than the readers may be used to.
- Identify who is making the final decision with regard to temporary assignment authorization.

Announcing Shutdown of Branch Facility

To:

From:

Date:

Regarding: Owensboro, Kentucky plant

In order to target resources more effectively in a competitive market, ABC Corporation will close the Owensboro, Kentucky plant. June 12 will be the final day this plant will be in operation.

All manufacturing and support operations in that facility will cease as of that date. Affected personnel who wish to discuss ABC's standard severance packages, or possible reassignment options involving relocation, should contact Jane Phillips in Human Resources.

Alternate Version:

ABC Corporation has decided to close the Owensboro, Kentucky plant. June 12 will be the final day of operation for this facility.

This decision was made in response to the declining market for large-format floppy disks and overcapacity in our other small-format floppy disk plants in Temecula, CA and Del Rio, TX. Production of DLT drives will be transferred to Temecula.

The closure will position us to concentrate company resources on our core business of small-format data storage devices. Personnel wishing to apply for relocation openings to one of the above facilities should contact Jane Phillips in Human Resources.

DEVELOPING A CUSTOMIZED MEMO? BE SURE TO . . .

- Specify the date on which operations will conclude.
- Detail any appropriate reassignment options. If none exist, however, you should not build up unrealistic expectations among your readers.

Announcing the Shutdown of the Company's Physical Fitness Facility

To:

From:

Date:

Regarding: Closing of the ABC Corporation fitness center

The ABC Corporation physical fitness center will be closing effective January 1st.

A study of the center's attendance log has shown that usage of the gym has declined steadily over the past year. Because of this, and because of the financial constraints that face the company in the current market environment, the expense of operating the center can simply no longer be supported.

Ellen Chen is heading up a group that may be able to gain a discount for membership at the local YMCA. If you're interested in joining, please contact Ellen directly.

Alternate Version:

Due to budgetary limitations and decreasing use of the facility, the company fitness center will be closed effective January 1. The center will continue to offer its full range of services and facilities until that date.

Although many of us would have preferred for the company to have found a way to continue offering the fitness center, we shouldn't lose sight of the new and old workout opportunities that exist. Ellen Chen is working on negotiating a company discount for employees who wish to join the local YMCA, and informal company exercise programs—such as the softball team and the lunchtime walking club—are still open to everyone. Sign up now!

DEVELOPING A CUSTOMIZED MEMO? REMEMBER TO . . .

- Specify the date of the facility's closing.
- Outline any appropriate alternatives employees may wish to pursue on their own.

Attrition (Some Employee Departures Will Not Result in Job Vacancies)

To:

From:

Date:

Regarding: Staffing issues

A reminder: Not all vacancies will automatically result in a new job opening. Approval from the Executive committee is required before recruiting can commence on any opening, regardless of how that opening has come about.

Current approved job openings will continue to be posted at the commissary bulletin board. Please contact Dorothy Henderson in Human Resources for more information.

Alternate Version:

Managers please note: Any and every vacancy arising due to a voluntary employee departure must be reviewed with Graham Clark or Vera Nettles before any recruiting effort to fill the vacant position begins.

Transfers from other departments, temporary reassignments, and revised scheduling arrangements must be considered before a new hire is authorized. Many positions that become vacant due to attrition will not be filled with full-time employees during the current fiscal year.

Thanks in advance for your help.

DEVELOPING A CUSTOMIZED MEMO? REMEMBER TO . . .

- Identify who is in charge of final staffing decisions.
- Keep the tone brisk, professional, and to the point.
- Make it clear that there are no exceptions to the necessity for review of recruiting proposals by designated superiors.

Changes Forecast in Work Hours

To:

From:

Date:

Regarding: Change in work hours

We want to help you spend less time behind the wheel!

ABC is considering making a change in the work schedules of some positions.

Your supervisor will be contacting you to go over proposed changes in individual positions. For the most part, arrival and departure times will be staggered to avoid the worst of the commuting delays. Thanks in advance for your input . . . and for helping us take a flexible approach to scheduling issues.

Alternate Version:

ABC Company will soon be revising the company's work schedule to allow employees to spend less time on the road driving to and from work.

For some employees, this will mean a slightly earlier arrival time; for others, it will mean a somewhat later arrival time. Please see your manager for details on the new program, which will take effect January 1, and how it may affect you.

DEVELOPING A CUSTOMIZED MEMO? REMEMBER TO . . .

- Outline the primary benefit to employees of the new schedule.
- Specify when the program will take effect.

Departments Being Merged; New Responsibilities Outlined

To:

From:

Date:

Regarding: Department mergers

Effective March 1, the Research and Product Scale-Up departments will merge. This move will make the most of team members in both departments, and will enable ABC to react more quickly to changing market conditions. Be as flexible and supportive as you possibly can during the transition period.

John Smith, current Director of Research, will assume the position of Director, Research and Scale-Up. Richard Feldman, who has been filling in as acting Director of Product Scale-Up, will be transferring to Del Rio to fill the position of Plant Manager vacated by the retirement of Myra Steward. Please join me in congratulating John and Richard on their promotions and wishing them continued success in their new positions.

Alternate Version:

Effective March 1, the Research and Product Scale-Up departments will merge. John Smith will be heading up the new unified department; he will need your help, support, and input as he begins to focus this exciting new team on its new goals.

Please keep an open mind with regard to reassignments and new duties; John wants to help everyone work to achieve the highest level of performance possible, and in the beginning that will mean looking closely at areas of possible overlap in the new department.

DEVELOPING A CUSTOMIZED MEMO? REMEMBER TO . . .

- Identify the person who is coordinating and overseeing activities within the new department.
- Ask for the help and support of team members during the transition phase.

Downsizing/Rightsizing on the Horizon

To:

From:

Date:

Regarding: Reorganization

On January 15th I will be meeting with all department heads to discuss the proposed company-wide reorganization initiative. Please be sure your schedule is free that day.

I realize the changes being considered are likely to lead to much discussion and speculation, but I urge you to avoid encouraging irresponsible talk. I will make every effort to keep people informed as our plans take form, and I will do so in as prompt and accurate a manner as I possibly can. I expect that we will announce our final reorganization plan within a week of our initial meetings, a plan that will be the cornerstone of future growth for our organization.

Alternate Version:

Beginning the week of January 15th, the company's reorganization plans will be considered and evaluated by the Board of Directors. Final results of these meetings will be relayed to ABC employees as soon as possible, probably within one week. No one, least of all the members of the Board, wants this process to be drawn out any longer than is absolutely necessary.

In the period before the final reorganization plan is announced, please avoid irresponsible speculation or inappropriate discussions with fellow team members. These activities will only make all of our jobs harder. Thanks in advance for your cooperation.

DEVELOPING A CUSTOMIZED MEMO? REMEMBER TO . . .

- Consider leaving this memo unwritten if you do not detect evidence that productivity is suffering as a result of suspicion and speculation about the upcoming reorganization.

- Offer as clear a timeline as you can if you do decide that this memo is in order. People will want to know when they can expect changes to be announced.

Hourly Workers' Schedule: Change of Hours to be Announced

To:

From:

Date:

Regarding: Change of hours (effective May 1)

In accordance with ABC Corporation's reorganization measures, all hourly team members will be working new schedules starting May 1. The Executive Committee has been studying all elements of work scheduling closely. Revised schedules are being posted this afternoon in the employee lounge.

The new work patterns will require a period of adjustment. Please bear with us during this time, and feel free to talk to your supervisor or to me if you have any questions or concerns.

Alternate Version:

A new schedule for hourly workers is being finalized as part of ABC's reorganization program. The new schedule, which will help us all make the most of the resources at our disposal, will take effect May 1 and is available for review today in the employee lounge.

Once the new system is in place, we'll need everyone's help to make it work smoothly. Please bring questions or problems about the new schedule directly to me. I will do my level best to help resolve any difficulties we encounter during the transition to the new hourly schedule.

DEVELOPING A CUSTOMIZED MEMO? REMEMBER TO . . .

- Let people know when the new hours will take effect.
- Tell readers whom they should contact if they have questions.
- Specify where the new work schedule can be found.

Hourly Workers' Schedule: Fewer Hours Available

To:

From:

Date:

Regarding: Change in hours

Our new schedule has been adjusted to reflect an average of 32.5 hours per week per hourly worker. Additional hours will be assigned from time to time, but they are likely to be considerably less common than they have been in the past, and they will be assigned to hourly team members possessing the most seniority.

If you have any questions please do not hesitate to consult your supervisor.

Alternate Version:

The new hourly-employee work schedule incorporates an adjustment to an average total of 32.5 hours per week. Although some workers may be in a position to receive on-the-spot assignments that will raise the weekly total somewhat, overtime hours will not be granted during the company's reorganization campaign.

Although significant variations from the 32.5 hour average are not expected in the near future, you should know that you will be notified when additional hours become available.

DEVELOPING A CUSTOMIZED MEMO? REMEMBER TO . . .

- Offer all relevant information you can on additional hours and overtime pay. These are the issues people will be most curious about.
- Be prepared to handle in-person questions and objections concerning benefits.

Increased Hours Due to Reorganization Plan

To:

From:

Date:

Regarding: Time commitments

The reorganization plan for ABC Corporation will mean longer hours for all salaried staff members. Production management staff in particular (and yes, that includes me) must be ready to commit to extra time when the need arises.

This is, as you know, a period of challenge for our company. I realize that these added hours will require some adjustment by all team members. Bear in mind, however, that our efforts during these times will serve to build a stronger company—and greater job security in the long term—for everyone here.

Thanks in advance for helping us hit our numbers this quarter.

Alternate Version:

This probably won't come as much of a surprise, but . . . .

The current reorganization plan means each and every one of us is going to have to put in some late hours over the next few months. Although this principle applies to all senior managers (myself very much included), it's of particular importance for people in the production management area to bear in mind. We've got a big job ahead of us. It's going to take a few late nights for us to do it.

Many thanks for your help and support during what will be a challenging, but highly rewarding, quarter.

Developing a Customized Memo? Remember to . . .

- Point out, if at all possible, that you, too, will be sharing in the added responsibilities.
- Thank team members in advance for their help during a trying time.

Importance of Overcoming Resistance to Change

To:

From:

Date:

Regarding: Hectic times

The past few weeks have been demanding for all of us at ABC Company. The new initiatives that have been put into place will demand commitment from us all—and they will also require us to embrace change, rather than avoid it. Change can be frightening and confusing at first, but it can also be highly rewarding.

If you need to discuss the new roles, responsibilities, and objectives that have arisen at ABC recently, I hope you'll feel free to schedule time to talk to your supervisor, to Mark Anderson in Human Resources, or to me.

Thanks for your continued hard work during a challenging and exciting period.

Alternate Version:

Rapid changes can leave us feeling confused and perhaps insecure about when and what the next change will be and how it will affect us. I realize we've been through a tough time lately, but please bear in mind that flexibility in difficult circumstances is a key to growth in today's economy.

You're here because we think you can do a great job in helping us deal with a complex, quickly changing market situation. If you'd like to go over any of the new initiatives in our organization, please feel free to ask questions, in public or in private, of your supervisor, of Mark Anderson in the Human Resources Department, or of me.

DEVELOPING A CUSTOMIZED MEMO? REMEMBER TO . . .

- Explain, without apology, that change is part of the current economic environment your organization faces.
- Identify who the reader can turn to for advice and support.

New Space Assignments Due to Reorganization Plan

To:

From:

Date:

Regarding: A move in the right direction

In a move to provide a more efficient and organized work environment, we will be reorganizing many of our offices and work spaces over the next two weeks.

Most of you will remain in the same buildings you are in now, although the placement of workspaces may change A few groups will be restationed closer to the production offices in the west wing of the plant. It is our hope that these moves will make ABC a better workplace for everyone. Thanks for your patience during the transition period.

Alternate Version:

We've decided to make the most of our working space!

After careful study, a working group assigned to make a thorough review of our existing office space use has recommended a new layout—one that will be implemented this week and next. A copy of the new floor plan will be distributed shortly.

Although the new office plan will result in fewer than half of us being relocated to new quarters, it will allow closer contact between the Editorial and Production departments, an objective which has been the topic of much discussion recently.

Ellen Jackson is coordinating the Big Move; if your workspace is one of the areas affected by the new floor plan, please see her as soon as possible to discuss storage and transfer procedures.

DEVELOPING A CUSTOMIZED MEMO? REMEMBER TO . . .

- Detail when the move is scheduled to take place. People also will want to know when the process is likely to be complete.
- Highlight increased efficiency and other benefits associated with the move.

Responding to a Dismissed Worker's Request for Information on Employment Opening

To:

From:

Date:

Regarding: Request for information on new openings at ABC Corp.

It was good to talk to you on the phone again the other day.

Although a check with the good people in Human Resources confirms my suspicion that there's no new hiring going on here right now, I did appreciate the chance to catch up on what you've been doing and what you hope to do next. I'll keep my ears open around here—if anything that seems appropriate to your objectives opens up, you can bet I'll give you a call.

Best of luck with the search.

Alternate Version:

It was good to hear from you again. I hope all is well with you and yours.

I have taken a close look at the company's hiring requirements—which are, as you know, still guided by some tight budgetary restrictions. Right now, I can find no opening that suits your work experience or would point you toward the kind of income level you mentioned. I did appreciate the chance to look over your resume, however, and I'll certainly keep it close at hand for the other hiring managers here to review.

I will continue to keep an eye open and keep you posted if anything appropriate comes along. Good luck with the search!

> DEVELOPING A CUSTOMIZED MEMO? REMEMBER TO . . .
>
> - Respond as promptly as possible to the person's request for information about new openings.
> - Keep the tone open and accessible, but not overfamiliar.
> - Promise—if you can honestly do so—to keep the person informed about appropriate new openings.

Response to Worker's Request for Information Regarding Upcoming Downsizing Measures

To:

From:

Date:

Regarding: Information on the upcoming downsizing

I was glad to get your note the other day. I understand your concern about the possibility of reorganization measures.

From what I can gather, the plan should begin to emerge more fully near the end of this month. In the meantime, I think the best strategy for all of us is to focus on the job at hand and remember Bill's promise about giving lengthy advance notice to anyone and everyone affected by any changes.

I know that doesn't give your team members the yes-or-no answers they want, but that is what you and I have to work with at the moment.

Alternate Version:

Thanks for your recent note. I understand your concerns, and I know you're under a certain amount of pressure to talk to your people about some issues that greatly concern them.

The truth is, though, nothing's been finalized yet, and any speculation about what may or may not be under consideration as part of the reorganization plan just wouldn't be appropriate. If I hear of anything that directly affects your people, I will do my level best to pass important information along in a timely way. Remember, we have been promised significant lead time on any personnel-related decisions. I believe we should continue to count on that commitment.

DEVELOPING A CUSTOMIZED MEMO? REMEMBER TO . . .

- Respond as promptly as possible to the person's note, even if you have no new facts to report.
- Make it clear that you will not speculate about pending management decisions.
- Reinforce—if you can honestly do so—any reliable commitments you have received concerning timeframes and advance notice on personnel decisions.

Restrictions on the Use of Company Facilities

To:

From:

Date:

Regarding: Company facilities: New restrictions implemented

Effective immediately, the ABC Corporation gym will limit its hours to lunch periods and one hour after work. We will also discontinue the lunch time aerobics classes unless we can get a volunteer to teach the course. If you're interested in helping out in this score, please give me a call as soon as possible at extension 2375.

The company daycare center will remain open—however, it will shorten its hours. It will no longer be open for members who work the night shift.

Alternate Version:

Please be advised of the new hours for the company gym and the child-care center, which will be in effect beginning January 1 (schedule attached). Members of shifts who are affected by the reduced hours of operation at these facilities may want to check in with Polly Vinson in Human Resources for information on local healthcare programs and day-care services.

Changes in this quarter's budget allocations have made revisions in these programs essential. If you would like to volunteer to coordinate the lunchtime aerobics workout series, which is scheduled to be phased out during the same time period, please get in touch with Jane at the gym.

DEVELOPING A CUSTOMIZED MEMO? REMEMBER TO . . .

- Highlight any appropriate volunteer activities that may make the closure less difficult.
- Specify when the changes will be taking place.

Staff Cutbacks

To:

From:

Date:

Regarding: Personnel

Due to recent financial setbacks, ABC Corporation will be forced to initiate staff cutbacks immediately. You are affected by these cutbacks, and will be notified personally today by your supervisor about the next steps you'll need to take.

We understand that this is a serious step. Several programs have been implemented to aid those affected. Job search assistance programs, health care continuation packages and lists of several certified outplacement programs have been gathered and will be made available to all employees affected by the cutbacks.

Alternate Version:

A reduction in force is necessary at ABC Company. I'm writing this memo to everyone in the company to let people know exactly how it will be handled.

If you do not receive a written notice from your supervisor at this morning's meeting, you are not among those who will be placed on the reduction-in-force list.

If you *do* receive a written notice from your supervisor this morning, you should know that you now have a three-month period in which to take advantage of outplacement counseling services, employer database access, and resume preparation, courtesy of ABC Company. If any other option than a reduction in force were open to the firm, that would have been pursued—but the demands of the marketplace have dictated that we make this change.

We are hopeful that today's action will be the turning point for our company. We hope to be in a position to consider employees affected by today's action as first-preference applicants for new positions that arise at ABC in the future.

Thank you for your understanding and support during a difficult time for everyone at ABC.

Developing a Customized Memo? Remember to . . .

- Avoid making any specific commitments about future employment.
- Follow the memo up *immediately* with in-person meetings with all affected parties.

Chapter 3

Personnel and
Human Resource Issues

The Human Resources department is sometimes the final arbiter when it comes to resolving personnel-related issues. From time to time, though, the department supervisor can be put in the position of being primary interpreter of company policy, as well as mediator and peacemaker.

This chapter offers some helpful tools for dealing with issues that are likely to arise in these areas. Included are suggestions for: dealing with employee abuse of company policies or privileges; handling insubordination and other types of inappropriate behavior; announcing guidelines for everything from hiring to firing; implementing drug, alcohol and smoking policies; handling discrimination and sexual harassment issues; dealing with problem employees; and mediating disputes.

Abuse of Company Comp Time Policy

To:

From:

Date:

Regarding: Comp time

Comp time hours are granted on a one-for-one basis at the discretion of one's immediate supervisor, and must be scheduled at least three working days prior to the desired date.

Taking comp time in advance of expected extra hours, taking more comp time hours than those worked or authorized, and/or "calling in" a comp time decision are not allowed.

Abuse of this system jeopardizes the continuation of the program. Excessive abuses can also be considered grounds for dismissal. Please help me ensure that this system is used fairly and honestly—so it can continue for everyone.

Alternate Version:

Let's remember: Comp time requests must be approved in advance by the employee's supervisor.

A recent check of comp time records indicates that a number of employees arrange for comp time on an "informal" basis with supervisors and then complete paperwork after the fact. There are also reports that managers authorize comp time without calculating the irregular or off-peak hours at all, simply estimating the amount of time due to the employee and giving verbal assent to a request for that amount of comp time.

The system is there for a reason: We need to be able to keep track of who's taking comp time and why. Please fill out the forms beforehand, supplying all the relevant times and dates.

DEVELOPING A CUSTOMIZED MEMO? REMEMBER TO . . .

- Outline the specific unauthorized activities you wish to stop.
- If your memo is intended for more than one person, avoid mentioning the names of people who are abusing the policy.

- Make it clear that times and dates of past overtime work must be specified.

Abuse of Company Leave Policy

To:

From:

Date:

Regarding: Company leave policy

ABC Corporation grants leave, both paid and unpaid, for employee absences that are not covered under normal vacation and sick day provisions. Types of leave available are extended sick leave, family and medical leave, maternity leave, leave of absence, and educational sabbatical. Each category must be used only by eligible employees, subject to the discretion of that employee's manager, acting in accordance with existing law.

Stop by Human Resources for more information on ABC policy concerning all forms of company leave.

Alternate Version:

There's been some confusion about the company policy on extended leave by employees.

Some employees who have used up their sick and personal days have applied for (and, erroneously) received permission for paid leave in other categories, despite the fact that these employees are not eligible for the leave in question.

Extended medical leave is a paid leave program available to those who face serious illness or must undergo medical procedures over an extended period of time. Extended family leave is a paid leave program available to those who must care for a newborn child or an infirm relative. Details on both programs are available through Midge Wallace.

Employees who do not require leave for a real emergency are not eligible to use leave time to supplement sick and personal day allowances. Please follow these guidelines—and see me or Midge if you have any questions.

- Make it clear that leave decisions are not up to the individual employee.
- Provide appropriate contact information or advice on tracking down the specifics of company policy.

Abuse of Overnight Service (Sending Personal Packages)

To:

From:

Date:

Regarding: Overnight delivery service abuses

Just a reminder: Overnight delivery service is contracted as a means of delivering high priority business correspondence and materials to authorized destinations. Company employees may use this service for personal articles, provided the cost is covered at the time of posting.

The Shipping and Receiving office has set aside the time between 12:30 p.m. to 1:30 p.m. for processing personal overnight packages. Please help out by not sending personal articles as company business, or asking the Shipping and Receiving personnel to process a personal package at other than the posted time. If you have any further questions about this policy, please contact Bill Emory at extension 2203.

Alternate Version:

Please remember! The ABC corporate overnight shipping account is for company shipments only. Use of the company overnight shipping account number to ship personal packages may be grounds for disciplinary action.

A regular review of overnight shipping records is underway. Senders will be asked to justify any shipment that appears to be personal, rather than business-related. If you wish to send a personal package and charge it to your own credit card or to a third-party account, please see Bill Emory for details on how to do this.

DEVELOPING A CUSTOMIZED MEMO? REMEMBER TO . . .

- Make it clear that the firm does not subsidize personal use of the overnight service.
- Outline the procedures (if any) available for paid employee access to overnight service.

Addressing a Pattern of Insubordination

To:

From:

Date:

Regarding: Repeated insubordination

I was glad you and I had a chance to talk yesterday. I hope our conversation and agreement marks the return of your usually strong job performance.

I honestly believe we can avoid the disciplinary measures I outlined—by following through on the goals we discussed. Please help me to help you meet those goals. As I mentioned, I have been impressed with your work in the past and I hope you will feel free to see me any time you have questions or concerns. Let's work together on this issue and put it behind us.

Alternate Version:

I think our talk yesterday was an important one, and I hope it leads to a more harmonious working environment between the two of us.

I wish I didn't have to reiterate this, but I'm going to: Failing to carry out specific requests that are clearly within your job description, misleading me about the status of tasks that have been assigned to you, and using inappropriate language in the workplace when I want to discuss these problems, are all grounds for disciplinary action and possible dismissal.

I want to help you reach your very highest level of performance, but I need your help and cooperation. If you want to suggest other ideas that will help you achieve that goal, let's discuss them.

- Use the memo to supplement a face-to-face meeting, not to replace it.
- Avoid taking a harsh, accusatory tone.
- Consider making no direct mention of the specific problems that gave rise to the discussion (see the first memo above). Emphasize what has worked in the past, and make it clear you want to work with the employee to return to those days.
- Conclude with an open-minded expression of your trust in future progress.

Addressing a Single Instance of Insubordination

To:

From:

Date:

Regarding: Yesterday's discussion

I just wanted to touch base with you again about our talk yesterday concerning your public disagreement with Sally over use of the office fax machine. I realize this was an isolated incident, and not your usual pattern. Still, it concerns me. I want to make sure we don't have problems like this in the future.

I hope you'll feel free to come to me first—as we discussed—if there's something that's bothering you. I'm here to help.

Alternate Version:

What happened today really wasn't like you at all.

Your remarks during the discussion about the use of the fax machine seemed to me to be out of character, but they were nevertheless completely inappropriate. If there's a stress-related problem or other difficult non-work-related subject you want to discuss, please come see me so we can talk about it. If there isn't, let me remind you that incidents like today's simply can't be repeated.

- Use the memo to supplement a face-to-face meeting, not to replace it.
- Make it clear that you understand that the incident in question does not reflect the employee's usual behavior.
- Let the person know you're available to discuss any problem.

Addressing a Subordinate's Inappropriate Racial Remarks

To:

From:

Date:

Regarding: Recent inappropriate remarks

As we discussed yesterday, the inappropriate remarks made by you in the cafeteria could have serious repercussions. This memo will serve to document our discussion and the possible consequences of your actions.

ABC Corporation is a company that does not tolerate discrimination in any form. Racist or prejudiced comments, such as those you made, disrupt the workplace and damage company morale. Any more racial comments along these lines will be cause for disciplinary action that may include dismissal. As we agreed, barring any further inappropriate comments along these lines, I will treat this as an isolated incident, one that we both agree must not be repeated.

DEVELOPING A CUSTOMIZED MEMO? REMEMBER TO . . .

- Express your company's position clearly: There is no room for racially abusive language in the workplace.
- Make it clear that disciplinary action will accompany any future problems in this area, and be willing to follow through on this promise.
- Keep a copy of the memo for your records. You may eventually need to document your warnings to this employee.

Addressing a Subordinate's Inappropriate Behavior; Importance of Reviewing Company's Sexual Harassment Policy

To:

From:

Date:

Regarding: Inappropriate behavior in the workplace

Our discussion today reviewing the company's policy on sexual harassment was an important one. Please carefully review the handbook I passed along and come see me if you have any questions.

The incident with Jill that we discussed must not be repeated, and no other such incidents will be tolerated. I value your significant contributions on the job at ABC, but I cannot overlook our company's stated policy of not permitting sexually harassing behavior of any kind.

Alternate Version:

As we discussed today, I feel you should take some time to review the company's sexual harassment policy, which I am forwarding to you.

Sexual harassment in any form is not tolerated at ABC Corporation. I trust the incident we discussed will not be repeated, and that you will take a close look at the negative effects of your behavior toward Jill. Whether or not you believed your remark to be lighthearted in nature, the fact is that it represents behavior I cannot allow.

You've done fine work here, and I see you as an asset to our department. However, I have to let you know that any further behavior along these lines will result in disciplinary action.

DEVELOPING A CUSTOMIZED MEMO? REMEMBER TO . . .

- Express your company's position clearly: There is no room for sexual harassment in the workplace.
- Make it clear that disciplinary action will accompany any future problems in this area, and be willing to follow through on this promise.

- Keep a copy of the memo for your records. You may eventually need to document your warnings to this employee.

Call for Keywords Relating to Qualifications for New Hires (Computerized Resume Search Requirements)

To:

From:

Date:

Regarding: Keywords for resume search

As you know, we're looking for new technical salespeople. We'll be using a powerful new search engine to track down just the right resume in a massive nationwide database.

The only way to use the search feature is to supply particular keywords. Could you take a few minutes to develop a short list of words that reflect particular technical disciplines we should be searching for—in addition to the word "sales"? (See the attached list of keywords developed for hires in the Accounting department.)

Thanks!

Alternate Version:

We're expanding, and Human Resources is implementing a computer search protocol to aid in identifying qualified engineering job applicants. To help us build a comprehensive database, I need you to assemble a list of keywords unique to the requirements of the new positions in your area.

For instance, an adhesives department quality control technician position might include keywords such as "gas chromatography," or "viscosity test." To help focus our recruitment efforts, I'd like to develop lists reflecting all seven job titles included in this department..

Please return your lists to me by next Thursday, and feel free to stop by for a demonstration of this powerful new data retrieval technology.

- Offer appropriate examples, either in the body of your letter or in the form of an attached list.
- Play it safe—reinforce the fact that you're using the list to track down new hires, not to replace existing staff.

Change in Official Orientation Program

To: All Supervisors

From:

Date:

Regarding: Orientation

Human Resources has analyzed the feedback forms submitted by new hires over the last quarter. As a result of the many constructive comments we received, we are making some changes to the orientation schedule for new hires.

Please review the proposed program outline and return your comments to me by next Tuesday.

First impressions mean a lot—let's make ours reflect the very best aspects of working at ABC!

Alternate Version:

We're strongly considering changing our employee orientation process to incorporate suggestions made during a poll of recent hires.

Attached please find the outline of the new employee orientation process we've developed, based on the feedback we've received. If you have comments or suggestions about the best ways to implement or improve this program, please let me know with a return memo no later than the end of the day on Tuesday.

DEVELOPING A CUSTOMIZED MEMO? REMEMBER TO . . .

- Express why you've decided to change the orientation program.

- Let people know when you expect to receive their feedback and suggestions.

Change in Pay Status

To:

From:

Date:

Regarding: Pay status

Congratulations on exceeding your quota again this quarter! Since your arrival here at ABC Corporation, you have consistently surpassed the goals set up for you.

As we discussed, you will find that your next paycheck reflects a transfer to full-time status, and a corresponding pro-rated increase in your base salary. We appreciate all your efforts. Keep up the great work!

Alternate Version:

As you and I discussed during our recent meeting, this pay period will be your first since moving from full-time employment to the new schedule you and I arranged. I've made the changes you requested in your tax forms; accordingly, you will notice some changes in withholding allowances when you receive your check.

Feel free to contact me if you have any questions on this.

DEVELOPING A CUSTOMIZED MEMO? REMEMBER TO . . .

- Explain why the change in pay status is taking place.
- Use the memo to reinforce or amplify points covered in a previous face-to-face meeting.

Change in Paycheck Disbursement Schedule:
Options to Consider

To:

From:

Date:

Regarding: Paycheck disbursement

In response to concerns voiced about paycheck disbursement, the practice of issuing weekly paychecks will end. We now have the option of switching to one of the following disbursement schedules:

- Full payment of the month's wages on the first business day of the month, or,
- Two payouts of 50% of total monthly pay on alternating Tuesdays.

What do you think? Please forward your comments on these options to me by January 7.

Alternate Version:

ABC Company has decided to change payroll services. Beginning on February 1, we will be issuing all employee checks through Baron Payroll and Deposit.

Baron offers us two options for the disbursement of checks, neither of which reflects our current policy of passing out paychecks on a weekly basis. Starting in February, we will be able to receive checks on either the first business day of the month (one full month's wages) or every alternate Tuesday (two weeks' wages).

Which system do you prefer? Let me know so that I can make a recommendation on which payment schedule to adopt. If you have strong feelings one way or the other, please drop me a line no later than January 7th.

Thanks!

DEVELOPING A CUSTOMIZED MEMO? REMEMBER TO . . .

- Outline the specifics of the check disbursement options open to employees.

- Let people know the latest date when they may forward comments to you.

Company Guidelines: Keeping the Workplace Drug Free

To:

From:

Date:

Regarding: Drug-free workplace

We are proud to support a drug-free workplace at ABC Corporation.

If you have questions about our policy—or if you wish to learn more about the health plan, which offers a wide variety of counseling services for individuals who face drug or alcohol dependency in their own lives or on the part of a family member—please feel free to review the appropriate materials, which are available in the employee lounge or through the Human Resources office.

Alternate Version:

ABC Company is committed to maintaining and supporting a drug-free work force.

Use of alcohol or illicit drugs during work hours is prohibited; employees who report for work under the influence of alcohol or illicit drugs will be subject to disciplinary action.

While these guidelines are not subject to revision, ABC also offers programs through the company health plan designed to assist those who want to take action to reverse a problem with drug or alcohol dependency. SAS Services is under contract to offer free and strictly confidential counseling to any ABC Co. employee who asks for it.

- Express your company's position clearly: There is no room for drug or alcohol abuse in the workplace.
- Let employees know how to gain access to the information they need.

Company Guidelines: Policy on Drug Testing

To:

From:

Date:

Regarding: Drug testing

As outlined in the President's Message of July 6, 19XX, ABC Corporation is committed to making a drug-free workplace a reality. Even though the vast majority of the employees who work here have no history of or inclination toward illicit drug use, our current "zero-tolerance" policy requires random testing of employees—including workers at all management levels—on a periodic basis.

You have been selected for testing as part of this program. May I ask that you contact Mary Harris in the Human Resources department as soon as possible in order to allow her to schedule your test?

Alternate Version:

When you signed on as an employee of ABC Company, you agreed, as part of your employment contract, to take part in the company's ongoing drug testing program. You are scheduled for an examination as part of this program this week.

Please report to Mary Harris in Human Resources as soon as possible for information on scheduling your test.

- Keep the message concise and to the point. Even if you have suspicions concerning a particular worker's drug use, do not use this memo as an excuse to raise issues likely to cause conflict.

- If possible, appeal to past (and accepted) organizational policies or initiatives in this area.

Company Guidelines: Policy Prohibiting Sexual Harassment

To:

From:

Date:

Regarding: Sexual harassment

ABC Corporation is proud of its status as a workplace free of sexual harassment, and is committed to maintaining that status. We do not tolerate abuses in this area.

Employees who wish to file a grievance related to sexual harassment may do so by contacting either James Bush or Melanie Tollefson. Upon notification of a complaint of sexual harassment, ABC will review the matter closely and respond promptly, sensitively, and appropriately.

Alternate Version:

ABC Company is firmly committed to developing and fostering a work environment free from sexual harassment of any kind.

Harassment is expressed via lewd language, unwarranted physical contact, inappropriate overtures from a superior that link employment or compensation with sexual overtures, or other offensive behavior. Any employee who feels that he or she has been subject to harassment may record a strictly confidential protest by contacting either James Bush or Melanie Tollefson. Upon notification of a complaint of sexual harassment, ABC will review the matter closely and respond appropriately.

Individuals employed by ABC company who are found to have engaged in sexual harassment will be subject to immediate disciplinary action, up to and including dismissal with cause.

Developing a Customized Memo? Remember to . . .

- Express your company's position clearly: There is no room for sexual harassment in the workplace.

- Let employees know whom to contact in the event that they wish to file a complaint.

Dealing with a Chronically Disorganized Subordinate

To:

From:

Date:

Regarding: Time management

In keeping with our discussion yesterday, I have put together a few ideas that I believe will help you organize your time more effectively. They're outlined on the attached list. I believe the most important is one we've already discussed, namely our daily morning meeting to review your to-do list.

I thought our talk was a very positive one, and I believe it will help you make great progress here. I look forward to meeting with you briefly at 8:00, beginning this coming Monday.

Count on it: These steps are going to make things a whole lot easier for you.

Alternate Version:

It was very good to talk to you yesterday. I think if we work together, we can help you reduce your stress levels at work . . . and help you get more done in less time.

As we discussed, I'd like to set apart a regular time for us to meet to take a look at your schedule and the priority of the various tasks that you're trying to accomplish in a given week. I've now had the chance to take a look at my own schedule—how would you feel about meeting for twenty minutes every Wednesday morning at 8:30?

I hope this time works for you. I think this weekly meeting represents a very good way for us to develop a new approach to time management for you. Please get back in touch with me and let me know whether or not you'll be available this Wednesday, or if we should set up another time.

- Strongly consider a regular face-to-face meeting schedule with this person to help him or her manage scheduling issues.
- Avoid berating the person for missed schedules, unrealistic time estimates, and the like. Focus on the positive; focus on the future.
- Keep the tone accessible and upbeat.

Dealing with Misuse of Petty Cash Funds

To:

From:

Date:

Regarding: Petty cash fund

Is the petty cash fund that is maintained in your work station being used for appropriate business-related expenditures?

Sometimes misuse of petty cash funds arise out of confusion about the fund's intent. If you have any questions on this matter, please feel free to let me know so that we can discuss them.

Alternate Version:

Please bear in mind: Managers who are authorized to disburse petty cash funds must enter the purpose for the withdrawal in the Petty Cash Ledger.

Petty cash disbursements are allocations of company funds, and as such must be handled responsibly. Use of the petty cash fund for inappropriate purposes is grounds for disciplinary action.

- Demonstrate that you are aware of the possibility of a problem. (In most cases, this will be enough to stop the abuse in its tracks.)
- Avoid direct accusations.
- Outline, if appropriate, the administrative safeguards that should be observed in disbursing cash from the fund.

Dealing with a Procrastinating Subordinate

To:

From:

Date:

Regarding:

We need to review the status of the Thompson report.

I know you've been busy, but this project is well beyond deadline. If there are significant problems in wrapping it up, I need to know what they are so we can all decide how to move forward.

Please take a few minutes today to summarize where you stand on this project, then pass it along to me. I want to review this no later than 4:00 tomorrow.

Thanks!

Alternate Version:

Everyone has a lot to do these days, and when the schedule gets backed up, it's easy to lose sight of what's been waiting for action. But the Thompson report was due on June 1, and as we approach the autumn, there's still no sign of it.

I'd like a written estimate of when you think this project is going to be wrapped up. Please get back to me on this as soon as possible, but no later than the close of business tomorrow.

Thanks!

DEVELOPING A CUSTOMIZED MEMO? REMEMBER TO . . .

- Set out a specific next step you want the subordinate to take.
- Detail a time—preferably within the next 48 hours—at which you will review the specifics of the stalled project.
- Avoid using the memo to rehash old problems.

Details of Recent Vandalism Summarized for Superior

To:

From:

Date:

Regarding: Vandalism at the new plant

After having assessed the damage done last week at the new plant in Weston, I found conditions were not as bad as we had first feared. Although a good deal of garbage had been strewn around the plant area, only two machines were affected, and the repairs required were minor. Fixing the damage will not be a major problem; however, insuring that we do not face incidents like this in the future may be more of a challenge.

Can we meet soon to discuss some security proposals I have been working on?

Alternate Version:

I estimate that the damage done to our Weston facility by vandals over the weekend will cost between $500 and $1,000 to repair. Discussions with Fidelity Business Resources lead me to conclude that the damage will not be covered by ABC's insurance policy.

Graffiti, broken windows, and an overturned dumpster were the primary means of "entertainment" for our visitors. I have some ideas on steps we can take to secure the facility more effectively; perhaps we can review these proposals together at your earliest convenience.

DEVELOPING A CUSTOMIZED MEMO? REMEMBER TO . . .

- Summarize the level of damage arising from vandalism.
- Suggest a future discussion of heightened security measures.

Discipline of Employee for Substance Abuse Problems

To:

From:

Date:

Regarding: Substance abuse issues

I am recommending disciplinary action against you based on my knowledge of your intoxication during work hours as a result of the use of illegal drugs.

Please sign and date one copy of the sheet I've left in your mailbox, then leave the workplace immediately. Before you report to work for the next time, please check with Mary Thomas in Human Resources concerning your formal status here.

Alternate Version:

You have been placed on probation as a result of testing positive during a recent drug test.

ABC policy requires that you:

- Take two weeks' unpaid leave, effective immediately.
- Meet with Sharon Young to set up a meeting with a counselor authorized through our company health plan, who will outline the programs available to assist you.
- Develop a written plan of action with your counselor and submit it to my office no later than June 1.

Once you submit your plan, a formal decision on your status at ABC will follow within three business days.

Failure to comply with the above guidelines will be considered grounds for dismissal with cause. This notice will be entered into your personnel records.

DEVELOPING A CUSTOMIZED MEMO? REMEMBER TO . . .

- Do not issue the memo if you are unsure about whether or not the employee is in fact using illegal drugs.

- Meet with superiors and legal counsel before issuing any memo reprimanding a subordinate for illegal drug use. Make sure your company's attorneys have reviewed the language carefully.

Expense Account Abuse

To:

From:

Date:

Regarding: Expense accounts

A discussion with Rose in the Accounting department leads me to believe that there has been a steady, substantial rise in the monthly expense account totals for your department. Inasmuch as budgetary guidelines—and my personal instructions to you—have led to less authorized travel, auto, and hotel use by employees reporting to you, I cannot rule out the possibility of abuse of the system.

Please see Rose immediately to review the numbers she has flagged. I would like to see a report from you on my desk by tomorrow morning evaluating this situation and suggesting a plan of action.

Alternate Version:

An audit Rose and I conducted last week led us both to the conclusion that ABC Corporation has some serious problems with expense account use and monitoring.

Twenty percent of the expense accounts we reviewed did not have adequate receipts or other paperwork. In addition, fifteen percent of the reports we reviewed were for items that clearly were not authorized under current budget guidelines.

Until new guidelines are sorted out, Rose or I will authorize any and all expense account approvals. Managers who wish to issue a check on an expense report for a particular employee should provide an item-by-item breakdown of each expense, complete with appropriate receipts.

- Make it clear that research—and not a simple "gut feeling"—lies beneath your concern.
- Call for a meeting to review the problem in depth, or formulate specific guidelines meant to curb future abuses.

Guidelines for Company Parties: No Alcohol Allowed!

To:

From:

Date:

Regarding: Company party

Just a reminder as we approach the holiday season—ABC Corporation pursues a strict no-alcohol policy at all company social events. (Hey, we're going to have so much fun that we won't *need* alcohol when we get together.)

Thanks for helping us maintain a safe and enjoyable party environment for everyone while we deck the halls.

Alternate Version:

We're going to have a great Christmas party—and we want you to join us!

ABC Company is holding an alcohol-free party this year on December 20 in the employee lounge at 5:15 pm. Please help us maintain a responsible and enjoyable party atmosphere for everyone by leaving alcohol at home so we can all look forward to a safe and happy holiday season.

Developing a Customized Memo? Remember to . . .

- Put the accent on fun.
- Say when and where the party will take place.

Guidelines on Documentation Needed from New Hires

To:

From:

Date:

Regarding: Documenting new employees

If we don't have the paperwork, we can't issue paychecks!

Please remember that photocopies of formal identification (passport, driver's license, or birth certificate) are necessary for us to process all new hires. Questions? Feel free to give me a call.

Thanks!

Alternate Version:

Please remember that all new hires must provide photocopies of formal identification before we can process the internal paperwork necessary to issue initial paychecks.

Typically, a photocopy of a birth certificate will do the trick. See Wendy Chu in Human Resources for a list of the types of identification that will allow us to minimize or eliminate delays, comply with applicable regulations, and keep employee files accurate. If you have any questions on this, or on any aspect of the process of entering new hires into the ABC payroll system, please feel free to give me a call.

DEVELOPING A CUSTOMIZED MEMO? REMEMBER TO . . .

- List the types of identification that will allow the process to move forward.
- Let people know whom they can contact if there are problems.

Handling an Ongoing Dispute Between
Antagonistic Subordinates

To:

From:

Date:

Regarding: Good workplace relationships

Anger and recrimination use up energy. I believe you're each too smart to waste yours pursuing a workplace feud.

The discussion we all had today marks the beginning of a new working relationship—and I'm counting on you both to make the most of it. If there are obstacles that you feel are not being addressed properly, do yourselves a favor: Take some time out and *listen* to what the other person has to say . . . before you launch an attack.

I'm confident both of you are ready to do what it takes to work harmoniously together—and to improve performance in your department.

Alternate Version:

I want to take this opportunity to remind both of you of the importance of acting on the suggestions we discussed earlier today to develop a more harmonious working relationship.

You can substantially minimize instances of conflict by:

- repeating the key points of the other person's message before responding;
- committing difficult problems to paper for later review, giving yourselves a "cooling-off" period; and
- working together to develop at least three viable alternatives for action before referring a question to me.

These steps will help you to move forward to higher levels of productivity and job satisfaction. I'm counting on you both to follow through on these three points as we discussed them.

DEVELOPING A CUSTOMIZED MEMO? REMEMBER TO . . .

- Use the memo you write as a complement to an in-person meeting with the principals, not a replacement for it.
- Avoid "if-there's-a-problem-come-and-see-me-about-it" formulations— unless you're willing to referee the Fight of the Century on an ongoing basis!

Importance of Completing Required Forms

To:

From:

Date:

Regarding: Forms

Just a reminder: Please complete all necessary forms when processing orders for the new Gizmo system. If any information is missing, it may not be possible for us to finalize new orders. Nobody, after all, wants to keep customers waiting—or go through the same order request twice!

When in doubt, make use of the Gizmo checklist you received earlier this quarter—and then doublecheck the form you're filling out for accuracy.

Thanks!

Alternate Version:

A modest investment of time and attention will pay off handsomely when it comes to filling out the paperwork related to the new Gizmo system.

By completing all the spaces requesting information, and doublechecking all your entries for accuracy before you pass along your request, you'll reduce delivery delays to our customers and help us customize new Gizmo options we hope to offer in the near future. You'll also save yourself a lot of time.

Thanks for getting us the facts we need to serve everyone better!

DEVELOPING A CUSTOMIZED MEMO? REMEMBER TO . . .

- Highlight the benefits of filling out appropriate paperwork—reduced delay to customers, for instance, or less time spent in bureaucratic gridlock.
- Thank your reader for his or her help and attention.

Information Not Yet Received
for Processing New Hire

To:

From:

Date:

Regarding: Information still needed for Paulo Rosa's records

I'm still missing the information I need to process Paulo Rosa's entry to the payroll system.

Time is marching on! Can you please check in with him today and let him know I need all the items on the enclosed list as soon as possible in order to process his first paycheck?

Thanks!

Alternate Version:

I still have not received Paulo Rosa's employment records. Can I get them today?

He will not receive his paycheck nor any of his benefit packages until my files can be completed. I understand there have been lots of new hires lately, and things must be hectic for you right now. But payday is coming up soon, and I know we don't want Mr. Rosa to have to wait for his first check.

Thanks!

> DEVELOPING A CUSTOMIZED MEMO? REMEMBER TO . . .
>
> - Isolate an impending deadline (say, today) that makes sense given your current time constraints (say, getting this week's payroll out).
> - Thank the person for his or her attention.

Informing Subordinate Pay Calculations are Correct

To:

From:

Date:

Regarding: Pay question

I have reviewed your pay rate as you requested. My calculations show that your current compensation is in fact correct—assuming 30 days (rather than 4 weeks, as I think your numbers may have reflected). But thanks for doublechecking!

If you would like to review the calculations with me please feel free to see me at your earliest convenience.

Alternate Version:

I had the chance to look over your pay stub; it's correct, but I think I understand where the misunderstanding arose. If I understand your calculations, you assumed that a month's worth of compensation should be equal to four weeks of pay. But there are actually slightly more than four weeks in the "average" month—if there is such a thing around here.

Anyway, it looks like everything checks out.

DEVELOPING A CUSTOMIZED MEMO? REMEMBER TO . . .

- Tactfully isolate the mathematical wrong corner your reader appears to have taken.
- Keep the tone nonconfrontational.

Informing Subordinate that Disciplinary Action is Imminent

To:

From:

Date:

Regarding: Disciplinary action will be taken

As I discussed with you yesterday and the week of January 1, 19XX, your attitude toward your fellow staff members has been unacceptable. This morning, despite the warnings, I heard you make several abusive and insulting comments to Ellen in the employee lounge.

This is the second official notice concerning your inappropriate language and attitude. If this problem persists I will be forced to put you on suspension.

Alternate Version:

This confirms our discussion this morning about your remarks to Ellen and others in Customer Service.

We need to find a way for you to develop a less antagonistic style of communication, and we need to do it now. I look forward to your proposed suggestions at our morning meeting in my office tomorrow; in the meantime, please remember that future irresponsible and inappropriate language will result in disciplinary action.

DEVELOPING A CUSTOMIZED MEMO? REMEMBER TO . . .

- Issue the memo only as a last resort—and be ready to follow through on any threats you make.
- Base your memo, if at all possible, on conversations or interactions you yourself have observed.
- Beware of using direct quotes in your memos—you may find yourself lured into a game of "I didn't say that."

Issuing a Job-in-Jeopardy Notice for Habitual Tardiness

To:

From:

Date:

Regarding: Warning: Job in jeopardy

Even after repeated written warnings and three private counseling sessions you continue to arrive late for work. The average is now four work days out of five.

If there is one more instance of this abuse of trust, I will be forced to terminate your association with this company.

I will be available to discuss this matter with you anytime today.

Alternate Version:

Your job is in jeopardy.

Your continued late arrival in the mornings has been the topic of many discussions between us. Even a series of written warnings appears not to have made it clear that ABC Corporation takes prompt morning arrival very seriously.

If there isn't an immediate, permanent change in this area, I will be forced to begin termination procedures.

DEVELOPING A CUSTOMIZED MEMO? REMEMBER TO . . .

- Issue the memo only as a last resort—and be ready to follow through on any threats you make.
- Combine the memo with a face-to-face meeting outlining the seriousness of the situation.
- Follow your organization's policies for procedural and legal protection in pre-termination situations.

Issuing a Job-in-Jeopardy Notice for Habitual Early Departure

To:

From:

Date:

Regarding: Warning: Job in jeopardy

I assumed after our many meetings on the topic—November 17, 19XX, December 14, XX, and January 3, 19XX—that you understood the importance of remaining at work until the end of your designated shift.

To assure you of the seriousness of this warning, I must tell you now that one more early departure not caused by a legitimate emergency will result in your termination.

Please remember: We must all abide by the same guidelines.

Alternate Version:

Despite repeated meetings between the two of us on the subject (the most recent of which took place on January 4th), you ignored the company regulations on departure times and left work without permission yesterday at 4:15 rather than 5:00.

This morning I confirmed with you that no emergency prompted your early departure.

This is the sixteenth documented instance of unauthorized early departure on your part. Please consider this memo your formal notice that a single additional early departure without permission will lead directly to your termination with cause.

DEVELOPING A CUSTOMIZED MEMO? REMEMBER TO . . .

- Issue the memo only as a last resort—and be ready to follow through on any threats you make.
- Combine the memo with a face-to-face meeting outlining the seriousness of the situation.
- Follow your organization's policies for procedural and legal protection in pre-termination situations.

Issuing a Job-in-Jeopardy Notice for Poor Performance

To:

From:

Date:

Regarding: Warning: Job in jeopardy

After three counseling sessions and repeated written notices over a period of four months, your batch processing speed remains at 25% of quota.

I will be forced to terminate your association with ABC Corporation if you cannot show significant improvement in this area by the end of next week. I strongly suggest that you meet with me at 4:00 today to discuss strategies for improving your performance.

Alternate Version:

This memo constitutes your formal notice that your job is in jeopardy. One week from today, I will review your work levels. The following performance standards will determine whether or not you continue at ABC beyond that point.

- One week from today, you need to have averaged no fewer than sixteen batches entered per hour over five work days, starting today. (The department average is eighteen batches entered per hour.)
- One week from today, you need to have averaged no more than a three percent error entry rate based on random sample methods. (The departmental average is one and one-half percent.)
- One week from today, you need to have accurately completed logs reflecting the totals and relevant time information requested about your work for each day. As you know, all members of the department are required to file these logs before punching out for the day.

If you meet these targets by the end of next week, you will still have a job at ABC Company. If you don't, your connection to the company will conclude on Friday, January 30th, at the close of business.

DEVELOPING A CUSTOMIZED MEMO? REMEMBER TO . . .

- Issue the memo only as a last resort—and be ready to follow through on any threats you make.
- Combine the memo with a face-to-face meeting outlining the seriousness of the situation.
- Follow your organization's policies for procedural and legal protection in pre-termination steps.

Lunch Periods that Run Beyond Allotted Time

To:

From:

Date:

Regarding: Lunch hour

A friendly reminder: Barring emergencies (or unusual situations preapproved by your supervisor) lunch hour starts promptly at twelve and ends promptly at one. This is a fair standard, and it's one I need everyone to observe.

Thanks in advance for your cooperation.

Alternate Version:

Yesterday, seven people returned from lunch at 1:20 or later. Similar problems have been reported for most of this month. I know the weather is nice, but I must still ask you to follow our policy on lunchbreak periods.

Unless there's prior approval from one's supervisor, the hour between noon and one is the time we break for lunch. ABC respects your right to your time during this period by not scheduling any work-related activities for employees . . . other than front-desk personnel who work irregular shifts to cover the lunch hour. Please respect them—and our organization's standard for promptness—by returning at one sharp.

DEVELOPING A CUSTOMIZED MEMO? REMEMBER TO . . .

- Identify the organization's formal, accepted lunch period.
- Make appropriate allowance for unusual situations and emergencies.

New Smoking Policy

To:

From:

Date:

Regarding: New company policy on smoking

With the exception of the area outside the employee dining room and the canopied area near the front entrance of the building, ABC Corporation is now a smoke-free work environment.

Persons wishing to smoke in these designated areas should check with a supervisor regarding the guidelines for cigarette breaks.

Thanks for smoking *only* in authorized outdoor areas.

Alternate Version:

Effective immediately, ABC Corporation will limit smoking to designated outdoor areas only. Please see your supervisor for details on our policy regarding scheduling cigarette breaks.

Absolutely no smoking will be permitted in the building under any circumstances!

Developing a Customized Memo? Remember to . . .

- Specify, if appropriate to your setting, the company's formal policy on obtaining permission for cigarette breaks.
- Describe where smoking is permitted.

Overview of Company Probationary Period

To:

From:

Date:

Regarding: Probation period

Welcome to the company! I wanted to clear up a matter some new employees have asked about; it's covered in detail on page 16 of the current employee handbook. As I mentioned during our recent telephone conversation, all new staff members are subject to a three-month probationary period.

At the end of this time you will be notified of your status by your supervisor, who will provide you with your first formal written review. During this probationary period, all new hires fall under the category of "temporary contract assignment."

If you have any questions on this policy, please don't hesitate to contact me.

Alternate Version:

You may have noticed that your formal pay-assignment status, describes your position as "temporary contract assignment." This is a standard designation for every employee hired into a position that results in full-time work with our company.

For the first ninety days of your employment here, you are working under probation. At the conclusion of that period, your supervisor will issue her first written review of your performance at ABC, and will make a recommendation concerning your full-time status.

Of course, I have every confidence that your first ninety days here will come off without a hitch. If you have any questions on the probationary period policy, please don't hesitate to talk to me or to your supervisor.

DEVELOPING A CUSTOMIZED MEMO? REMEMBER TO . . .

- Explain, if appropriate, that the standard is applicable to all new hires.
- Let the person know whom to contact with questions about the probationary period.

Request for Justification of Expense from a Subordinate

To:

From:

Date:

Regarding: Your last expense report

I need more information about some of the items you've claimed for reimbursement on your expense report.

The large number of "miscellaneous" charges is confusing to me. Can you itemize these more specifically? I'm putting a hold on this request until we have the chance to go over this.

Alternate Version:

Some of the items you listed on your expense report don't make sense to me.

I've issued authorization for the majority of the items you listed, and a check for $234.75 will be released to you this week. However, the charges you listed as "miscellaneous"—totaling $119.54—seem to me to need a little more detail. Some of the items in this category feature receipts, but no descriptions; others are identified, but are missing the receipts. Can you file a revised expense request that supplies the missing items?

DEVELOPING A CUSTOMIZED MEMO? REMEMBER TO . . .

- Specify, where applicable, which expenses have been approved for reimbursement.
- Alternatively, if the entire amount requested appears to require more explanation, make that clear to the reader.

Responding to a Complaint of Sexual Harassment

To:

From:

Date:

Regarding: Your letter of June 10, 19XX

This is just a note to let you know that I received, and was deeply concerned by, the allegations in your letter of the tenth. ABC has a strong and rigidly enforced policy prohibiting sexual harassment in the workplace; it also has a tradition of fairness that requires an objective review, by a neutral third party, of all such allegations.

I will be in touch very shortly to let you know the status of the review concerning your complaint.

Alternate Version:

I received the letter you wrote outlining the potentially serious problems that have arisen in your relationship with your superior, Mel Dennehy.

Our organization is one in which inappropriate behavior on the part of a superior will not be tolerated. I want you to know that ABC Corporation takes accusations of sexual harassment very seriously indeed, and that the incidents you outline will be reviewed promptly, objectively, and professionally. You may expect to hear from this office no later than July 1 on the status of your appeal.

DEVELOPING A CUSTOMIZED MEMO? REMEMBER TO . . .

- Consider contacting legal counsel for advice on how to proceed.
- Acknowledge receipt of the letter immediately.
- Outline the steps you are taking to review the specifics of the person's complaint.
- Demonstrate that you take the complaint seriously.
- Make no judgment concerning the truth or falsehood of accusations that have not yet been reviewed.

Revision of Company Employee Handbook

To:

From:

Date:

Regarding: Employee handbook

You will soon be receiving a new copy of ABC Corporation's Employee Handbook. It has been revised throughout, but it incorporates some particularly important changes regarding the role of the company ombudsman and the use of certain off-site facilities. Please discard the old edition of the Handbook and replace it with the current version.

Alternate Version:

Enclosed please find a new copy of the Employee Handbook. Please note that Chapter Six has been revised to reflect recent changes in the operating hours of certain company facilities, and that the section on the ombudsman's role has been expanded significantly to address concerns raised in recent months.

Please replace your old edition of the handbook with this one.

Developing a Customized Memo? Remember to . . .

- Point out which portions of the handbook are new.
- Remind employees to get rid of outdated handbooks.

Subordinate Sleeping on the Job

To:

From:

Date:

Regarding: On the job alertness

As you know from our conversation yesterday, I'm concerned about your well-being and safety (and, of course, the level of your work performance), since you're tired enough to fall asleep in your cubicle. I was more than a little anxious about your drive home last night!

Please contact me if we need to review your schedule again. In the meantime, I need your assurance that you'll use a sick or personal day if you're too tired to come in to work.

Alternate Version:

I realize that this has been an unusual week for you, what with the family commitments you've made, and I certainly accept your promise that the "nap" incident won't be repeated. All the same, I wanted to drop you a note to suggest that, the next time you find yourself stretched too thin because of unusual outside events, you talk to me about taking a personal day—or arrange for other time off so you can get your bearings.

Is it a deal?

DEVELOPING A CUSTOMIZED MEMO? REMEMBER TO . . .

- Take a concerned, helpful tone.
- Avoid accusations or threats (especially if the incident is a first-time occurrence).
- Use the memo as a follow-up to an in-person meeting on the subject.

Suggesting an Employee Take Advantage of a Stress-Reduction Program

To:

From:

Date:

Regarding: An upcoming program

Yesterday, after our discussion about stress on the job, I promised to follow up with any interesting articles or seminar listings I was able to track down. I found one you might want to consider.

I'm strongly considering attending the "Managing Workplace Stress" seminar next month that's outlined in this brochure—would you consider going along with me?

Alternate Version:

What's the meaning of life?

Is there consciousness after death?

How do you pick a winning lottery ticket?

Is there anything to be done about workplace stress?

How can you track down the answers to big questions like these? Well, on three out of four of the above questions, I came up empty. On the last one, though, I had something of a brainstorm that I thought people might be interested in.

The enclosed pamphlet on "Managing Workplace Stress" looks intriguing to me, and I thought I'd pass it along to anyone and everyone given to pondering the elusive answers to life's seemingly impenetrable questions.

Developing a Customized Memo? Remember to . . .

- Take a gentle, tactful approach (by, for instance, offering to attend a seminar yourself, or pointing out a program of general interest).
- Consider using appropriate humor, as in the second example.

Summarizing, for Superior, Details of Recent Theft

To:

From:

Date:

Regarding: The recent theft of September 2, 19XX

The most recent report from the local authorities on the theft of our equipment indicates that this incident was of one of many robberies occurring on the same evening.

According to the police, significant leads have been uncovered, and they hope to make an arrest by the end of next week. I have been promised by Detective Steele that I will be kept informed on this score; I'll keep you posted.

Alternate Version:

The recent robbery at our warehouse resulted in an estimated $4,200 inventory loss. I've developed an itemized list for the insurance people (see attached summary), and will pass along information on property damage to the facility as soon as I receive it.

The police have informed me that there were two other robberies of local businesses on the same night, presumably by the same "perps." I assured them that we were very interested in filing charges if they track down the people responsible for the break-in.

I'll keep you posted.

Developing a Customized Memo? Remember to . . .

- Pass along all appropriate information arising from police investigation.
- Make a commitment to pass along new information as it becomes available.

Unauthorized Presence on Restricted Site Without Manager

To:

From:

Date:

Regarding: Restricted facilities

Please remember: The temporary structure located behind the parking lot is a confidential research facility open only to authorized personnel. ABC Corporation has a contractual obligation to maintain internal security over this area.

Those who work in this facility should continue to store all confidential materials properly at the conclusion of the workday—and . . .

- Be sure the door is securely locked whenever there is no one inside the facility.
- Keep an eye out for unauthorized personnel who may stray near the building out of curiosity.

Thanks in advance for your help on this.

Alternate Version:

If you're reading this, it's because you're one of a very few managers with access to the temporary work structure behind the parking lot. Please bear in mind: As long as the Acme project is being researched, this site is *not* open to all ABC team members.

Last week, several of our employees disregarded the posted signs and began to make their way through the research workplace with no manager present. James Burton noticed their presence on-site and asked them to leave; fortunately, all confidential materials had been properly stored before this incident occurred.

Our agreement with Acme Company requires that only senior managers who have signed a confidentiality agreement be granted access to this facility! Thanks for helping us follow through on this commitment.

DEVELOPING A CUSTOMIZED MEMO? REMEMBER TO . . .

- Clearly identify the site that is restricted.
- Stress the importance of existing commitments to confidentiality and security.

Unauthorized Purchases

To:

From:

Date:

Regarding: Unauthorized purchases

Your use of the company credit card to purchase a new set of posters for the employee lounge was not discussed with me or any other manager.

I need a commitment from you that this type of expenditure will not be repeated. Can I count on you to review these matters with me in the future?

Alternate Version:

Unless I'm mistaken, you and I never discussed the recent purchase of posters for the employee lounge.

Leaving aside for the moment the fact that the employee lounge already had a set of decorative posters, I want to remind you that purchasing authority under the company credit card is strictly limited to purchases previously authorized in writing. The posters cannot now be returned, but I would like you to understand that no further abuses of this kind will be tolerated.

Developing a Customized Memo? Remember to . . .

- Keep the tone brisk and to the point.
- Make it clear that future purchases must be authorized ahead of time.

Warning Regarding Unsatisfactory Performance Level

To:

From:

Date:

Regarding: Batch orders

Is there a problem we should discuss? I've been reviewing your performance levels over the past three months, and I've noticed your output in processing batch orders has declined significantly during that time.

I'd like to get together with you for lunch today about ways we can work together to help you get back to the level of performance that will stand you in good stead at evaluation time. Are you free?

Alternate Version:

My records indicate that, over the past three months, your input speed has fallen an average of fifteen percent a month.

This trend represents a serious and continuing performance problem on your part, and I want to talk to you in person about the reasons that may be behind it. Although this memo doesn't constitute a formal job-in-jeopardy notice, you should know that if I don't see marked improvement in your performance soon, I'll have no option but to issue such a notice.

Can we get together tomorrow morning at 8:30 to review your work?

DEVELOPING A CUSTOMIZED MEMO? REMEMBER TO . . .

- Clearly identify the quantifiable area of work performance that is slipping.
- Avoid generalities (such as "You're going to have to develop into a better team player").
- Offer one-on-one help and try to schedule a face-to-face meeting to help the person improve.

Warning Subordinate About On-the-Job Alcohol Consumption (and Possible Loss of Job)

To:

From:

Date:

Regarding: A warning

Yesterday, I received word that you had consumed alcohol on the premises and reported for work while under the influence. This is a serious breach of company policy that cannot be repeated.

I have forwarded information on treatment programs you may want to consider in dealing with alcohol abuse, and would like to discuss these programs with you today. In the meantime, please consider this your warning that future incidents of this kind will place your job in jeopardy.

Alternate Version:

We've got a problem, and you have to decide what we're going to do about it.

Consumption of alcohol on the premises—and being intoxicated in the workplace—are grounds for dismissal at ABC Corporation. We should talk immediately about the treatment programs available to you under the company health plan. If we cannot work together to formulate a next step for both you and the company, your job here will be in jeopardy.

- Offer, if you can, information on treatment programs available.
- Make a "one-more-incident-and-you're-out" pledge only if you are willing to follow through on this threat.

Warning to Subordinate Regarding Chronic Problems of On-the-Job Sleeping

To:

From:

Date:

Regarding: Sleeping on the job

This is your second written notice about the issue of falling asleep during work hours. Further problems in this area will lead to disciplinary action.

A copy of this note will be placed in your permanent personnel file.

The time has come for us to work together solve this problem once and for all. I would like to meet with you today at 3:30 pm to discuss strategies for achieving this goal.

Alternate Version:

The incident this afternoon marks the fourth time over the past three weeks that you have fallen asleep on the job.

This is your formal written notice that such lapses are unacceptable, and will, if they continue, be considered grounds for termination with cause. Take whatever steps you must take to rearrange your schedule and ensure that you can perform capably and alertly during your working hours here, or you will face the loss of your job.

I'd like to meet with you today at 3:30 to discuss how we can overcome this problem once and for all.

- Take a firm stance that will let the reader know that repetition of the pattern will lead to disciplinary action.

- Offer one-on-one help and try to schedule a face-to-face meeting to help the person improve.

Warning: Continued Inappropriate Behavior Toward Other Workers Will Place Job in Jeopardy

To:

From:

Date:

Regarding: Insulting remarks

Your coarse language and rude remarks this afternoon to Mark and Ellen, which I heard first-hand, were totally inappropriate. Please do not attack the motivation, competence, and educational backgrounds of your colleagues in this manner ever again.

This is not the first time you have used unreasonably harsh terms in your interactions with others on the job. Consider this a formal warning: future outbursts of this kind will lead to disciplinary action, up to and including termination with cause.

Alternate Version:

Your remarks to Mark and Ellen this afternoon questioning their competency, commitment, and education, were uncalled for. So was the language you used.

As I mentioned to you the last time you made insulting and derogatory remarks to fellow employees, this type of behavior is totally unacceptable and will not be allowed to continue.

I am not interested in a rehash of why you made the remarks you did, or whether or not you considered them to be justified. I am interested in making sure that you realize that any future problems in this area will result in formal disciplinary measures, including suspension without pay or termination.

DEVELOPING A CUSTOMIZED MEMO? REMEMBER TO . . .

- Avoid focusing on the precise words the employee did or did not say. (This may lead to a debate over accuracy that dilutes the larger message.)

- Issue threats of separation from the company only if you are prepared to follow through on them.

Warning: Continued Racially Motivated Remarks Will Place Job in Jeopardy

To:

From:

Date:

Regarding: Inappropriate workplace language

This note marks the second time you will have received a warning not to use racially discriminatory language on the job.

Future incidents of this kind will lead to disciplinary action and place your job in jeopardy. Please do not employ racially derogatory terms in this workplace.

Alternate Version:

If you persist in making insensitive and offensive remarks of the sort you shared this morning during the coffee-break period, you will be subject to disciplinary action.

ABC Company is committed to a tolerant, inclusive, nondiscriminatory workplace. If you cannot temper your remarks and show greater sensitivity in your dealings with your fellow workers, you will face formal disciplinary actions from this office.

Developing a Customized Memo? Remember to . . .

- Consider contacting your legal counsel for advice on how to proceed.
- Avoid focusing, in this memo, on the precise words the employee did or did not say. (This may lead to a debate over accuracy that dilute the larger message.)
- Issue threats of separation from the company only if you are prepared to follow through on them.

Accommodations for Disabled Employees, Diversity Training, Sexual Harassment Policies, and Other Potential Problem Areas

In our litigious world, companies are increasingly being forced to contend with potentially disastrous issues concerning employment of and access for the disabled, racial insensitivity, sexual harassment, and worker grievances.

How do you handle sensitive situations that can adversely affect both employee satisfaction and company performance? It isn't easy, but this chapter may help. The memos here include responses in a variety of areas, from reporting the problem to responding to it. Specific topics addressed include acting on complaints of insensitivity, harassment or discrimination; dealing with ineffectual employees; and implementing diversity training.

Announcing Diversity Training Session

To:

From:

Date:

Regarding: Diversity seminar

ABC Corporation will be conducting a mandatory diversity training session this week. It will take approximately two hours. All employees—including senior management—will be required to attend.

Please check in with Ann Delacorte in Human Resources to discuss the dates and times of these events, and sign up for a slot.

Alternate Version:

There will be a mandatory diversity training session this week. All employees of ABC Company are required to attend.

The two-hour session will take place at 10:00 on Tuesday and 1:00 on Wednesday. Please select one of these two dates and forward your choice to Ann Delacorte in Human Resources.

Thanks!

Developing a Customized Memo? Remember to . . .

- Let people know how long the seminar will last.
- Identify the contact person.

Notification of Status of Subordinate's Request to Review a Serious Problem

To:

From:

Date:

Regarding: Your request for a meeting

I got your recent note, and am certainly willing to set aside time to talk with you about departmental issues you feel need to be discussed.

You mentioned the need for confidentiality and discretion in your memo; certainly, I understand the need for these from time to time. You may rest assured I will give your problem a fair hearing.

Alternate Version:

It was good to hear from you today. I'd be happy to meet with you tomorrow to discuss any problems you think may be important to review in your department.

I want you to know that you can count on me to hear you out on a confidential basis, and to give you my best advice on how to proceed.

DEVELOPING A CUSTOMIZED MEMO? REMEMBER TO . . .

- Retain a copy of the memo. (This is good policy in all cases, of course, but particularly important when you are interested in developing a "paper trail" demonstrating your accessibility and interest in addressing sensitive problems.)
- Emphasize your understanding of the sensitivity of the issues the employee faces.

Reporting to Superior Regarding Complaint of Insensitivity to Needs of Disabled Employee

To:

From:

Date:

Regarding: Volmer memo

You asked me to look into Mark Volmer's recent memo concerning his discussion with Mary Ellen Casey about water faucet accessibility. I've spoken to Mary Ellen about the importance of sensitivity in this area, and the legal ramifications of not providing a way for Mark to get water.

A small table with a few paper cups set up next to the faucet will make the faucet easy for Mark to use, and represent a minimal expenditure of time and effort. Perhaps we could try something along those lines.

Unless I hear otherwise from you, I'll assume it's all right to get started on this.

Alternate Version:

As you may know, Mark Volmer has a physical disability that precludes him from using the company water faucet as it's currently set up. Mary Ellen's recent remarks to him led him to believe that we would take no measures whatsoever to accommodate his disability. Whether or not this was a misunderstanding on Mark's part, I've spoken with Mary Ellen about developing sensitivity in this area. There is a legal requirement to comply with Mark's request.

Mark has suggested that we set up a table with some paper cups next to the faucet. I thought I should talk to Mary Ellen about how we might implement this—and discuss any other options that may be worth looking at. I'll keep you posted.

DEVELOPING A CUSTOMIZED MEMO? REMEMBER TO . . .

- Retain a copy of the memo. (This is good policy in all cases, of course, but particularly important when you are interested in developing a "paper trail" demonstrating your willingness to respond sensitively to the needs of disabled workers.)
- Make it clear that you will make reasonable accommodations to the needs of the disabled worker, as required by the Americans with Disabilities Act.

Reporting to Superior Regarding Complaint of Racial Insensitivity

To:

From:

Date:

Regarding: Mel Simpson

As you asked, I've reviewed Marcia's complaint concerning derogatory language on Mel's part, and I think it's one I should review more closely and then discuss with you as soon as possible.

I am still tracking down people who may have heard the remarks she describes, and I believe I will have enough information for us to go over by tomorrow morning. Can we meet first thing?

Alternate Version:

I've looked into Marcia's complaint about Mel on a preliminary basis, and I think we may need to talk things over in detail once I've put everything together.

Marcia's complaint contains some points that deserve closer review. I'm particularly concerned about her reports of ethnic slurs made during the recent staff meeting. Apparently, these remarks were overheard by at least three other people, although there is no way to tell whether or not they bear any ill will against Mel.

I believe it's important that we talk this over. When can we get together?

Developing a Customized Memo? Remember to . . .

- Request an in-person meeting to review your findings.
- Emphasize the importance of a thorough review of the situation.

Reporting to a Superior Regarding an Apparently Legitimate Complaint of Sexual Harassment

To:

From:

Date:

Regarding: Melanie Vanderbilt

Melanie has filed a formal complaint alleging sexual harassment against Ellis Peterson. After briefly reviewing the situation and discussing it in detail with Melanie, I believe we have an obligation to make a more detailed inquiry, and to get the advice of legal counsel as to how we should proceed from there. Obviously, this is a sensitive situation, one that I have discussed only with Melanie thus far.

Can we get together soon to talk about this?

Alternate Version:

After discussing Melanie's sexual-harassment complaint against Ellis (a copy of which I've forwarded to you), I believe we should carefully discuss how to proceed, perhaps after consulting with legal counsel.

I have not spoken about this situation with anyone other than Melanie; she is interested in maintaining complete confidentiality about the entire incident for the time being, but she does want to know how we plan to respond.

We should take the time to go over her complaint point-by-point in person. Can we meet soon?

DEVELOPING A CUSTOMIZED MEMO? REMEMBER TO . . .

- Make it clear that you understand the sensitivity of the situation.
- Suggest that the organization consider engaging qualified legal counsel.
- Request an in-person meeting.

Reporting to a Superior Regarding Disabled Employee's Request For Accommodation

To:

From:

Date:

Regarding: Jane Whitcomb

Jane has requested that we come up with some system that will allow her easier access to the accounting information on the second floor. As it stands, her only option is to wheel her chair through the loading dock at the rear of the building and use the freight elevator.

I have worked out some ideas that may make things easier for Jane. Can we take a few minutes to discuss them?

Alternate Version:

Jane has asked for help in accessing her work on the second floor without having to use the freight elevator.

Suppose we set up a terminal downstairs exclusively for Jane's use, one that allows her continuous access to the accounting department's mainframe information? If we take this step—and perhaps expand Bert's job description to incorporate occasional trips upstairs to obtain key documents for Jane—I feel we will have gone a long way toward making the workplace accessible for her.

What do you think?

DEVELOPING A CUSTOMIZED MEMO? REMEMBER TO . . .

- Retain a copy of the memo. (This is good policy in all cases, of course, but particularly important when you are interested in developing a "paper trail" demonstrating your willingness to respond sensitively to the needs of disabled workers.)
- Make it clear that you will make reasonable accommodations to the needs of the disabled worker, as required by the Americans with Disabilities Act.

Reporting to Superior Regarding Employee Grievance

To:

From:

Date:

Regarding: Complaint from Ben

We should talk soon. Ben has filed a formal grievance against Josh, and I think you'll want to take a look at it before I proceed. There are some serious allegations here that, if true, raise some troubling questions about the environment in Josh's department.

When can we get together?

Alternate Version:

Ben has filed a formal grievance against Josh alleging improper pressure to work overtime hours on short notice and lack of concern for certain safety issues. I haven't had the chance to review the complaint in detail or confirm its particulars, but I did want to talk to you before I spoke to Josh about this.

Have you got a few moments so we can go over this in person?

Requesting Specific Adaptation for Disabled Employee

To:

From:

Date:

Regarding: Brent's request

After doing a little digging, I've found out that a new set of mirrors for the bathrooms would allow Brent to see clearly from his wheelchair. The mirrors are not all that expensive—$76.00—and could be installed quite easily by Frank in Operations.

Doesn't this seem like a worthwhile expenditure? It would certainly make life a good deal easier for a key contributor.

Alternate Version:

Brent has asked me to look into the possibility of altering the mirrors in the restrooms and the employee lounge; his wheelchair is too low to the ground for him to see his reflection clearly.

I've looked into the possibility of having larger mirrors installed; the total cost would be $76.00, which seems reasonable enough given the daily use of these facilities by Brent and any future employees who may also have special needs.

What do you think?

DEVELOPING A CUSTOMIZED MEMO? REMEMBER TO . . .

- Retain a copy of the memo. (This is good policy in all cases, of course, but particularly important when you are interested in developing a "paper trail" demonstrating your willingness to respond sensitively to the needs of disabled workers.)

- Make it clear that you will make reasonable accommodations to the needs of the disabled worker, as required by the Americans with Disabilities Act.

Responding to Complaint of Insensivity to Needs of Disabled Employee

To:

From:

Date:

Regarding: The matter of treating our disabled staff equally

Thank you for your letter notifying me of the possible discrimination by some of our staff toward those with disabilities.

I want to assure you that such behavior will not be tolerated under any circumstances. Managers who do not comply with ABC Company policy (and federal law) in this area are subject to serious disciplinary action.

I am planning a meeting with all of the supervisors on Monday at 11:00. I would like to meet with you personally beforehand, so that you can go over your experiences and insights on this matter in detail with me.

Alternate Version:

I took your report concerning possible discriminatory attitudes toward disabled employees very seriously indeed, and I am conducting a full review of the matter.

ABC is firmly committed to making its workplace one that anyone and everyone can work in constructively and harmoniously. I plan to speak to all those who may have been involved in the incident you describe, and to develop a full report for the president on what happened, as well as how ABC should respond.

Thank you very much for keeping me informed.

- Retain a copy of the memo. (This is good policy in all cases, of course, but particularly important when you are interested in developing a "paper trail" demonstrating your willingness to respond immediately to a problem supervisor.)
- Make it clear that there is no room for discrimination in your organization's workplace.

Responding to Complaint of Racial Insensitivity

To:

From:

Date:

Regarding: Your recent note

Thank you for contacting me about the possibility of racially insensitive comments by managers at the recent picnic.

The remarks you passed along are a matter of deep concern to me; I am committed to carrying out ABC Corporation's stated policy of zero tolerance for racial prejudice in the workplace. I am conducting a review of this event, and will be in touch with you soon about my findings. In the meantime, let me ask you to keep in touch about any other incidents of this nature that you may learn of or encounter directly.

Alternate Version:

I appreciate your getting in touch with me concerning your complaint of racial discrimination here. You should know that we take any reports of discriminatory activity very seriously indeed at ABC Company, and I intend to conduct a thorough personal investigation of the issues you've raised.

This review will be as complete, prompt, and fair as I can possibly make it, and I will keep you posted on its progress. In the meantime, I want to assure you that no effort will be spared to ensure that ABC Corporation continues to meet the highest standards of nondiscrimination in its dealings with every one of its employees. Please keep in touch on this and related issues.

DEVELOPING A CUSTOMIZED MEMO? REMEMBER TO . . .

- Express your organization's commitment to fostering racial sensitivity.
- Make it clear that you are interested in hearing about other problems in this area that the employee may encounter or discover.

Responding to a Disabled Employee's Request for Accommodation

To:

From:

Date:

Regarding: Workplace accessibility

I got your note about possible changes in the ABC workplace. Many thanks for taking the time and trouble to put these recommendations together.

The ideas you've outlined seem to me worth considering in depth. I'd like to share them with Mark Robbins in Human Resources and develop a detailed response to the points you've raised. I will be getting back to you before March 1 to pass along Mark's reactions to your ideas.

Once again, many thanks for putting this together. I look forward to speaking with you soon.

Alternate Version:

Thanks for your recent note concerning possible accommodations in the workplace.

ABC Corp. is committed to maintaining an accessible, easy-access workplace. I want to share the ideas and concerns in your letter with people in our Human Resources and Maintenance departments and see what they have to say about the points you've raised. I will be back in touch before March 1, 19xx, to let you know what recommendations they have.

I appreciate your taking the time to contact me about this, and I hope you'll continue sharing ideas about how we can work together to make ABC Corp. accessible for everyone.

DEVELOPING A CUSTOMIZED MEMO? REMEMBER TO . . .

- Respond promptly—even if (as above) you do not yet have a formal response to the points raised.
- Keep a copy of your memo.
- Set a date by which you will be able to address the suggestions in detail.

Responding to Report of Incompetent or Impaired Supervisor

To:

From:

Date:

Regarding: Your letter

Thank you for the time and initiative you showed in writing your recent note.

The points you raise are potentially troubling ones. ABC Corporation is committed to a workplace in which all employees, whether managerial or not, perform up to the highest standards of efficiency and competence.

I want you to know that I'm concerned about the issues you addressed in your letter. I'll be conducting a personal review of this situation, and I will be in touch in short order to discuss what I find out.

Alternate Version:

Thanks for your recent note.

As you know, ABC Corporation has a long-standing policy concerning drug and alcohol abuse in the workplace. I realize that you were passing along only informal observations about your supervisor, and I realize, too, that it takes a certain amount of courage to write the letter you wrote.

I want you to know that I will personally take responsibility for reviewing the performance issues you described in your note to me. I hope to be able to meet with you soon to discuss my findings.

- Avoid any opinion concerning the accuracy or inaccuracy of the points raised by the employee.
- Let the employee know that you will be back in touch soon. (Then do so!)

Responding to an Employee Grievance (Negative Answer)

To:

From:

Date:

Regarding: Your formal grievance of August 9, 19XX

I was glad that you felt comfortable sharing your misgivings about the new no smoking policies that ABC Corporation will be putting into effect next month.

While I appreciate the disappointment that may be caused by the new arrangement, I think you can understand that this decision was made after a good deal of careful thought. While I cannot reverse the decision on our company's smoking policy, I would like to meet with you this week to discuss any ideas you may have that will help make this transition period easier for everyone.

Alternate Version:

Thanks for taking the time to share your views with me on the new no smoking policy. I understand that this may be a frustrating time for employees of ABC Corp. who smoke cigarettes.

Although we have no plans to reinstitute an indoor smoking area again in the near future, I do want to suggest that you and I get together to discuss any ideas you may have concerning the scheduling of smoking breaks in your department—an issue you raised—and any other issues you feel may be worth reviewing in this transitional period.

DEVELOPING A CUSTOMIZED MEMO? REMEMBER TO . . .

- Express your thanks for the time and effort shown in developing the formal protest or grievance.

- State clearly what your organization's position is on the issues raised by the employee.
- Leave open an opportunity for the employee to share opinions and insights with you in the future.
- If appropriate, thank the employee for his or her patience.

Responding to an Employee Grievance (Positive Answer)

To:

From:

Date:

Regarding: Your grievance filing of 6/2/XX

We've had the chance to review the above filing, which argued that you were due back pay for the period March 15–April 1 of the past year. Our finding is that there is a gray area in the way pay and benefits are computed with regard to vacation time carried over into a sabbatical from work.

This matter has gone on for longer than any of us would like. We'd never really run into a situation like this one, which I hope will explain the delay in finally resolving this matter.

Our judgment is that you are in fact entitled to the pay you specify. Thank you for your patience.

Alternate Version:

After a review of the above filing, which argued that you were due back pay for the period March 15–April 1 of the past year, we have concluded that, although there is no precedent for awarding the funds you are seeking, there is no compelling reason to deny them, given the circumstances of your sabbatical.

Although this news probably took longer to reach you than you would have liked, we hope that you will understand the importance of looking closely and objectively at unusual questions that affect pay and benefits procedures.

Thank you for the patience you showed while we reviewed this issue.

Developing a Customized Memo? Remember to . . .

- Express your thanks for the time and effort shown in developing the formal protest or grievance.
- State clearly what your organization's position is on the issues raised by the employee.
- If appropriate, thank the employee for his or her patience.

Dealing with Non-Customer Outsiders such as Vendors, Consultants, and Members of the Media

Employees must have clear policies to guide them through their interactions with outsiders. Your team members must also understand that they are expected to act tactfully, sensitively, and diplomatically in all situations. These 60-second memos cover possible problems with vendors, explain how to deal with consultants, and shed light on key publicity issues—like what to do when members of the media come calling unexpectedly.

Directing Subordinate to Obtain Multiple Bids on New Project

To:

From:

Date:

Regarding: Bids on McPhee project

I know the folks at Lanta won't be crazy about any decision we make to change vendors, given the long history we have with them. But the McPhee project is big—and complicated—enough to make me want to get an idea of what other vendors could offer us.

Please develop a list of potential vendors for this project that we can discuss together.

Thanks!

Alternate Version:

I think the McPhee project is important enough for us to try to track down multiple bids and review them carefully.

The people at Lanta, of course, have argued that they're capable of supplying everything we need, and they've made a point of emphasizing their years of reliable service to us. All the same, I think it's important that we get an idea of the pricing and delivery options available to us from other people.

Can you assemble a list of possible vendors for us to review together? Once we have that set up, you can go ahead with the requests for bids.

Thanks!

Developing a Customized Memo? Remember to . . .

- Request, if appropriate, a review of the vendors being considered.
- Thank the person in advance for his or her help.

Directing Subordinate to Sever Connection with Long-Term Vendor

To:

From:

Date:

Regarding: Lanta problems

I'd like you to call Brent Lee and let him know we won't be paying for the latest shipment of widget alternators from Lanta. These widgets contain the same faulty calibrators we discussed with him in detail in March and April.

If he asks, please let him know we're looking for new suppliers. (Can you develop a list of candidates for us to discuss on Monday?)

Alternate Version:

The latest shipment of widget alternators from Lanta contains exactly the same flaw we discussed in detail with them last month and the month before.

Although we've done a great deal of business with them in the past, I don't see that as a reason to continue to do so when they refuse to address fundamental product problems. Please prepare a list of new vendors to consider—and call Brent Lee at Lanta to tell him we will be returning this shipment and looking for a new supplier.

DEVELOPING A CUSTOMIZED MEMO? REMEMBER TO . . .

- Explain the product or service problem that has led you to determine that your relationship with this vendor is not working.

- Request, if appropriate, help in developing a list of new candidates.

Explaining Role of Consultant

To:

From:

Date:

Regarding: Jerry Hopkins's visit next week

A computer consultant, Jerry Hopkins of Priam Associates, will be visiting us next week to help us select the best new computer system for our organization.

Jerry will be asking everyone some basic questions about what we do, so we can find the best tools to help us do it better. Please take a few moments with him to review what you would like to see in the next system we purchase.

Thanks!

Alternate Version:

As most of us know, ABC has outgrown its current invoicing and accounting information management system. I've arranged for a consultant, Jerry Hopkins of Priam Associates, to visit the premises next week to take a look at what doesn't work now—and to help us find a system that does.

Jerry may well have some questions for you about what you think would make life easier for you as you approach your work in the Accounting department. Please take this opportunity to give him the information he needs to help us determine which new system is the right one for us.

Developing a Customized Memo? Remember to . . .

- Let employees know when the consultant will be on the premises.
- Encourage open and honest responses to the consultant's queries.

Government Regulatory Agency Investigating

To:

From:

Date:

Regarding: Visits from state officials

Over the next few weeks, ABC Corporation will be working with officials of the state's Consumer Protection Agency to discuss the design and release of our WidgetMaster 2000 product. Paul Kelly is acting as liaison with the Agency; I'd like to ask all team members who worked on this project to meet with Paul as soon as possible so that he can arrange meeting times with state officials.

Thanks in advance for your cooperation.

Alternate Version:

The state Consumer Protection Agency has asked us to provide information concerning the WidgetMaster 2000. They've also asked for the opportunity to speak with members of the design and marketing teams who worked on this project.

In order to help members of the Agency complete their review, we will need to access files from the third and fourth quarters of 19XX. Please forward any information you have on this project to Paul Kelly, who is serving as liaison with the Agency. I'd like to ask employees in the design and marketing area who worked on the WidgetMaster to meet with Paul as soon as possible in order to coordinate the times at which they will be meeting with Agency representatives.

Thank you!

Developing a Customized Memo? Remember to . . .

- Identify the liaison person.
- Thank employees in advance for cooperating with your guidelines.

Notice: Expect Unfavorable Media Attention;
Guidelines for Response

To:

From:

Date:

Regarding: Media inquiries

Please remember: Ellen Anthony, in our Corporate Public Relations office, is the *only* person authorized to deal with media queries concerning the data protection mechanism in the WidgetMaster 2000 unit.

Any media inquiries about this product—including, but not limited to, questions about a possible recall—should be forwarded to Ellen. She can be reached at extension 2101.

Alternate Version:

There are likely to be some press inquiries over the next few days concerning the data protection mechanism in the WidgetMaster 2000.

All media inquiries on this matter should be referred to Ellen Anthony in our Corporate Public Relations office. Please do not respond to any questions from media representatives concerning this product. Instead, refer all reporters to Ellen at extension 2101. Customer requests for refunds on these items will be processed as quickly as possible.

DEVELOPING A CUSTOMIZED MEMO? REMEMBER TO . . .

- Identify the person authorized to handle media queries.
- Issue the memo early—leave your organization enough lead time to make a difference.

Notice to Expect Unfavorable Media Attention

To:

From:

Date:

Regarding: WidgetMaster 2000 media attention

Sometimes the media is fair and balanced when it pursues stories about companies considering recall decisions; sometimes it isn't. We'll find out which set of circumstances we're looking at when the first print and broadcast stories about the WidgetMaster 2000 units show up this weekend.

Every ABC employee should know that we are doing all we can to identify and rectify any problems with this unit. I look forward to talking with everyone about the specifics of the media coverage our company receives next week. In the meantime, please be prepared for some energetic headlines.

Alternate Version:

We are likely to receive some fairly intense media attention over the next few days concerning the WidgetMaster 2000. I wish I could predict with confidence that all the coverage you see and hear will be balanced, but I'm afraid I can't.

I would like everyone to know that we are looking very closely at the potential problems in this unit. I've scheduled a company meeting on Monday morning, August 3, to discuss reactions to the print and broadcast stories that will have aired by that point.

I look forward to talking to everyone then about how ABC is responding to this matter.

DEVELOPING A CUSTOMIZED MEMO? REMEMBER TO . . .

- Let employees know about issues that will soon be addressed in the media.
- Beat rumormongers to the punch by scheduling an "airing out" session.

Obtaining Authorization before Releasing
Statements to Media

To:

From:

Date:

Regarding: Authorization for written media statements

If you're reading this memo, it's because you're one of the key managers who have been designated as a media contact for reporters seeking information concerning the WidgetMaster 2000.

Please remember that any written statement you intend for release to the press on this matter *must* be approved by the president's office before release. Please pass along drafts of your statement to Bernard Williams (ext. 2403).

Thanks!

Alternate Version:

Just a reminder: Any written statement to the media concerning our WidgetMaster 2000 unit must be approved by the president's office, via Bernard Williams (ext. 2403) before being distributed.

Thanks in advance for helping us stay "on message" during this period.

DEVELOPING A CUSTOMIZED MEMO? REMEMBER TO . . .

- Identify the proper contact person.
- Thank employees in advance for their cooperation.

Outlining Official Company Response for Media and Others

To:

From:

Date:

Regarding: Queries on the WidgetMaster 2000 unit

So—how do you respond to customers, members of the media, and others who ask about whether we're recalling the above unit?

Here's what you should say:

"ABC Corporation is currently conducting an internal review of the WidgetMaster 2000 unit, and has made no determination concerning a recall of this product. Customers who wish to exchange their WidgetMaster product for another model are free to do so, and may make arrangements for such an exchange by calling 1-800-555-5555."

Thanks in advance for helping us stay "on message" with regard to inquiries about the WidgetMaster 2000.

Alternate Version:

You are likely to receive calls and fax inquiries concerning our plans for a recall of the WidgetMaster 2000 unit this week.

Until further notice, the response to give to those who ask about this issue is as follows:

"ABC Corporation is currently conducting an internal review of the WidgetMaster 2000 unit, and has made no determination concerning a recall of this product. Customers who wish to exchange their WidgetMaster product for another model are free to do so, and may make arrangements for such an exchange by calling 1-800-555-5555."

Please use this response in your dealings with customers and outsiders! Thanks.

Developing a Customized Memo? Remember to . . .

- Outline a specific, detailed message that should serve as the basis of all responses to outsiders.
- Thank employees in advance for their cooperation.

Problem with Product Defect: Guidelines on Working with Media Consultant

To:

From:

Date:

Regarding: Verne Preston

You've been scheduled for a meeting with Verne Preston, a senior media consultant who will help prepare you for some potentially tough interviews concerning the WidgetMaster 2000 recall. Are you free to meet with him this coming Monday, August X, 19XX at 10:00 am? We've reserved Conference Room A for an hour.

Alternate Version:

Verne Preston is the Senior Vice President of Maxim Communications Consulting, one of the nation's premier media consultants. He will be on hand to help all of our senior managers as we prepare ourselves for (possibly intense) media queries in the wake of the recent decision to recall our WidgetMaster 2000 unit.

You have been scheduled for a session to review and enhance media skills with Verne. The time we've set aside is this coming Monday, August X, 19XX, at 10:00 am in Conference Room A. If this is not a good time, please let me know as soon as possible.

DEVELOPING A CUSTOMIZED MEMO? REMEMBER TO . . .

- Make the issue "how to deal with an intense interviewer" (rather than "improving your substandard media relations skills").
- Specify where and when the session will take place.

Problem with Product Defect: Guidelines on Working with Regulatory Agency

To:

From:

Date:

Regarding: Working with state officials

Please remember: Only James Collins, Keesha Zaire, Mike Baynes, and Sandra Cortez are authorized to work with members of the state Consumer Protection Agency as they review our release of the WidgetMaster 2000 unit. If you are approached by a state official in this matter, please refer him or her to one of the above team members.

Thanks for your help.

Alternate Version:

The following team members, and only the following team members, are authorized to work with the state Consumer Protection Agency as it conducts its inquiry into the WidgetMaster 2000 unit.

> James Collins
> Keesha Zaire
> Mike Baynes
> Sandra Cortez

If you are approached by representatives of the Agency with regard to this matter, please politely refer them to one of the above ABC team members.

Thanks in advance.

Developing a Customized Memo? Remember to . . .

- Identify the team members who will be dealing with governmental officials.
- Thank employees in advance for their cooperation.

Problems with Vendor: Do Not Assign Purchase Orders

To:

From:

Date:

Regarding: Lanta problems

You've probably heard all about the product quality problems we've been having with this vendor on recent shipments. Until you hear from me that we've resolved the (significant) issues that have arisen in the last few deliveries, I'd like you to make sure no purchase orders for this vendor are issued through ABC. Team members who have questions about this policy can feel free to contact me directly.

Thanks!

Alternate Version:

There have been some real problems with the Lanta organization. Despite our long-standing relationship with this supplier, and despite many attempts on my part to get them to improve product quality, we keep running into the same problems over and over again.

Effective today, I'd like you to make sure that no ABC purchase orders are issued to this vendor until you hear otherwise from me. Employees who want to discuss this further can do so by contacting my office. If you haven't heard from me by the end of the month on this matter, why not give me a call so we can discuss the status of this vendor.

Developing a Customized Memo? Remember to . . .

- Make it clear that no further purchase orders are to be issued until you give the word.
- Let your reader know who is handling internal queries on this issue.

Problems with New Vendor: Business May be Severed

To:

From:

Date:

Regarding: Nineveh Systems

Well, this vendor certainly seemed like the right one to choose at the time. I must admit, I've got my doubts now.

The current slipped schedule is wreaking havoc with my cash-flow projections. I'd like you to contact these people and let them know that if we don't have the units we ordered by the fifteenth of this month, we're going to have to cancel all our current orders.

Alternate Version:

Maybe we made a mistake in deciding to go with Nineveh for our widget input regulators.

They're now a full month late in delivering our most recent order. Please get in touch with them today and let them know that the units we ordered must show up in our warehouse no later than the fifteenth of this month—or we're going to have to cancel all the orders we've passed along this quarter.

DEVELOPING A CUSTOMIZED MEMO? REMEMBER TO . . .

- Specify what you want from the vendor.
- Authorize the employee to warn of specific future actions if the vendor does not come through for you.

Reporter to Visit Premises for Feature Story

To:

From:

Date:

Regarding: Visit of *New York Tribune* reporter

Maureen Soderstrom, consumer reporter for the *New York Tribune,* will be visiting our site this coming Wednesday, August 23, to speak with Ms. Gallaway.

Please treat our guest with courtesy and respect . . . and let the president do the talking for this interview. In the unlikely event that Ms. Soderstrom asks you to comment on any ABC product or service issue, please refer her to me.

Thanks in advance for your help.

Alternate Version:

This Wednesday, Maureen Soderstrom, the head consumer reporter for the *New York Tribune,* will visit our facility to conduct an interview with Ms. Gallaway.

Obviously, it is in everyone's best interest to be unusually attentive to issues of courtesy and professionalism during this visit. I'd like to ask that any questions Ms. Soderstrom may ask about ABC products or services be tactfully referred to me.

Thank you for helping me to make this visit a success for the president and for all of us.

DEVELOPING A CUSTOMIZED MEMO? REMEMBER TO . . .

- Mention the name of reporter and the organization for which he or she works.
- Specify when the reporter will be visiting.

Reporting Changes Suggested by Consultant

To:

From:

Date:

Regarding: Recommendations of Mel Weaver

Mel Weaver of DataGroup has some interesting recommendations on our computer system. He feels we should spend a modest amount on an upgrade now, and hold off on the switchover to all-new hardware and software for another two years, in order to take full advantage of what will be available then.

Let me know when a good time to review this in person would be.

Alternate Version:

Mel has had the chance to review our data management system; he is proposing that we upgrade the current technology, rather than purchase a brand new computer immediately. His reasoning, outlined in the report (enclosed), is that by making do with the existing system for another two years, we can take advantage of much more powerful information management systems and software packages that will be available in the spring of 19XX.

We should talk about this report in detail, I think. Do you want to get together this week?

DEVELOPING A CUSTOMIZED MEMO? REMEMBER TO . . .

- Concisely outline the "bottom line" impact of the proposals (some consultants may be less than skilled at this).
- Suggest a future meeting to discuss the recommendations in detail.

Responding to Request for Information from Government Regulatory Agency

To:

From:

Date:

Regarding: Requests for information from Consumer Protection Agency

You may receive, over the next week, requests for information on the WidgetMaster 2000 recall from representatives of the state Consumer Protection Agency. (Such inquiries are often conducted after a high-profile recall.) Please refer all such calls to Jennifer DiGiorgio (ext. 2359).

Thanks in advance for your help on this.

Alternate Version:

Over the next week, we are likely to receive requests for data on the WidgetMaster 2000 recall from the state Consumer Protection Agency.

These requests are not anything to get alarmed about—it's not at all uncommon for the Agency to review actions such as recalls—but they do need to be handled correctly. Any and all inquiries from state officials on this matter should be referred to Jennifer DiGiorgio (ext. 2359), who is acting as our liaison.

Thanks.

DEVELOPING A CUSTOMIZED MEMO? REMEMBER TO . . .

- Identify the contact person.
- Reassure readers, if it is appropriate to do so, about the nature of the inquiry governmental officials will be making.

Specific Reporter Likely to Call Staff Members: Do Not Cooperate

To:

From:

Date:

Regarding: Calls from Yvonne Hopkins

Hopkins is a reporter from the *Baltimore Eagle* whose career has been founded on attacking leading companies in our industry. She is an equal opportunity antagonist: She hates any and all companies with any connection to widgets.

Her inquiries may be flattering from a certain point of view, but they're best referred to a single contact within the organization. Please do not respond to any of Ms. Hopkins' questions if she should happen to contact our company. Refer her to Bill Harrison in Public Relations (ext. 2543).

Alternate Version:

Yvonne Hopkins is an ambitious reporter with a history of unbalanced, antagonistic, and misleading articles concerning our company (and the widget industry in general). Please do not respond to any questions she asks. Instead, refer her call to Bill Harrison in our Public Relations office. Bill can be reached at extension 2543.

<small>Developing a Customized Memo? Remember to . . .</small>

- Identify the person who is handling any calls known to originate from the reporter in question.
- Consider restricting circulation of the memo to front-desk or reception personnel. (Employees eager to settle some personal grudge with the company may look forward to making contact with an antagonistic reporter.)

Upcoming Meeting with Important Vendor: Problems to Be Reviewed

To:

From:

Date:

Regarding: Meeting with Dan Morrison of Lanta Associates

I've got a meeting scheduled tomorrow with Dan—our sales rep at Lanta—to discuss some of the recent quality problems. Can you drop by at around 2:00 to sit in and offer some of your insights on what we've been running into? The meeting shouldn't last more than half an hour.

Thanks!

Alternate Version:

Dan will be dropping by tomorrow at 2:00 to discuss the problems we've been having in product quality levels in recent shipments from Lanta. The meeting should take 30 minutes.

We're going to need to take a look at the sample units you unpacked last week, and at the checklists we're using before authorizing units for reassembly. Can you make a point of attending this meeting, so Dan can get a handle on the problems we need him to look at?

<small>Developing a Customized Memo? Remember to . . .</small>

- State when the meeting is going to take place.
- State how long you expect the meeting to last.

Upcoming Radio/Television Broadcast on Company Likely to Affect Company Morale

To:

From:

Date:

Regarding: Media Coverage

Any ideas on strategies we can use to counter the possible negative impact on company morale that may occur when the *Loose Copy* profile appears?

I'd be very interested in hearing your ideas as soon as possible. Can we meet on Wednesday morning to discuss this?

Alternate Version:

As you know, a flurry of media coverage on the WidgetMaster 2000 recall is likely to result in some unflattering stories next week. Some of our people may experience a sense of disillusionment after they see the coverage.

Not all of what they will hear is balanced and objective reporting, but I think we'd be unwise to pretend that there are no lessons to be learned from the recall. I'd like to get your ideas on the best ways we can counter any negative morale issues. Can you get back to me with some proposals by the close of business on Wednesday?

DEVELOPING A CUSTOMIZED MEMO? REMEMBER TO . . .

- Set a deadline for submission of proposed ideas.
- Act quickly once you receive them, so that you can have a plan in place that will help "inoculate" employees before the unflattering coverage appears.

Vendor Expects Unrealistic Payment Terms: Guidelines for Counterproposal

To:

From:

Date:

Regarding: Lanta request for payment terms

Citing last year's delayed payments, the powers that be at Lanta are agitating for a fifteen-day turnaround on payments. This is completely unrealistic, and I'd like you to meet with Lanta's senior sales manager, David Welton, to let him know as much.

They want, I believe, to secure a thirty-day turnaround commitment. Forty-five is the outside limit.

Alternate Version:

Our recent meeting with David Welton, senior sales manager at Lanta, has left us at a crossroads of sorts. They expect payment within fifteen days of delivery, and have cited last year's cash flow crunch—during which some bills, including Lanta's, had to be put aside—as the reason.

Payment problems or no payment problems, fifteen days is completely unrealistic. I'd like you to arrange a written proposal setting out our position: forty-five days. If they won't accept new orders under that arrangement, let them know that we're going to start looking around for a new vendor.

DEVELOPING A CUSTOMIZED MEMO? REMEMBER TO . . .

- Identify who the contact is at the vendor.
- Set out the terms you want your employee to secure.

Vendor Has Placed Our Organization on Credit Hold; Guidelines for Resolution

To:

From:

Date:

Regarding: Lanta

I think you and Lance in Accounting need to take a few moments to look at our current cash situation and determine how much we can/should pass along to the good people at Lanta. They've refused to ship an important order because of late payments.

Can we get together to discuss this before the close of business tomorrow?

Alternate Version:

The people at Lanta now say they won't ship completed units until they receive payment from us on back orders.

Can you get together with Lance in the Accounting department and ask him to help you come up with an estimate on how much we should offer to pass along, given our current cash constraints? I'd like to hear from you both by the end of the day tomorrow.

DEVELOPING A CUSTOMIZED MEMO? REMEMBER TO . . .

- Let the employee know who he or she will be working with in your organization.
- Ask for prompt action and specify a completion date.

Vendor Short-Shipped Us; Hold Payment Until Resolved

To:

From:

Date:

Regarding: Lanta

Our order for 6400 widget reregulator units from the above vendor came in considerably short of the mark. Only 3000 units arrived!

Obviously, I'd like to get this worked out before we process the invoice. Can you please put a hold on it until you hear from me?

Alternate Version:

The most recent shipment of widget reregulators from Lanta was less than half of what we ordered!

Our purchase order requested 6400 units; yesterday, a shipment of 3000 arrived, complete with an invoice that seemed to indicate no more were on the way. We can't track down any messages from Lanta on this over the past week.

Would you please put this invoice on hold until we're able to sort this out?

Developing a Customized Memo? Remember to . . .

- Specify the discrepancy between the invoice and the purchase order.
- Make it clear that payment should be held up until further notice.

Chapter 6

Vacation Scheduling, Benefits Policies, Overtime, and Leave

As much as we would like our employees to work for the pure joy of contributing to important company goals, the fact is that a job's benefits have a heavy impact on attitude and morale. This chapter examines many issues affecting employees with which a manager may have to contend. Included are suggestions for handling such areas as overtime, paid or unpaid leave, vacation time, flex-time, salary and benefits, and your reasons for denying specific requests in these areas.

Announcing Flex-time Policy

To:

From:

Date:

Regarding: Flex time

ABC Corporation has a new set of scheduling policies that will allow employees a much greater degree of autonomy in establishing individualized schedules. If you'd like to find out more about working "off hours," or working at home, please contact Penny Vinson in Human Resources (extension 2453).

Alternate Version:

The times they are a-changing . . .

Our new approach to scheduling issues means that ABC Corporation employees have greater latitude when it comes to designating nonstandard work hours, and can, in certain circumstances, win approval for work at home. To find out more about this new program, please see Penny Vinson in Human Resources (ext. 2453). She can bring you up to date on what the new policies are and how to take advantage of them.

DEVELOPING A CUSTOMIZED MEMO? REMEMBER TO . . .

- Briefly outline your new approach to scheduling.
- Let the reader know whom to contact.

Approving Overtime Pay

To:

From:

Date:

Regarding: Sally Watson's overtime hours

The three hours of overtime pay Sally is claiming for the thirteenth of January are all right; she was working in my department at that time to help me wrap up the Peterson project. Please process these hours with her next pay statement.

Thanks!

Alternate Version:

Sally's request for overtime hours on the thirteenth of January may seem a little unorthodox, as her department was taking part in an out-of-state seminar during that time. These hours are legitimate, though; I gave her some work to do on the Peterson project, work which she completed after the seminar from her hotel room and faxed to me that evening.

Please process this overtime request in Sally's next pay statement. Many thanks.

DEVELOPING A CUSTOMIZED MEMO? REMEMBER TO . . .

- Briefly explain the circumstances behind the overtime request.
- Make it clear when the additional pay hours should be processed.

Correcting Error in Pay

To:

From:

Date:

Regarding: Your pay statement of June 10, 19XX

I don't know whether you noticed this, but your most recent paycheck featured an underpayment!

There was an error of $150.43, based on an error in entering your pay status during our transfer to the new accounting system. Please accept my apologies on this; the missing funds will be applied to next week's check.

Alternate Version:

Oops!

A review of last week's payroll records indicates that you were underpaid by $150.43, thanks to a confusion in your pay status arising from our switchover to a new accounting system.

I am sorry about this slipup; the proper amount will be added to next week's check.

DEVELOPING A CUSTOMIZED MEMO? REMEMBER TO . . .

- Apologize for the error.
- Explain when the erroneous payment will be corrected.

Deadline for Submitting Required Benefit Application Forms

To:

From:

Date:

Regarding: Benefit forms

Don't forget: The date for passing in the forms that will allow you to enroll in the new BensonCare Health Plan is January 30, 19XX. If you're interested in changing your current coverage, you must get your enrollment forms to me no later than 5:00 on that date.

Thanks in advance for helping me help you take advantage of the new program.

Alternate Version:

A friendly reminder: If you are interested in switching over to BensonCare Health Plan, the deadline for doing so is January 30, 19XX.

Please fill out the forms that were passed out during our recent meeting with Anna Greeley of BensonCare and return them to me by the above date. Otherwise, I will not be able to process your request for enrollment!

DEVELOPING A CUSTOMIZED MEMO? REMEMBER TO . . .

- Specify the date by which the paperwork must be submitted.
- Keep the tone friendly and nonconfrontational.

Dealing with Excessive Accumulated Leave

To:

From:

Date:

Regarding: Excess leave

You've accumulated four weeks of personal and vacation time so far this year. I thought you might appreciate a reminder about our current policy prohibiting "carryover"—no leave from one year can be transferred to the following year.

In other words, you may want to talk to your supervisor as soon as possible about scheduling vacation and personal time, before your accumulated leave evaporates at the end of the day on December 31!

Alternate Version:

A word to the wise: You've built up four weeks of personal and vacation time—but, under our new human resources policy (outlined last month in the employee newsletter), this time cannot be carried over to next year.

I thought you'd want a reminder, before we proceed too far into the summer, so that you could schedule your leave and use as much of it as possible before December 31. Of course, all vacation and leave issues should be finalized with your supervisor.

DEVELOPING A CUSTOMIZED MEMO? REMEMBER TO . . .

- Explain why scheduling decisions should be made soon—and what will happen if they aren't.
- Refer the employee to his or her supervisor for clearance on specific scheduling issues.

Denying Overtime

To:

From:

Date:

Regarding: Your overtime request

I appreciate your willingness to help out on an overtime basis with the Peterson project, but the project just isn't all that time-sensitive. I don't think the schedule justifies those hours from a budgetary point of view.

May I keep you in mind for future overtime hours that may come up?

Again, many thanks for stepping forward.

Alternate Version:

Thanks for your recent note. Although I appreciate your willingness to pitch in after hours on the Peterson project, there's really not enough time pressure on this item for me to authorize overtime hours. As you know, though, there are any number of projects that do require overtime help from time to time; I'll keep you posted if we need help on such "crisis" jobs.

Again, many thanks for volunteering.

DEVELOPING A CUSTOMIZED MEMO? REMEMBER TO . . .

- Thank the person for volunteering for extra hours.
- Leave the door open for future overtime work.

Denying Request for Change in Work Schedule

To:

From:

Date:

Regarding: Your letter of June 10, 19XX

Thanks for taking the time to share your views with me on your work schedule.

You raise some important points that have given me a great deal to think about. All the same, I'm not in a position now to adjust your hours. I hope, though, that we can continue to look closely at this issue together. Perhaps we can review the matter again at the end of the year, as part of your annual evaluation process.

Again, many thanks for letting me know where you stand on this.

Alternate Version:

I appreciate your taking the time to get in touch with me with regard to your schedule. Thank you for outlining your ideas on this.

Although I'm not able to approve the proposed schedule you outlined, I'm eager to help you make the greatest possible contribution at ABC Corporation. I do think it's important that we continue to look closely at where, how, and when you perform your job. Perhaps you could keep a file containing your ideas on this score.

Let's stick with the current schedule for the time being, and then review this issue at the end of the year.

DEVELOPING A CUSTOMIZED MEMO? REMEMBER TO . . .

- Thank the person for taking the time to suggest the change.
- Make reference, in general terms, to a time at which the issue may be examined again.

Denying Request for Change in Work Venue

To:

From:

Date:

Regarding: Your letter of May 10, 19XX

I wish I had a positive answer to your letter requesting work-at-home status, but I don't. The current guidelines within which I have to operate don't authorize me to let people work off-site.

The outlook may change in the near future, however. Can we take a look at this again at the end of the year?

Alternate Version:

Although I understand the concerns you raise in your letter, I'm not in a position now to authorize a work-at-home situation for you. The number of employees seeking to arrange such working situations is quite large, and I'm afraid the people in Personnel have decided to take a very conservative approach to this issue. My feeling is that we should revisit this after the conclusion of the current fiscal year.

Thanks for your input—and for your understanding of the ramifications of a fairly complex human resource issue.

DEVELOPING A CUSTOMIZED MEMO? REMEMBER TO . . .

- Outline, where appropriate, the organizational hurdles you face in addressing the issue.
- Suggest a review of the matter at a point in the future.

Denying Request for Leave

To:

From:

Date:

Regarding: Your request for leave during the month of August

Even if the time taken were categorized as "unpaid leave," your departure would leave a huge hole in the schedule. I'm afraid I can't authorize this request.

The only suggestion I can make, considering the time available to us, is that we find a way to use available vacation and personal days to allow you some time off. Do you want to discuss this?

Alternate Version:

I wish we'd had the chance to talk about this a month or so earlier. As it stands, the schedule is looking very unforgiving indeed.

Even on an unpaid basis, I'm afraid I can't authorize a request like this on such short notice. All I can suggest is that we find a way to make the most of the weekend time and remaining vacation days available to you during this period. I'm certainly willing to discuss this with you.

DEVELOPING A CUSTOMIZED MEMO? REMEMBER TO . . .

- Deliver the bad news directly and in no uncertain terms. (You don't want the message to be misconstrued.)
- Propose, where possible, a discussion of a compromise involving unused sick, personal, or vacation days.

Denying Request for Vacation Time

To:

From:

Date:

Regarding: Vacation request

I'd like to be able to okay your request for two weeks of vacation in the early part of September, but I can't.

This is, as you know, the busiest time of the year for our department. I'd be happy to talk about another schedule, but I'm afraid September is out of the question.

Can you drop by my office to discuss this today?

Alternate Version:

Thanks for passing along your recent request. I'm eager to find a way to make this work for both of us—but I'm afraid September is one of the least likely times for vacation leave. This is by far the busiest month of the year for our department. We need to work together to identify another start date.

When can we get together to talk about this?

- Deliver the bad news directly and in no uncertain terms. (You don't want the message to be misconstrued.)
- Suggest a meeting to discuss the question in more detail—or propose alternate dates yourself.

Employee Is Still on Probation and Is Ineligible for Benefits Package

To:

From:

Date:

Regarding: Benefits

I got your note concerning health-care benefits; I think there has been a misunderstanding, and I apologize for any role I may have played in it. Your health care benefits will not be in effect until your manager upgrades you to full-time employee status, and, under the terms of your probation period as a new hire, that can't take place before August 16.

If you have further questions about the company benefit program, please feel free to contact me.

Alternate Version:

Thanks for your recent note concerning the company health plan.

I'm sorry if I didn't give you all the information you needed on this. You are still, technically, on initial-hire probation here at ABC Corporation; your benefits package will not be activated until your manager upgrades you to full-time status, and that can't take place until August 16. Once you're entered as a full-time employee on the company payroll system, you will become eligible for all appropriate company benefits, including the health plan.

- Let the employee know when he or she will be eligible for the benefits program in question.

- Apologize, if it is appropriate to do so, for any communication problems.

Family-Leave Policy

To:

From:

Date:

Regarding: Family leave

ABC Corporation offers employees with family obligations the opportunity for unpaid leave to attend to pressing domestic matters. If you'd like to learn more about this policy—which can help you deal with challenging times at home—please see Diane O'Shaughnessy in Human Resources, or call her directly at (ext. 2453).

Alternate Version:

Sick parents—newborn babies—recuperating spouses. They're all a part of life. They shouldn't have to cost you a job.

We want to help. ABC's family leave policy means that you can attend to the needs of the people you love without jeopardizing your job here.

If you'd like to learn more about our policy of providing unpaid leave to employees who must attend to matters at home that involve family members, please contact Diane O'Shaughnessy in Human Resources (ext. 2453).

DEVELOPING A CUSTOMIZED MEMO? REMEMBER TO . . .

- Briefly outline the benefits of the program.
- Let the reader know whom to contact for more information.

Filling Out Leave Forms

To:

From:

Date:

Regarding: Leave forms

Please remember: No leave or vacation period is finalized until your manager has signed off on it, in writing, on Form 23-B. If you need a copy, or have questions about leave, please contact me.

An informal "all clear" from your supervisor is not enough. Before you head out the door, please be sure all the paperwork is in order and forward it to me. Then . . . have a great time!

Alternate Version:

Before you pack that suntan lotion, toss your airline tickets into your coat pocket, set up your carry-on bag, and hop in the car to head to the airport, ask yourself: is there anything I've forgotten?

Please remember: Any and all vacation and leave periods are considered "off the books" until and unless the supervisor of the employee in question signs Form 23-B and returns it to the Human Resources office. Questions? Feel free to give me a call.

DEVELOPING A CUSTOMIZED MEMO? REMEMBER TO . . .

- Identify the forms that must be filled out, or steps that need to be followed, before leave can be granted.
- Let the employee know who is handling questions on this issue.

Guidelines: Overtime

To:

From:

Date:

Regarding: Authorized overtime

Why chance it?

Why take the chance that your overtime hours won't end up on your paycheck? When in doubt, check with your supervisor. If he or she does not authorize your overtime work, you won't get paid for it!

Questions? Feel free to ask me or your manager—or see Chapter 6 of your employee handbook.

Alternate Version:

Hourly employees: Please bear in mind that overtime pay is subject to the approval of departmental managers. If you are working on a project that appears to require overtime, and your supervisor does not approve the hours ahead of time, there is a very real chance that your hours will not be paid.

Play it safe: Get your supervisor to sign off on overtime hours before you do the work!

I am available to help you resolve questions on overtime; feel free to drop by my office so we can set up a time to talk.

DEVELOPING A CUSTOMIZED MEMO? REMEMBER TO . . .

- Let the reader know who can answer questions about overtime status.
- If appropriate, point the reader toward a company resource (such as an employment-related bulletin board or employee handbook).

Policy for Vehicles Leased by Company

To:

From:

Date:

Regarding: Company-leased vehicles

If you're planning to use a company-leased vehicle to conduct ABC business, please remember that two, and only two people per department are authorized to drive these autos: the departmental manager, and one *previously designated* alternate driver. For more information on this policy, please contact me at extension 2651.

Alternate Version:

Before you head out on the road on company-related business, please bear in mind the restrictions on who may and may not drive vehicles leased by the company. In keeping with our agreements with our insurance provider, *only* department managers and one *previously designated* alternate driver may use these automobiles. Both people, of course, must have valid driver's licenses.

If you would like to designate (or change) an alternate driver, or if you have questions about the company's policies on automobile use, please feel free to call me at extension 2651.

Developing a Customized Memo? Remember to . . .

- Let the reader know who may (and may not) drive company-leased vehicles.
- Identify the contact person for information regarding the policy.
- Offer the possibility of more detailed review of the specifics of the policy.

Referring Employee with Benefits Inquiry to Personnel

To:

From:

Date:

Regarding: Your question on dental benefits

I'll admit it—I'm stumped. I think your best bet in resolving the issue of exactly what your dental benefits cover is to refer the question to Cindy Jones in Personnel. She can be reached at extension 2567.

Sorry I can't be of more help here.

Alternate Version:

I wish I knew the answer to your question about dental benefits, but I don't. May I suggest that you get in touch with Cindy Jones in Personnel? She's got a much better background in this area than I do. You can reach Cindy by calling her at extension 2567. She's usually available for calls between the hours of ten and noon.

Developing a Customized Memo? Remember to . . .

- Admit that you don't know the answer to the question posed.
- Offer as much detail as you can on the best way to get in touch with the person who *can* answer the question.

Requesting Leave

To:

From:

Date:

Regarding: Leave request

Something's come up at home, and I need to take time to attend to it.

Legal problems my family encountered as a result of a libel suit we filed some years back have forced my mother to deal with a countersuit. I wish

I'd had more advance notice about the deposition she will be giving next week, but I didn't. She wants me to be with her during this time, and I'm hard pressed to refuse.

I'd like to request a week's unpaid leave, beginning next Monday.

Alternate Version:

There's a family problem I've only learned about recently—my mother has some legal problems arising from a libel proceeding she initiated some years ago. She found out about the countersuit yesterday, and apparently her deposition is scheduled for next week.

She'd like me there for support and advice during this process, and I'd certainly like to be by her side as she deals with this. How do you feel about a week of unpaid leave for me, beginning next Monday? Things seem quiet enough here at the moment . . .

What do you think?

DEVELOPING A CUSTOMIZED MEMO? REMEMBER TO . . .

- Briefly outline the reason for your request for leave.
- Specify the date at which you would like the leave to begin.
- Specify the length of the leave you're requesting.

Union-Related Topics

The presence of union employees can bring a special set of problems. Union guidelines may prohibit a manager from handling a situation in the way he or she would with a nonunion workforce. In addition, actions taken by a union can directly affect a company's performance.

This chapter looks at the impact unions can have, and offers some ways to deal with specific situations. Included are memos on procedures to be followed during work stoppages and labor negotiations; when handling union grievances; when setting out regulations for union employees; and when issuing guidelines for nonunion employees during a union action.

Confidentiality Concerning Current Offer from Union

To:

From:

Date:

Regarding: The Union offer as of February 24, 1996

A gentle reminder—we have entered an *extremely sensitive* phase of our negotiations with the Widget Rotators' Union, an offer we will be reviewing as a group in short order. Any unauthorized discussion of the latest offer from the union over the weekend could be catastrophic.

Do not discuss the offer with any employee who is not on the executive committee.

Alternate Version:

Please remember: All members of the ad-hoc review committee are free to review the current status of negotiations with *each other* over the weekend, but discussions with other employees or outsiders (especially members of the media) are strictly forbidden.

And remember: Only the chief negotiator is authorized to deliver official commitments to union representatives.

Thanks for your cooperation.

DEVELOPING A CUSTOMIZED MEMO? REMEMBER TO . . .

- Make it clear that the present negotiations are sensitive.
- Keep the memo focused clearly on its main point: Outsiders must not be exposed to sensitive information.
- Outline, if appropriate, who is authorized to respond to union officials.

General Memo: Change in Operations During Strike or Work Stoppage

To:

From:

Date:

Regarding: Effective immediately . . .

. . . management personnel will be handling all reception, phone desk, and shop floor activities due to the current labor dispute. Since we will be operating with a short staff, our operating hours will be 10:00 am to 3:00 pm, Monday, Wednesday, and Friday.

Appropriate messages on our phone equipment will inform customers and other callers of the change.

Please check the board in the main lobby for the latest information on work assignments.

Alternate Version:

Due to the current labor dispute involving the Widget Rotators' Union, the operating hours of ABC Corporation will be modified, and a significant number of duties will be temporarily reassigned. A copy of the new work schedule and key assignments is on display in the main lobby.

This schedule and revised assignment list will be in effect on a temporary basis, while we negotiate the current contract with the Widget Rotators' Union. Thank you for your patience and support during this period.

For more information on the latest developments and schedule changes, please check the board in the main lobby.

DEVELOPING A CUSTOMIZED MEMO? REMEMBER TO . . .

- Outline the most important new changes.
- Let readers know where they can find information on recent assignment changes—or, alternatively, whom they should contact.

Impending Strike Action or Work Stoppage

To:

From:

Date:

Regarding: Meeting with Steamfitters' Local will be held tonight.

The ongoing negotiations with the Steamfitters' Local are not progressing as well as any of us had hoped.

As a precautionary measure, all department heads must prepare an emergency work schedule that provides adequate coverage for all essential activities with existing nonunion personnel. Please review your department's operations immediately.

Further changes—including work reassignments for managerial employees—are very likely to be on the way. I will provide you with updates as often as I can.

Alternate Version:

As you may know, our talks with the Steamfitters' Local are not going well at the moment.

There is the distinct possibility that ABC Corporation will be facing a temporary work stoppage from union members in the near future. Altered schedules and reassigned duties during any such stoppage will allow us to continue operations with existing nonunion personnel, but we'll need everyone's cooperation and support to get through this challenging time.

Updates on the negotiations will be supplied as the situation warrants.

DEVELOPING A CUSTOMIZED MEMO? REMEMBER TO . . .

- Acknowledge the difficulty of the current situation, and let people know that temporary changes are on the horizon.
- Commit, if you can, to provide regular updates.

Meeting with Union Representative; Strategies for Avoiding Strike or Work Stoppage

To:

From:

Date:

Regarding: Upcoming contract negotiations

The upcoming negotiations with the Widget Rotators' Union this weekend take place at an unfortunate time for our firm. The revenue situation we face requires that we make every possible effort to avoid a plant shutdown. We must, of course, make the best deal possible—but we must also strive to bring the talks to a successful conclusion for both sides.

I'd like your reactions to the attached strategies for developing a workable agreement with the union. Please remember that these notes are confidential, and should not be distributed to anyone.

Alternate Version:

Attached please find a confidential list of concessions that the Board of Directors has prepared, as well as a series of strategies for timing the offers. We believe that judicious negotiations carried out along these lines should result in a new agreement with the Union. Please review the attached summaries carefully—keeping in mind at all times that they are strictly confidential—and contact me if you have any questions concerning the strategy and objectives of the upcoming talks.

DEVELOPING A CUSTOMIZED MEMO? REMEMBER TO . . .

- Restrict circulation to the most trusted team members.
- Emphasize the importance of confidentiality in your communications.

Request for Input on Evaluating Latest Offer From Union

To:

From:

Date:

Regarding: Request for input on latest union offer

The widget rotators' local has submitted a new offer for settlement of the ongoing contract negotiations. Please review the summary and reply to me with your comments by the close of business tomorrow.

Thanks!

Alternate Version:

Here's a summary of the latest offer for settlement put forward by the Widget Rotators' Union. Please bear in mind that the attached summary is highly sensitive and must be treated with the utmost discretion.

Please contact me no later than the close of business tomorrow with your comments.

Developing a Customized Memo? Remember to . . .

- Restrict circulation to the most trusted team members.
- Emphasize the importance of confidentiality in your communications.

Review of Regulations: Union Employees Only to Perform the Following Tasks

To:

From:

Date:

Regarding: Outline of union members' responsibilities

In your mailbox, you will find a list of the tasks to be performed only by union staff members.

If you do not hold a union position in the company and need any of these tasks completed, please contact your supervisor. If you are a union member, please take note of the following responsibilities, especially those that relate to your position.

Alternate Version:

Important! Our recently concluded contract negotiations with the Widget Rotators' Union leaves us with a *legal obligation* to insure that a new list of tasks are carried out only by union employees.

The summary sheet outlining these tasks is attached. Please review it carefully and inform your people of any new work schedules or assignments. We have *no alternative* to following these guidelines, so please stop by my office if you have any questions on implementing the new work guidelines.

Temporary Change in Job Description for Nonunion Employees During Strike Action or Work Stoppage

To:

From:

Date:

Regarding: Temporary change in job description

Certain changes in your job description, effective only during the current labor dispute, are being made. I'd like to take a few moments with you today to discuss them. Can we meet at 3:00 pm?

Thank you for your support at this difficult time.

Alternate Version:

As you may know, ABC Corporation is re-evaluating work assignments during the current work stoppage. Your job description is being revised, on a temporary basis, to include some front desk duty and occasional administrative help—and to de-emphasize certain other elements of your normal routine, such as accounting and payroll support.

Thanks in advance for your help and flexibility during a challenging time.

- Emphasize that the changes in question are temporary.
- Thank the team member for his or her support and assistance.

Union Election Schedule

To:

From:

Date:

Regarding: Union election schedule

The referendum concerning whether or not shop employees of ABC Corporation will be represented by the Widget Rotators' Union will take place this Monday, August 1, 19XX. Voting (open to eligible shop employees) will take place between 8:00 am and 6:00 pm in the employee lounge.

Wherever you stand on this issue, the fact is that this issue will affect every ABC employee. Don't let others do your deciding for you!

Alternate Version:

However you feel about the issue of union representation in our organization, we urge you to take full advantage of the privilege of expressing your opinion. The upcoming binding ballot process will determine whether shop employees will be represented by the Widget Rotators' Union.

Under current law, once this question has been addressed, it cannot be voted on again for a significant period of time. Eligible employees may vote in the employee lounge between 8:00 am and 6:00 pm on Monday, August 1.

DEVELOPING A CUSTOMIZED MEMO? REMEMBER TO . . .

- State when and where the election will take place.
- Make it clear that only eligible employees may participate.

Union Files Formal Grievance with Regard to Downsizing Efforts

To:

From:

Date:

Regarding: Union issues

As the document I've forwarded indicates, we are facing a formal grievance from the Widget Rotators' Union concerning access procedures to the storeroom and the safety of the materials stored there. Rather than issue a simple denial of the points raised, I think we should appoint Ellen Beresford to conduct a full review and issue a detailed accounting of her findings no later than September 1.

Any thoughts?

Thanks in advance for your input.

Alternate Version:

Every formal grievance—including the one we now face concerning our restructuring campaign—must be handled according to the following guidelines:

- An initial response, acknowledging receipt and assigning a case officer, must go out by the next working day after a complaint is filed.
- The union must receive a status report covering all open actions each week.
- As a rule, grievances should be resolved within thirty days of filing, if at all possible.

Bearing all this in mind, Ellen, I'm asking you to handle this union grievance. If there are any complaints that appear to require my special attention, please do not hesitate to contact me.

Thanks!

Developing a Customized Memo? Remember to . . .

- Set a clear timeline for response.

- Leave no doubt as to who is responsible for moving the process forward.
- Thank the person with whom you are working (or to whom you are delegating the task).

Union Files Formal Grievance with Regard to Work Schedule

To:

From:

Date:

Regarding: Formal union complaint

I've just received a formal grievance from the Widget Rotators' Union concerning the overtime schedule we plan to implement this fall. I want to develop a response by no later than September 1.

Can you meet with me as soon as possible so we can discuss how to address the issues they've raised?

Thanks for putting this at the top of your list.

Alternate Version:

The union has filed a grievance.

At issue is whether or not newly hired union employees must be offered overtime hours during their probationary period with ABC Corporation. This is a gray area that was, as I recall, left essentially unresolved during our most recent contract negotiations.

I'd like you to . . .

- Call the union immediately (i.e., before the close of business tomorrow). Acknowledge receipt of the grievance and explain that you'll be acting as case officer.
- Check with our attorneys at Badger, Settle, and Runn to find out how they feel about this union claim.
- Discuss the overtime issue with Peggy Meecham in Personnel.

- Develop a recommendation and a draft response and forward it to me by August 28.

Other than informing the appropriate union officials that you're actively pursuing this grievance, please *do not* discuss this matter with any union personnel.

Thanks!

DEVELOPING A CUSTOMIZED MEMO? REMEMBER TO . . .

- Set a clear timeline for response.
- Thank the person with whom you are working (or to whom you are delegating the task).

Union Files Formal Grievance with regard to Workplace Surroundings; Guidelines for Response

To:

From:

Date:

Regarding: Union complaint

The recent surge in orders has led to a full facility as we bring the temporary third packing line up to speed. The permanent plant expansion has been approved and should break ground on December 1.

That having been said, we nevertheless face a formal complaint from the union relating to the tight quarters in the plant. Can you take a few hours to discuss this with Melvin Pryor in Personnel, and then get back to me tomorrow with recommendations on how we should respond?

Thanks.

Alternate Version:

I've just received a formal grievance from the Widget Rotators' Union concerning the "cramped" conditions in the shop.

Responding promptly and responsibly to these grievances is an important priority for our organization. On this and future grievances relating to workplace operations, please be sure to:

- Immediately (i.e., within one working day of receipt of the grievance) contact union representatives to acknowledge receipt of the grievance and inform them who is in charge of responding (you).
- Contact our attorneys and forward a copy of the grievance, along with any appropriate references to the labor agreement. Ask for their written recommendation as to how we should respond.
- Conduct informal open-minded interviews with appropriate floor personnel.
- Report back to me quickly (in this case, no later than August 15) so we can discuss your notes and the recommendation of the attorneys in drafting a response together.

Thank you!

Developing a Customized Memo? Remember to . . .

- Set a clear timeline for input to the response.
- Thank the person with whom you are working (or to whom you are delegating the task).

Update on Status of Labor Negotiations

To:

From:

Date:

Regarding: Update on Labor Negotiations

The union talks appear to be going well. With any luck, we should be able to hammer out an agreement that will make everyone happy.

We do not have an expected completion date for the talks as yet, but I will continue to keep you informed concerning the status of the negotiations.

Alternate Version:

A quick update: Talks with the Widget Rotators' Union are proceeding in a constructive fashion, but there is a long way yet to go.

I am confident that with continued perseverance and commitment from both sides, the result will be a negotiated agreement between labor and management that works for everyone. All the same, there are many sensitive issues that must still be resolved. I will keep you informed on the status of our talks as events warrant.

DEVELOPING A CUSTOMIZED MEMO? REMEMBER TO . . .

- Clear the release of the memo with the proper authorities in your organization.
- Avoid any mention of specific topics under discussion in the negotiation (unless appropriate officials in your organization decide that it is to your advantage to go into detail on a particular topic).

Chapter 8

Sales Department Performance

From targeting customers, to selling them on a product or service, to keeping them happy and informed, salespeople are called on to satisfy a variety of needs, as well as to meet the company goals that have been set for them. Their success or failure in these areas has an immense impact on the company's performance as a whole.

This chapter covers many of the areas that come into play for department managers and sales staff. You will learn ways to handle specific issues such as poor sales performance; problems with individual work habits; commissions, bonus structures, and incentives; special offers to customers; sales conferences and seminars; telemarketing issues; and sales quotas. In addition, there are memos designed to help your salespeople do the work of wooing, winning, and keeping customers; guidelines for submitting reports or improving sales techniques; and strategies for improving sales performance.

Allocation of New Territory

To:

From:

Date:

Regarding: New growth in our sales department

As we discussed in our recent sales meeting, there are going to be some major changes in sales territories. The new breakdown is reflected on the map in my office and in the main conference room.

Questions? Please feel free to get in touch with me directly.

Alternate Version:

It's finally happened!

As discussed in our recent meeting, we've acted on our decision to reassign certain sales territories. Although no adjustment of boundaries in a situation such as this one is likely to make everyone happy, I am confident that the new arrangement is fairer and likely to lead to greater efficiency when it comes to scheduling travel time.

The decision on allocating the new territories was a difficult one, but it was not made without a great deal of thought and deliberation. If you have suggestions on how we can make the new system work better, please drop by my office any time so we can discuss them.

DEVELOPING A CUSTOMIZED MEMO? REMEMBER TO . . .

- Ask for input on making the new arrangement work.
- Avoid asking "what people think" of the new setup.

Average Unit Purchase Down: Strategies for Improvement

To:

From:

Date:

Regarding: Improving our purchase power

Can we post an even better quarter than the one we just completed? I think so.

At our next sales meeting, let's brainstorm about some ways we can increase the widgets-per-new-customer figure.

I look forward to discussing this with you in detail on Monday.

Alternate Version:

The current quarter's sales numbers are in. They show that our new prospecting program really is paying off, because the number of new customers we're bringing in is slightly *above* our target for the period. Congratulations!

One number that could benefit from a little more of our focused attention is the average number of units purchased per new customer. The average new customer is now purchasing seven widgets per transaction. If we can get that up to eight by asking about accessory widgets, or by suggesting alternate uses for widgets in the customer's business, we'll hit our target in this area next quarter—and pick up some bigger commission checks at the same time.

Any ideas? Let's review them at the next sales meeting.

Developing a Customized Memo? Remember to . . .

- Focus on the positive wherever possible.
- Encourage people to develop ideas for group review.

Call for Written Endorsements from Current Customers

To:

From:

Date:

Regarding: Endorsements

Could you take fifteen minutes today to help us develop some materials that will help us put together a top-notch flyer? Call up your best customer and ask him or her for an endorsement. If the person asks for time to compose one, ask if you could quote something great he or she said about ABC Corporation during your last meeting. In either case, we'll need written approval from your contact to use his or her remark on the flyer.

We're hoping to get final copy by the end of this week, so make the call(s) now! Thanks.

Alternate Version:

We're putting together a new flyer that could help bring loads of new business to the company . . . and increase everyone's chance of hitting the yearly bonus level.

I'm enclosing a list of past endorsements from ABC customers that should help you get the wheels rolling.

Please pass along *at least one* endorsement from a favored customer no later than close of business Friday. (Of course, the more endorsements you pass along, the better our flyer will look—and the greater our chance of exceeding our target!)

I really appreciate your taking a few minutes out of the day to check in with a top-level customer on this.

Developing a Customized Memo? Remember to . . .

- Explain how the endorsements will help the organization.
- Encourage immediate action (politely), perhaps by highlighting an impending deadline.
- Thank salespeople in advance for their help.

Change in Bonus Structure

To:

From:

Date:

Regarding: A new bonus structure to start next month

Here's the lowdown on the new bonus program we talked about at our recent meeting.

As the summary sheet indicates, the new program makes it easier for you to attain bonus amounts in the X, Y, and Z product categories. It also reduces the amount of paperwork necessary to become eligible for bonus amounts.

I'm very excited about the new bonus plan, and I hope you will be, too. If you have any questions about the new plan, please feel free to drop by my office.

Alternate Version:

The new fiscal year brings with it a new—and, I think, much more exciting- bonus structure for sales reps at ABC Corporation.

The bottom-line advantages: You need to sell fewer units than in the past to reach the new bonus levels, and there's less paperwork necessary to become eligible for the bonus levels. You'll find all the details on the summary sheet in your mailbox. Questions? Drop by my office so we can discuss them.

Developing a Customized Memo? Remember to . . .

- Emphasize the aspects of the new program that you feel will benefit the salespeople.
- Let salespeople know whom they can contact with questions.

Change in Commission Structure

To:

From:

Date:

Regarding: New commission structure

In the separate summary sheet, you'll find all the details on the new commission and compensation arrangements we discussed at the last sales meeting.

As excited as I am about this new compensation program, I realize that it's likely to be a while before it becomes second nature for you. Please feel free to drop by my office as we make the transition to the new plan . . . so we can discuss the best ways to make the new structure pay off for you.

Alternate Version:

The new commission system (see the separate summary) is the result of a great deal of careful planning. It allows you greater scheduling flexibility than the old compensation structure, significantly greater income potential for those willing to work to develop brand-new accounts, and a lucrative bonus program for those who meet their targets in the deluxe widget program.

I realize people may have questions about the new system. I'm eager to talk the new plan over with you; drop by my office so we can set up a time to review the details.

Developing a Customized Memo? Remember to . . .

- Emphasize the aspects of the new program that you feel will benefit the salespeople.
- Let salespeople know whom they can contact with questions.

Cold Calling Techniques: Room for Improvement

To:

From:

Date:

Regarding: Cold calling strategies

A seminar I attended recently in Bigcity reminded me of the importance of prospecting on a regular basis. (That's "calling people we don't know and asking them for business" in layman's terms.)

I want to try an experiment, beginning this Monday morning. Let's take the first thirty minutes of each day and spend it at the phone calling brand-new potential customers. Let's keep track of all the dials and contacts you make—and see how many appointments result by the end of the week.

Questions? Comments? Talk to me during this afternoon's sales meeting or in my office at any time before we start the program on Monday morning.

Alternate Version:

I've just finished reading a superb book on personal sales management by Victor Highend called *Your Personal Sales Breakthrough*. There's a copy in my office for anyone who'd like to check it out.

One of Highend's most inspiring points is that superstar salespeople find a reason to prospect (usually by phone) every single solitary day, no matter what their current income level looks like. His theory is that sales cycles depend on what we did three months ago to determine current income levels—and that even a rosy quarter can be disastrous in the long term if there's no regular prospecting routine.

Highend suggests a *daily* calling ritual of at least twenty-five attempted calls to new, undiscovered customers-in-waiting. He's got the results to back it up, too.

Ready for a one-week experiment? Let's make the hours between 8:15 and 9:15 a new-customer calling period. (We're all here anyway, right?) Questions about Highend's system? Bring them up at the meeting this afternoon.

- Set out the period during the day you want to turn into "prospecting time."
- Consider framing the calling period as an "experiment."
- Let salespeople know whom they can contact with questions.

Customers Who Request Brochures: When to Send

To:

From:

Date:

Regarding: Brochures

The head office in San Disastro has reminded me that we are not, under any circumstances, to mail out brochures to first-time phone contacts . . . even if they ask for them.

Brochures are meant to be delivered in-person during first-time meetings with prospective customers, or mailed upon request to those potential customers with whom we have had at least one meeting.

Thanks for your help in observing this important standard. If you have any questions, please feel free to drop by my office.

Alternate Version:

Just a reminder—we are only authorized to send out brochures to potential customers with whom we have met at least once in person.

As you no doubt know, "send me some information" is perhaps the single most popular translation for "I don't want to talk about this" among the people we talk to on the phone. If someone is genuinely interested in receiving information about ABC Corporation, thank them for that interest and offer to drop the brochure by during a face-to-face meeting. If necessary, explain the company policy.

Questions? Comments? I'm here, and so are the brochures—to qualified leads only, by order of the head office.

Thanks for your cooperation.

- Explain why the policy exists in the first place.
- Clarify which people should receive printed information.

Daily Call Reports: Guidelines for Submitting

To:

From:

Date:

Regarding: Submitting your daily call reports

Please submit call reports to your supervisor by the end of each business day.

The more information we have on file about your calling patterns, the better the advice you'll get at quarterly review time. That means fatter commission checks!

Thanks in advance for filing these reports promptly and accurately.

Alternate Version:

Just a reminder—daily call reports must be handed over to your supervisor in person at the end of the business day. Please complete your call sheets in full before passing them along.

Keeping track of your own numbers, and working with your supervisor to analyze them, is an important part of monitoring your own progress toward your personal sales goals. Help us help you hit those targets! Fill out the sheets completely as you work during the day. Check them for omissions, errors, or overlaps before you pass them on. Then copy and forward them when you check in with your supervisor in person before leaving for the day.

Thanks!

- Highlight the benefits of knowing—and documenting—personal calling patterns.

- Let the salesperson know how often the reports should be forwarded, and to whom.

Decision to Change Advertising Campaign

To:

From:

Date:

Regarding: The new campaign for the Gizmo

A major shift in our nationwide promotional campaign for the Gizmo 2000 line is about to take place, and you ought to know all about it.

Please make a note to attend the all-company meeting in Conference Room B tomorrow for a preview of the new campaign. The show starts at 8:00 am sharp!

Alternate Version:

The new Gizmo campaign, targeted to women between the ages of 18 and 34, was designed by the folks at Miatt/Day/Chojo International Group—the same advertising firm that launched our successful Velex 1500 campaign last year. Many of the people you contact on the phone and meet with in person will be talking about this campaign. In order to learn more about it, you'll want to take advantage of a special sneak peek we've arranged for you.

The preview takes place tomorrow morning at 8:00 in conference room A. Everyone should be there!

DEVELOPING A CUSTOMIZED MEMO? REMEMBER TO . . .

- Specify when and where the new campaign preview will take place.
- Maintain an enthusiastic, upbeat tone.

Following Procedures on Special Consumer Offers

To:

From:

Date:

Regarding: Those strange calls you've been getting

I know, I know—In a perfect world, we all would have had a little more lead time to get ready for the questions people would start asking us about the double-your-money-back guarantee on the RetroWidget system.

As it stands, we've got to pass along the details on that guarantee, which has been a prominent part of the infomercial program that recently debuted in six major American cities (ours, alas, not being one of them). Please see the bulletin that's posted in the employee lounge for the steps the consumer must follow to become eligible for this refund program.

Thanks a lot!

Alternate Version:

The answer to the burning question of the week is: Yes, consumers are entitled to a double-your-money-back refund if they follow the steps set out on page 4 of the customer warranty for the RetroWidget program. (Copy enclosed.) You may want to keep a list of addresses and phone numbers handy in case you need to refer a customer to the appropriate facility for refund processing.

Please don't tell the customer we have no such offer, or that this office can process the double refund. (We can't.) Point the person toward the appropriate regional sales office.

Thanks!

DEVELOPING A CUSTOMIZED MEMO? REMEMBER TO . . .

- Let salespeople know where they can find the specifics of the offer. (Or, if you prefer, concisely incorporate the details in your memo.)
- Thank salespeople for their help in sending the right message to customers.

Information Concerning Sales Prospects Requested

To:

From:

Date:

Regarding: Sales prospects

Some prospects may be better investments of your time than others.

On the questionnaire passed out this morning, you'll find a list of questions about the people you've called this week for new business. Please make as many copies of this sheet as you need and complete it for every cold prospect you've called this week (not including today). Review your calling sheets so you can pass along accurate information.

Thanks for taking the time to assemble this information. I promise you, once you spot the improvement in your commission checks, you'll be glad you did.

Alternate Version:

We're trying to help you spend your time more efficiently and close more sales—so we're asking everyone in the sales department to take a look at the cold prospects you've called over the past week and to summarize some important information about them.

Please take a half-hour or so today to review your call sheets and answer the following questions about each cold prospect you contacted this week:

- When did I make my first-ever call to this prospect?
- How many times have I called this person over the past month?
- How many times have I called this person this week (not counting today)?
- How many messages have I left for this person this week?
- How many times has this person, or a representative of the prospect company, returned my call?

There are no "right" answers to these questions. We're assembling calling breakdowns for the department as a whole and for each individual sales rep so we can set up a system that will provide everyone with weekly summaries based on your daily calling logs. Our aim is to help you focus on those cold leads with the highest statistical likelihood of closing in fiscal year 19XX.

Can· you get this information to me by the close of business today? Thanks in advance for your help.

- Highlight the future income benefits of answering the questions you've laid out.
- Take a neutral, nonthreatening tone throughout.

Keeping in Contact with Current Customers: Minimum Standards

To:

From:

Date:

Regarding: Staying in contact with our customers

Our sales department guidelines require that we maintain regular phone and face-to-face contact with our customers. Please see the checklist on page 26 of the employee handbook for all the guidelines.

Nobody ever really "closes" a sale—sales have to be kept open through constant effort! Please review your customer base closely and find out when you last made contact with everyone on your "closed" list!

Thanks a lot.

Alternate Version:

"How's the Gizmo we shipped working out for you?"

That's the question you should ask your customers, either in person or during a face-to-face meeting, at least once every sixty days.

ABC Corporation sales standards require that we all contact current customers *at least* once every two months. (See the enclosed photocopy.) When was the last time you talked to each of your customers? Check your contact list and find out—then reach out and touch someone! By the way, if you get an answer that sounds less than promising, see me quickly so we can put together an action plan to help keep your customer satisfied!

DEVELOPING A CUSTOMIZED MEMO? REMEMBER TO . . .

- Highlight, if you can, company policies or high-level directives aimed at continuing customer contact after the sale.
- Emphasize that the sales process never really ends.
- Thank salespeople for their help.

Managing Partner's Directives to Consulting Partners: Importance of Pooling Leads for Personal Selling Campaign

To:

From:

Date:

Regarding: Swapping leads

I had a brainstorm over the weekend—suppose we all get together for a marathon personal lead-swapping session?

I'm interested in focusing on people we'd feel uncomfortable contacting in person, but whom another rep in the organization would do well to get in touch with. Hey, it's one way to hit a sales target, right? Why not scan your address book for likely candidates and meet with the other partners and me this coming October 15 at 1:00 pm in the conference room.

Alternate Version:

Let's get together to raid each other's personal databases—for the greater glory of the company revenue picture.

What I have in mind is a few hours during which we could all bring our address books and pass along the names of those past colleagues, business associates, friends and relatives we each would feel uncomfortable selling to as one individual to another—but whom ABC Corporation could contact on a referral basis.

Can we meet on October 15 at 1:00 in conference room A?

Developing a Customized Memo? Remember to . . .

- Allow people sufficient time to review their personal records.
- Specify when and where the meeting is to take place.
- Consider issuing a second "reminder" memo shortly before the lead-sharing meeting.

Mandatory Attendance at Annual Sales Conference

To:

From:

Date:

Regarding: Attending the annual sales conference

The annual companywide sales conference will take place on Tuesday, October 12 at 1:00 pm at the Sheraton Two Trees in Bigtown. The event will take place in the hotel's main conference room.

This is a *mandatory* event.

See you there!

Alternate Version:

What is it? The annual meeting of our national sales staff.

Where is it? The Sheraton Two Trees in Bigtown, in the main conference room.

When is it? Tuesday, October 12, at 1:00 pm sharp.

Sales reps from all over the country will be traveling hundreds of miles to attend this (mandatory) event, so it should be a great opportunity to catch up on market developments in our various sales areas. I look forward to seeing you there!

DEVELOPING A CUSTOMIZED MEMO? REMEMBER TO . . .

- Specify when and where the meeting is to take place.
- Let the reader know who else will be in attendance.

Mandatory Attendance During Visit by Officials of Prospect Company

To:

From:

Date:

Regarding: Visit by officials of the Very Large Corporation

The president of this major widget wholesaler, as well as its six regional vice presidents, will all be visiting our facility on Tuesday, January 31, at approximately 10:00 am.

Each and every salesperson should be in attendance on-site at this time!

Thanks in advance for your help in making this visit with the top officials of this industry leader a big success.

Alternate Version:

Some special visitors are coming our way.

Senior representatives of the Very Large Corporation will be visiting our facility on Tuesday, January 31 at approximately 10:00 am. They'll be accompanied by Eileen McCarthy, our national sales manager.

This visit represents a great honor—and a significant opportunity—for our company. Please help make our visitors from Very Large feel welcome . . . and let them know the kind of quality-first organization you work for.

Developing a Customized Memo? Remember to . . .

- Make it clear who should be in attendance and when.
- Specify when the visitors will be arriving.

Mandatory Availability for Customer On-Site Meetings Even During Off-Work Hours

To:

From:

Date:

Regarding: On-site meetings

Over the next week, it is quite likely that sales and support personnel will be asked to meet at the Macro Macaroni headquarters to help them with on-site review of their widgets, which have already been installed. These meetings are likely to take place during off-hours as well as standard business hours. Please do your best to make a contribution during this unusual period—and pitch in during off-hours if you are asked to do so. ABC will pay for all transport and lodging expenses.

Alternate Version:

Odds are that you've already heard about the servo problem that arose in the widgets that have been installed at the Macro Macaroni plant in Anytown, Massachusetts.

Over the next week, ABC Corporation will do its utmost to resolve this problem for Macro Macaroni, one of our most important and valued customers. You may be asked to make a trip to the Anytown plant to help the Macro Macaroni people get the widgets we shipped them up and running as soon as possible. Please show as much commitment and flexibility as you can if you are asked to make off-hours visits to the plant.

Thanks in advance for your help and support! ABC will pay for all transport and lodging expenses.

- Identify the customer who may need off-hours help.
- Specify where this customer is located.
- Give the reader some idea of how long the situation is likely to take to resolve (i.e., approximately one week, as above.)

Monthly Sales Reports: Guidelines for Submitting

To:

From:

Date:

Regarding: Submitting your sales reports

Your monthly sales reports need to be turned in to your superior no later than the *first business day of the new month!*

Help us help you keep your prospecting records and ratio information accurate and up to date. Please fill out your sales reports completely and accurately and pass them along to your sales manager on time, so the monthly departmental and individual summaries can be completed on schedule.

Alternate Version:

Our goal is to get the best, most accurate prospecting and sales information to you and to the department as a whole on time—so it's easy for you to work efficiently and monitor your own sales numbers. But we can't do that if we don't have your monthly sales report!

Please help us out. Pass your complete, accurate monthly sales report in to your superior no later than the second business day of the month.

Thanks!

DEVELOPING A CUSTOMIZED MEMO? REMEMBER TO . . .

- Specify when the sales reports are to be turned in.
- Keep the tone polite and enthusiastic, not accusatory.

New Accounts: Minimum Targets for Development

To:

From:

Date:

Regarding: New accounts

A friendly reminder: "Old Faithful" is a geyser—not a selling philosophy!

Don't get lulled into a sense of false security by your current list customers. Remember that each and every salesperson at ABC Corporation is expected to service existing accounts *and* bring in new business. One of the best ways to find new customers? Make prospect calls every single day!

Don't let the gusher run dry. Shoot for at least one brand-new account every month. That will leave you in a position of control over your career and your income now—and in the future.

Alternate Version:

Remember—the target for salespeople at ABC Corporation is to close one brand-new account *every month*. That's a realistic goal, and one that will help you win greater consistency in your selling routine if you work towards it consistently and make prospecting calls on a daily basis.

If you want to talk about how a more aggressive prospecting program may help you close that new business, please stop by my office. I've got some great audiotape programs that may help you develop or strengthen a winning prospecting routine.

Developing a Customized Memo? Remember to . . .

- Outline the target you want salespeople to hit.
- Briefly explain the best ways to attain that goal (by, for instance, making prospecting calls every day.)

New Product Release By Competitor

To:

From:

Date:

Regarding: Sprockets R Us

I have just returned from the latest trade show where Sprockets R Us unveiled its new product line. It's a doozy, and many of our customers are probably going to be talking about it.

I'd like to hold a meeting so that we can discuss some of the details I learned about the new releases. Let's get together at 10:00 tomorrow morning in my office.

Alternate Version:

I just got back from the big trade show in San Disastro, and I got a peek at the latest product release from Sprockets R Us.

In addition to an enhanced input-output ratio (finally up to the standard of our Gizmo 2000 model), the new Sprockets release features a number of snazzy options that we should probably discuss in detail. Let's go over everything—including our best responses to customers who ask how and when we'll be matching this product with a new release of our own—tomorrow at 10:00 in my office.

DEVELOPING A CUSTOMIZED MEMO? REMEMBER TO . . .

- Mention the competitor by name.
- State when and where you would like to meet to discuss the new release(s).

New Quarterly Department Sales Goals

To:

From:

Date:

Regarding: Sales goals are on the rise

We are committing ourselves to higher sales goals as of next month. Our departmental sales goal for the coming quarter has been adjusted to $2.3 million in gross sales.

Let's get together tomorrow morning at 9:00 in my office to talk about some strategies we can employ to reach this aggressive, but nevertheless realistic target.

Alternate Version:

After a review of the latest budget numbers, this quarter's departmental sales goal has been adjusted to $2.3 million. That's quite a target—but meeting aggressive targets is part of what we do best here.

I have every confidence that we can meet this goal . . . if we all keep monitoring our work closely. Let's talk about the new target—and any exciting new strategies you may be pondering to meet it—at tomorrow morning's sales meeting.

DEVELOPING A CUSTOMIZED MEMO? REMEMBER TO . . .

- Outline the new target you want salespeople to hit.
- Consider setting up a strategy meeting at which salespeople can discuss the best ways to work to meet the new goal.

Notice of a Salesperson's Probation for Poor Performance

To:

From:

Date:

Regarding: Official notice of probation period

This notice confirms your probationary status for failing to meet personal sales goals in three consecutive quarters. It is in accordance with clause 6(d) of your employment agreement with ABC Corporation.

Frank, I am eager to work with you to turn this situation around. I know you can do it. Let's talk this afternoon before you head home.

Alternate Version:

As of today, you are on probation for failing to meet established personal sales goals.

This is a serious situation, Frank—one that could result in termination if we don't find a way to turn things around. Fortunately, I'm convinced that you and I can develop a strategy that will get you back on the winning track you were traveling last year at this time. I can't make changes without a commitment from you, however. I hope and trust you'll be as good as your word yesterday and meet with me each morning at 7:45 so we can go over your goals for the day.

Company policy says I have to write this memo, and it is appropriate that I do so. All the same, I have a feeling this turnaround will be among the most dramatic in the history of our company. I look forward to helping you make that happen.

Developing a Customized Memo? Remember to . . .

- Clearly and unambiguously state the employee's probationary status.
- Express your confidence in the salesperson's ability to turn things around.

Obtaining Authorization for Incentive Plans

To:

From:

Date:

Regarding: Idea for new incentive plans

Are you interested in revising our bonus plan for salespeople? I think doing so could make a big difference for us.

My idea is pretty straightforward—a $2500 bonus for each salesperson who closes at least six new accounts in a single quarter. It would be easy to implement and, I think, highly effective.

Do you think it's worth a try?

Alternate Version:

I've got some ideas about how we can increase sales in our department that I'd like to discuss with you.

I think if we revamp the bonus program we can get some great results. Here's what I have in mind: We make any salesperson who closes at least six new accounts per quarter eligible for a $2500 bonus. *Only* sales reps who bring in this much new business over a three-month period would be eligible for the extra compensation.

What do you think?

Developing a Customized Memo? Remember to . . .

- Briefly outline the bonus plan you have in mind.
- Make it clear that you're looking for authorization to move forward with your idea.

Reallocation of Existing Territory

To:

From:

Date:

Regarding: New sales department responsibilities

We talked about it—and now it's official! Effective on the first of this month, Jane Miller will handle all sales arising out of the North Shore region. Peter Jones, who had previously been in charge of this territory, will inherit the mid-region territory left open by Gus's departure, and will still continue to sell in the metro Bigcity area.

If you have questions about who should talk to—or receive credit for—customers from the North Shore or mid-region areas, please feel free to check in with me or the reps in question.

Thanks!

Alternate Version:

As we discussed in this morning's sales meeting, Jane will now be handling the North Shore sales territory, while Peter, who used to handle the North Shore, will take on the mid-region territory left open by Gus's departure. Peter will still continue to handle accounts in the metro Bigcity area.

Please be sure to refer calls and inquiries to the correct sales rep!

DEVELOPING A CUSTOMIZED MEMO? REMEMBER TO . . .

- Say which rep is covering which territory.
- Consider developing a map that sets out the new allocations.

Repeat Sales, Repeat Customers: New Departmental Targets

To:

From:

Date:

Regarding: Repeat sales

As we discussed in our recent sales meeting, the goal for this year with regard to repeat business is to hold on to 85% of our current customers. The individual sales rep with at least one year at ABC Corporation who comes closest to retaining *all* of his or her current business will win a $1500 cash bonus next January!

Keep an eye out for an upcoming in-house seminar on how to hold on to current customers. It should be a valuable session.

Alternate Version:

It's that time of year! New budgets, new targets, and new goals. In 19XX, in addition to our overall revenue goal, we have specific goals for each sales rep in the area of repeat sales and repeat customers.

This year, our aim is for each rep to retain 85% or better of existing accounts. We'll be holding a seminar on how to hold on to business in today's competitive marketplace a little later this month—I'll keep you posted about dates and times.

The rep with at least one year's service who comes closest to holding on to 100% of current business will win a cash bonus of $1500 at the end of the year!

DEVELOPING A CUSTOMIZED MEMO? REMEMBER TO . . .

- Outline any appropriate incentives.
- Keep the tone upbeat and enthusiastic.

Research of Key Prospect Companies: Minimum Standards

To:

From:

Date:

Regarding: Research!

Keep up to date with events in your prospect company's industry! Take a gander *at least once a week* at the trade magazines available through my office. This material is what your likely prospect is reading every week . . . and you should be taking a look at it, as well.

Another good idea: check in by phone at the front desk of an "A" level prospect to ask for a brochure or annual report. These can be extremely informative.

Alternate Version:

Helpful hint: If you're not reading your prospect's industry or trade magazine, you're not doing your commission check any favors.

Attached please find a list of a half-dozen publications that are likely to be of interest to prospects in the widget reclamation and widget transport businesses—our most likely customers. ABC subscribes to these magazines for your benefit . . . so take advantage of them!

Please take the time to review what's going on in your prospect's industry *at least once a week.* You might also want to ask an "A-list" prospect whether or not you can take a look at the company's brochure or annual report.

DEVELOPING A CUSTOMIZED MEMO? REMEMBER TO . . .

- Describe appropriate resources available to your salespeople.
- Identify your organization's most likely customers.

Sales Quota Announcement (Department)

To:

From:

Date:

Regarding: Departmental sales quota

Our quarterly sales goal is $1.3 million. This is a major target, our biggest yet. I have every confidence that, with solid planning and good execution, we can work together to meet (or beat!) this quota. Let's talk about it at our first big strategy meeting of the quarter—in the conference room, this coming Monday, at 8:30 am sharp.

Alternate Version:

After a lengthy review of the market conditions facing ABC Corporation, the quarterly sales quota has been finalized. Our goal this quarter is to bring in $1.6 million dollars in total revenues. This is an aggressive but thoroughly attainable goal that will demand full commitment from all of us.

I've scheduled a strategy meeting to discuss the best ways to go about hitting this target for this coming Monday at 8:30 am sharp. I look forward to discussing our plans then!

DEVELOPING A CUSTOMIZED MEMO? REMEMBER TO . . .

- Give the specifics of the quota.
- Express confidence in your team's ability to meet its goals.
- Offer your help in developing strategies that will help the team hit the quota.

Sales Quota Announcement (Individual)

To:

From:

Date:

Regarding: Sales quota

As we discussed, your sales goal for the coming quarter is $113,000 in new business—a figure that represents nearly $17,000 in commissions.

I'm eager to help you meet this goal, and I have some strategies that I think will help you do so. Why don't we get together this Wednesday at 3:00 to review strategies for the coming three months?

Alternate Version:

It's official—your sales quota for the next three-month period is to bring in $113,000 in new business. This is an aggressive target, but it's a challenge I feel completely confident you can meet.

There's a lot at stake here. Meeting this target means $17,000 in commissions for you! Let's get together to talk about strategy for the coming three months. Why don't you drop by my office this Wednesday at around 3:00 so we can talk about your plans for meeting this goal?

DEVELOPING A CUSTOMIZED MEMO? REMEMBER TO . . .

- Give the specifics of the quota.
- Express confidence in the salesperson's ability to meet the goal.
- Offer your help in developing strategies that will help the salesperson hit the quota.

Senior Management Available to Add "Weight" to Sales Call

To:

From:

Date:

Regarding: Help on the big-account front

Just a reminder—both Janice Hutton and I are available to help you make presentations to big accounts. If you feel your meeting with an important prospect will benefit from our presence, swing by one of our offices so we can talk strategy.

Important note: Because of time restrictions, we'd like to reserve the "let-me-bring-my-manager-in" maneuver for accounts with the potential to bring at least $30,000 in total revenue to ABC on the very first purchase order. If the potential customer you're talking to fits this description, and you believe one or both of us would help you close the sale by showing up for a meeting, come talk to me so we can set up a time.

Alternate Version:

Sometimes a big account may come your way if you make it clear that you're willing to go the extra mile. If you think you're looking at a potential major customer who should be receiving that message, please feel free to consider a presentation in which I, Janice Hutton, or both of us, take part.

To make the most of everyone's time, we're trying to save the "let's-bring-my-manager-in" visits for those accounts that represent $30,000 or more in initial-purchase revenue. If you think we ought to meet one of your clients in this category, please feel free to drop by my office to talk about it.

Developing a Customized Memo? Remember to . . .

- Make it clear who is available to help out on sales calls.
- Outline any appropriate criteria (i.e., account size) for use of this approach.

Service Difficulties with Former Accounts: Outlining Steps Taken Since Computer System Problem

To:

From:

Date:

Regarding: Past computer-related service problems

Last month's shipping nightmare was, as you know, the result of inaccurately configured software installed on our mainframe system by DiskError Technology. The people most affected by the problem were our customers. I've enclosed a letter (in your mailbox this morning) that I'd like you send out under your signature to each of your accounts.

The letter explains what went wrong, what we did about it, and why it's extremely unlikely to happen again. I think we need to take the first step here and issue appropriate apologies for the temporary inconvenience this slipup caused our customers—whether or not they've called to complain yet!

Thanks.

Alternate Version:

Count on it: Our key accounts noticed that our computer system went haywire last month. Your customers have a right to know what went wrong, what we did to fix it, and whether something like that is likely to happen again. The answers:

What went wrong: We bought some software that was supposedly customized to our mainframe system. In fact, it was configured for another company, though nobody spotted that until it was too late.

What we did to fix it: We worked round-the-clock with the software company to fix the glitches and institute a glove-fitting, glitch-free operations system.

Why it won't happen again: The software company flew the team that originally designed this system out to customize our program specifically for us.

Please apologize to all affected customers and bring them up to date on where our system stands right now. Thanks!

DEVELOPING A CUSTOMIZED MEMO? REMEMBER TO . . .

- Summarize the basics of the technical problem.
- Give salespeople the information they need to explain the situation to customers and demonstrate that it was a one-time occurrence.

Special Consumer Offer: Expiration Date Has Passed

To:

From:

Date:

Regarding: Discount offer

A national print and broadcast promotion we launched last March appealed to a 25% discount for first-time subscribers. *This was an error.* The offer expired on August 1!

Several new customers have been frustrated to find full-price fees on their invoices; a few seem to have been told that the offer was still in effect. Please make sure any new customers you talk to get the most accurate information possible.

Thanks!

Alternate Version:

Remember—the 25% discount for first-time subscribers expired a while back (August 1, to be precise)! If you run into a caller who wants to take advantage of this offer, whether because of an old magazine ad or any other outdated promotional piece, please explain that the discount is no longer in effect.

Accounting cannot grant this discount to customers any more. We'll save everyone time and aggravation (and the hassle of revoking commission checks) if we make sure the current information is on the table.

DEVELOPING A CUSTOMIZED MEMO? REMEMBER TO . . .

- Clearly and unambiguously identify the focus of the consumer offer.
- Say when the consumer offer expired.
- Let salespeople know what they must explain to customers.

Telemarketing Department: Excessive Discussion of Personal Matters During Work Hours

To:

From:

Date:

Regarding: Office atmosphere

S.O.S.!

As we discussed at this morning's sales meeting, the level of background chat in the telemarketing room is making it difficult for people to close sales.

It's also keeping us all from operating at peak efficiency and moving toward our sales goals at the speed we deserve.

Please show everyone in the telemarketing room the professional courtesy of maintaining a professional workplace atmosphere. Save the socializing for off-hours and break times. Then go for it!

Thanks a lot.

Alternate Version:

Just a follow-up message on today's discussion during the sales meeting:

- Phones pick up background chatter. It's easy to be a lot noisier than you think you're being.
- We all benefit from a telemarketing room that's free of social talk and other distractions—because we're more likely to close sales in a quiet, professional room.
- Extended social discussions are great stress-relievers, and we all want to encourage them during break periods and other off hours.

Thanks for helping us make this work environment an efficient, high-energy one!

DEVELOPING A CUSTOMIZED MEMO? REMEMBER TO . . .

- Make it clear that there is a time and place for social discussions.
- Keep the tone positive and supportive.

Telemarketing Department: Improper Use of Computerized Dialing Equipment

To:

From:

Date:

Regarding: Harassment of telemarketing prospects

Please help us all stay on the right side of the law!

It is against ABC Corporation policy to use computerized dialing equipment to call prospects repeatedly in order to "punish" the person for a difficult or rude telephone response! This practice also conflicts with state law, which prohibits commercial telemarketers from making harassing or abusive telephone calls.

Any employee discovered using our computerized phone equipment to harass or annoy customers will be subject to immediate dismissal.

Alternate Version:

Do not—repeat, do not—use company phone equipment to harass prospects under any circumstances!

The act of hooking a troublesome prospect up to a "permanent redial" on our dialing equipment is inappropriate, contrary to ABC policy, and a violation of state law. If any employee of ABC is found to be engaging in such activity, he or she will be subject to immediate dismissal.

No kidding. This one could cost you your job. Don't do it.

Developing a Customized Memo? Remember to . . .

- Phrase your memo carefully—don't single out a particular salesperson who has engaged in this activity.
- Make it clear that abusive or harassing calling patterns are grounds for dismissal.

Telemarketing Department: Proper Use and Care of Phone Equipment

To:

From:

Date:

Regarding: Headset units

We've lost two phone headsets to "stomping disease" because the units were left casually draped over the backs of chairs at the end of the day. This is a great way to ensure that the units get knocked to the floor by the evening cleaning crew.

These are expensive, high-quality units that should be treated with care. Please store your headset in your desk drawer before you leave for the day. Thanks!

Alternate Version:

Please don't leave your headset units out when you go home at night!

These units are expensive and may be damaged unintentionally by the evening cleaning crew, which comes in at approximately 7:00. We've lost two headsets because they were left in a tangle on the backs of chairs, knocked to the ground, and accidentally stepped on.

Store your headset, as well as other equipment and materials that shouldn't be disturbed, *in your desk drawers* before you leave for the day.

Thanks!

DEVELOPING A CUSTOMIZED MEMO? REMEMBER TO . . .

- Explain exactly how the equipment in question should be stored and/or maintained.
- Keep the tone polite but direct. Skip the personal accusations.

Upcoming Department Meeting with Production/Design Person

To:

From:

Date:

Regarding: Visit by Chris Cairo

Everyone's been buzzing about the new Gizmo 4500 release we have planned for this coming August. Here's your opportunity to learn all the ins and outs of this exciting new product first-hand from the man who helped to design it!

Senior Widget Engineer Chris Cairo will be in attendance at our weekly sales meeting on Thursday, August 1, at 8:30 am. He'll be happy to answer any of your technical questions concerning the new Gizmo release—which may just turn the market upside down.

You know what your customers are going to want to know about this product, so take a few minutes to jot down the questions you're most eager to be able to answer yourself. Then see if you can stump Chris! (You can't.)

Alternate Version:

Great news! Senior Widget Engineer Chris Cairo, who played an important role in the design of the soon-to-be-released Gizmo 4500 unit, will be sitting in on our next sales meeting. Chris is in attendance to answer all of your questions about this exciting new product.

Prepare some questions you know your customers will want to have answered about the latest addition to the Gizmo family. Chris will be on hand to give you a rare peek inside the design process . . . and to help you learn how to help your customers get the most out of this new release.

The meeting is scheduled for Thursday, August 1, at 8:30 am. See you there!

DEVELOPING A CUSTOMIZED MEMO? REMEMBER TO . . .

- Let salespeople know what the technical person has done that relates to their work.
- Say when and where the meeting will take place.

Upcoming Sales Contest

To:

From:

Date:

Regarding: Hawaii!

Can you say "Aloha"?

Somebody's going to have to. Our winter sales contest is going to award the rep who brings in the most *new* business (based on total dollar volume of signed contracts) with an all-expenses-paid trip to Honolulu for one week!

The details are all laid out in the circular you'll find posted in the employee lounge. The short message, though, is simple: Find new customers, and then get ready to head for the sun and fun!

Alternate Version:

Winter's on its way. But somebody in this department isn't going to mind all that much.

Our sales contest this quarter awards one lucky rep—the one who brings in the most new business based on total dollar volumes of signed contracts—with an all-expenses-paid trip to Honolulu, Hawaii for one full week.

That's one way to take the chill out of the air!

See the enclosed circular for all the details . . . and then get out and track down the business that could send you to Honolulu while the rest of us are digging our cars out of the latest snowdrift!

Developing a Customized Memo? Remember to . . .

- Focus on the prize or benefit related to the sales contest.
- Keep the tone light and accessible.

Urging Salespeople to Use Product

To:

From:

Date:

Regarding: The Gizmo 4500

The new Gizmo 4500 model widget is getting ready to make some serious waves in our industry—and in your commission levels. Selected customers, industry experts, and retailers have responded with some very positive comments about this new item. You're going to sell a lot of them.

Why not give it a test drive?

A fully installed model of the Gizmo 4500 is on display in the Production area. Swing by during the day and see why people are talking.

Alternate Version:

Come check out the new Gizmo 4500!

A fully installed version of the breakthrough widget that's going to earn you uncounted commission dollars is on display in the Production area. This new item has been on the receiving end of more positive "buzz" than any release in our recent history. Come see what all the fuss is about—and flip a few of the switches your customers will be switching in huge numbers this quarter!

DEVELOPING A CUSTOMIZED MEMO? REMEMBER TO . . .

* Let salespeople know where they can find the new model.
* Assume an upbeat, enthusiastic tone.

Verifying Endorsements

To:

From:

Date:

Regarding: Endorsements

Effective immediately, ABC Corporation will require *signed letters on company stationery* from those willing to provide us with endorsements for our products and services.

If you have a verbal endorsement you want to pass along to our marketing department, please telephone your contact and ask for a signed letter (whether or not we use the person's name) on appropriate letterhead. The legal department has suggested that we protect ourselves in this way from claims that endorsements were somehow falsified or exaggerated.

Thanks for your help and cooperation!

Alternate Version:

I know I've been the one who's been lobbying ceaselessly for endorsements from satisfied customers, and we still need these items for the fall flyers, but . . . .

There's been an important shift in policy. Effective immediately, any endorsement we use must come in the form of a signed letter (even if we don't attribute the quote directly). The letter should be typed or printed on appropriate company stationery—or, in the case of a private individual, on a sheet of paper with complete contact information.

Thanks for helping us comply with these important new guidelines.

DEVELOPING A CUSTOMIZED MEMO? REMEMBER TO . . .

- Explain exactly what you need from salespeople before you can incorporate endorsements in marketing materials.
- Thank salespeople in advance for their help and cooperation.

Warning to Salesperson for Tardiness

To:

From:

Date:

Regarding: On-time arrival

There's a problem here. Despite our talk about the importance of on-time arrival last week, you've been in at least twenty minutes late the last two days running.

What's up? I don't want to have to issue a formal reprimand about this issue, but I feel you're leaving me little choice. When you show up late, you miss the morning sales meeting, get your own phone work off to a rough start, and send the wrong signal to others in the department. This habit is costing you money, and it could cost you a lot more.

If I can't count on your timely arrival, my next step has to be a disciplinary note that will go into your file—and that could lead to probation.

Alternate Version:

Didn't we make an agreement about your on-time arrival in the morning?

Despite our talk last week, this is the second day in a row you've arrived at least twenty minutes late. This pattern is costing you money—in terms of lost sales—and it's a demotivating factor for the department as a whole.

If I can't count on you arriving at 8:30, I'm going to have no choice but to issue a formal written warning. Please don't make me do that. It's the first step toward probation. Show up on time in the morning.

Developing a Customized Memo? Remember to . . .

- Emphasize that tardiness is hurting the salesperson's commission income.
- State exactly what you want the salesperson to do—show up on time—and outline the consequences for failing to do so.

Warning to Salesperson with Recordkeeping Problems

To:

From:

Date:

Regarding: Daily records

Help!

I'm still missing the daily call reports we discussed, as well as three sales reports. I'm concerned about these missing pieces, Pete, especially since you and I have discussed this problem in detail several times before.

I don't want to have to file a formal reprimand about this, but if you and I can't work this problem out together, you're going to leave me very little choice. Can I count on you to supply, at minimum, this week's call reports, and the missing sales reports? I'd like them first thing tomorrow morning.

Alternate Version:

We've gone over the importance of good personal recordkeeping several times since the turn of the year—most recently, last Friday. Even so, I have not yet received call reports from you for last week or the week past, and I am missing several individual sales reports.

I'll be honest with you, Pete: I'm concerned about this pattern. If I can't count on you to supply thorough, complete, and prompt personal calling records and sales reports, I'm going to have to issue a formal reprimand, and I don't want to do that.

I need, at the very least, this week's call report and the missing sales reports on the Wallace and Peridon accounts. Can I count on you to supply me with these by tomorrow morning?

DEVELOPING A CUSTOMIZED MEMO? REMEMBER TO . . .

- Let the salesperson know what you need—and when.
- Outline the consequences for failing to complete and pass along the needed paperwork.

Effective Customer Service

It is one thing to sell customers on what you have to offer; it is another thing altogether to keep them happy on a long-term basis. Only with effective customer service can a company hope to attract and retain loyal clients and customers. A great deal depends on a well-informed, efficient customer service staff.

This chapter will look at ways to handle a multitude of service issues, both general and specific. Topics covered include: providing guidelines for handling certain types of customer inquiries and needs; following up on customer problems and complaints; dealing with hostile customers; keeping representatives informed and well-trained on products, policies, and procedures; prioritizing work; and keeping management informed of key customer service issues.

Abusive or Hostile Customers: Some Guidelines

To:

From:

Date:

Regarding: Customers who make life tough

Let 'em yell! That's one of the main messages from our recent seminar on dealing with tough customers. When a customer has "built up some steam," attempting to get him or her to follow normal conversational standards of etiquette is usually counterproductive. Let the person vent— and work off some energy in the process. Other tips: never respond in kind; do show empathy and understanding; and assume personal control for keeping the individual informed about the status of his or her problem.

In your mailbox, you will find a summary sheet from the seminar. Use it in good health—and keep your cool, even when the other person doesn't!

Alternate Version:

Customers aren't really out to get us, of course. But sometimes it sure seems that way. You may find the following general guidelines on dealing with abusive or hostile customers helpful.

- Let them vent. (Yelling at people takes energy, so let your "tough customer" use some up. Don't try to interrupt.)

- Never respond in kind. (Sarcasm? Threats? Power plays? Forget about 'em—they backfire!)

- Tell them you understand how they feel. (Empathy and understanding- the more convincing, the better—can work wonders.)

- Explain exactly what you're going to do—and follow up appropriately. (Volunteer your name and let the person know that you are responsible for, at the very least, giving regular updates on the status of the problem.)

Feel free to talk to me about any issues you feel need to be discussed in greater detail in this area.

DEVELOPING A CUSTOMIZED MEMO? REMEMBER TO . . .

- Acknowledge that customers can sometimes be unreasonable.
- Encourage employees to let customers vent, rather than combat them point by point.

Cross-Selling: New Incentive Plan for Customer Service Representatives

To:

From:

Date:

Regarding: Service upgrades

"Would you be interested in upgrading your service for greater input-output performance?"

Before you conclude your calls from customers requesting help or technical advice, ask them if they're interested in upgrading to the new Gadget 6500 service (see enclosed circular featuring answers to the most common questions about Gadget 6500).

For every "yes" you hear (it will probably be about one of every twenty calls), you'll get a $100 cash bonus in your next paycheck! See your supervisor for details.

Alternate Version:

Want to make an easy hundred bucks?

Ask every incoming caller if he or she wants to enjoy the benefits of our new Gadget 6500 service. At the conclusion of the call, just ask, "Would you be interested in upgrading your service for greater input-output performance?" See the attached circular featuring answers to the most common questions about Gadget 6500 service.

For every upgrade you initiate (you'll probably turn around one out of every twenty calls), you'll get a $100 bonus! See your supervisor for details.

- Let your people know exactly what they should say to customers.
- Identify the contact person who can answer further questions.

Customer Refund Authorization Approved

To:

From:

Date:

Regarding: Your request for refund authorization

I'm glad you let me know about this. The customer is correct; the unit was faulty, and according to her warranty, she is completely entitled to a refund rather than a replacement product.

Would you mind drafting a letter to accompany the check apologizing for the problem? Let's go over it together before you send it out.

Thanks!

Alternate Version:

She's right!

I tested the unit. It is faulty, just as the customer claims. According to the terms of her warranty, the customer has the right to choose either a replacement product or a full cash refund. So we can go ahead and send the check out to her.

Before we do that, though, would you mind setting up a letter apologizing for the problem she had with this widget? Let's review it together and then send both check and letter at the same time.

I really appreciate your handling this for me! Talk to you soon.

DEVELOPING A CUSTOMIZED MEMO? REMEMBER TO . . .

- Praise the employee for having identified a problem.
- Identify the "next steps" (if any) you expect the employee to carry out.

Customer Refund
Authorization Denied

To:

From:

Date:

Regarding: Your request for refund authorization

I almost missed this one!

I was all ready to okay this refund request when I noticed that the date indicates that the purchase was made two years ago. We need to write a letter informing the customer that her warranty only allows her a refund during the six-month period after the purchase. Could you please put together a draft of that letter and check in with me so we can go over it together?

Thanks!

Alternate Version:

I'm afraid I can't authorize this request for a refund authorization. The customer's receipt shows that the purchase was made two years ago!

The warranty only allows for a money-back refund within six months of purchase. I suggest we avoid the potential fireworks of a phone call on this one and put together a letter advising the customer that we can't comply with the request.

Could you put together a draft for us to go over? Thanks for handling this.

DEVELOPING A CUSTOMIZED MEMO? REMEMBER TO . . .

- Employ a neutral, informal, and nonthreatening tone.
- Identify the "next steps" (if any) you expect the employee to carry out.

Dealing with Public Reaction to Unfavorable Press Reports Regarding Company and Products

To:

From:

Date:

Regarding: Questions about recent TV piece

The recent *Loose Copy* piece about ABC Corporation is going to lead to some angry calls from customers, potential customers, and members of the media. We've isolated the product defect in the widget shipment and are in the process of issuing a recall of all the affected machinery. This is the message to get across to callers and others who want to voice their displeasure over the recent interview.

If the customer believes his or her widget is likely to be affected by the recall, please get the person's contact information and the serial number on the widget and arrange for a return call. Outsiders who badger you, ask you questions about the widget recall to which you don't know the answer, or otherwise make life impossible should be referred to me, Ed Jackson, or Dwight Williams. Any representative of the media should be referred to my office.

Alternate Version:

Given the high profile of the piece that aired last night about our recent widget shipment, we can probably expect some tough sledding in the form of calls from agitated customers and members of the general public.

The message to get across is a simple one: We've isolated the product defect in the widget shipment and are in the process of issuing a recall of all the affected machinery. If a customer believes his or her widget is likely to be recalled, please take down all appropriate contact information (including the serial number on the widget) and promise a return call within 72 hours.

It's likely you're going to speak with some callers who are quite upset about the piece that aired. If someone starts getting out of hand, please refer that person to myself, Ed Jackson, or Wayne Williams. If you speak with a representative of the media, please forward that call to me directly.

Thanks—and keep the faith! This won't last forever.

- Set out, in appropriate detail, the "company line" for responding to agitated or unhappy callers.
- Let the employee know where to refer difficult or sensitive callers.

Delay in Reporting Customer Complaints on Critical Product Issue

To:

From:

Date:

Regarding: We missed one . . .

We should have spotted—I should have spotted—the technical glitch on the Gizmo 2100 launch long before the entire round of initial orders was shipped. The first three days of the month provided us with enough information from customer complaint calls to raise the red flag. We missed the call.

Let's all work together on future new product releases to show the kind of vigilance that will help keep problems like this from slipping past us!

Alternate Version:

After a meeting with the president of the firm today, it's quite clear to me that we stumbled a few weeks back when we failed to report promptly the widespread customer problems with the WidgetMaster 2100, currently under recall.

I believe the ultimate responsibility for this problem rests with me. I should have seen the pattern emerging earlier than I did, rather than assuming the difficulties that were being called in were all unrelated. In any event, I'd like to ask for everyone's help and vigilance in keeping an eye out for potential problems on new releases that may emerge via customer calls.

Let's all work together to make sure we keep something like this from happening again! I know we can do it.

DEVELOPING A CUSTOMIZED MEMO? REMEMBER TO . . .

- Assume appropriate responsibility. (Casting blame on your team members in this situation won't get you very far.)
- Express your continued confidence in the team.

Error in Advertising Campaign

To:

From:

Date:

Regarding: Error in mailing piece and magazine campaign

Oops!

Copy in our mailing and magazine advertisements indicates that the Model 1600 widget is available for $1.95. It's not. The actual price is $19.95—the price listed in the circular and magazine ads is a typo.

You may get some calls on this. Please apologize on behalf of the person who let the erroneous figure slip by (me) and inform the customer of the correct price.

Thanks!

Alternate Version:

You're likely to get some calls from people requesting a Model 1600 Widget at the low, low, price of $1.95. It would be wonderful if we could deliver a bargain like that to our phone customers, but the sad truth is the price is a typographical error.

Please apologize profusely for any misunderstandings created by this error in our mailing materials and magazine campaign—and then inform the customer that the Model 1600 is actually available for $19.95 . . . a bargain even someone who proofread the ad copy (that's me) can see is still magnificent.

Thanks for helping us straighten this out!

DEVELOPING A CUSTOMIZED MEMO? REMEMBER TO . . .

- Provide all the pertinent details related to the error as it appeared.
- Thank employees in advance for their help in rectifying the problem.

Filling Out Daily Call Log: Guidelines

To:

From:

Date:

Regarding: Daily call log

The only way we can figure out what people are calling us about is to review your incoming call log at the end of the day. Please fill it out legibly and completely—including the "problem" section—and pass it in before you head out the door.

Remember—if a call comes in, it wins a spot on your log!

Thanks for helping us serve customers better.

Alternate Version:

Please remember—each and every incoming call you receive from a customer should be summarized and initialed on your incoming call log!

Your supervisor will be reviewing all the call logs at the conclusion of the day. Please be sure your handwriting in the "problem" section is legible— and make sure your call log is an accurate reflection of *every* call you received during the course of the day.

Thanks!

DEVELOPING A CUSTOMIZED MEMO? REMEMBER TO . . .

- Set out the appropriate guidelines for keeping call records, and make it clear which calls should be recorded.
- Thank employees for their help.

Following Up on a Specific Customer Complaint

To:

From:

Date:

Regarding: Complaint from Mel Basso concerning audiotape program

Thanks for your note. I'm pretty sure the audiotape program the customer is referring to is another one he saw on television (and perhaps ordered), but I want to check our advertising to be sure. That means a trip to the archives to get the appropriate tape. Would you mind calling Mr. Basso—see his letter, photocopy enclosed—to let him know we'll be back in touch no later than the end of this week?

Thanks.

Alternate Version

Thanks for your note regarding Mel Basso's query about the audiotape he was shipped. I'm still uncertain whether or not the television advertisement he refers to specifically mentions that there are weight-loss benefits to following the audiotape program. I think he may be confusing the tape with another program he ordered, but I want to doublecheck the ad copy on the commercial to be double-sure. If there is a reference to weight loss, I'm pretty sure it's presented as a possible side benefit to the program, not its main focus.

I should be able to get to the archives tomorrow morning at the latest. Would you mind calling Mr. Basso (the number's on the photocopy of his letter) and letting him know we'll be in touch about this by the end of the week? Many thanks.

Developing a Customized Memo? Remember to . . .

- Make the current status of the complaint clear to the reader.
- Set out appropriate "next step" instructions for your reader to carry out.
- Thank the employee for his or her help.

Fulfillment Delay: How to Respond to Customer Queries

To:

From:

Date:

Regarding: What to tell customers

Yes, we will still make December 24th delivery dates for customers who order before December 15th. *Yes,* we are experiencing some shipping delays due to heavy volume. *No,* you shouldn't get into a protracted exchange about whether or not a particular shipment went via Priority Guarantee status.

What to do when customers call? If you can, simply apologize for the delay, confirm the outer date of the 24th for all pre-December 15th orders, and thank the customer for his or her patience. Feel free to come see me about the best ways to respond to unusually complicated (or emotional) calls.

Alternate Version:

Due to heavy order volume and the recent bout of the flu that's making its way through the shipping department, our fulfillment times are running a week or so longer than our usual targets.

You're likely to get some calls from customers about this, given the estimated turnaround times mentioned in our catalog. Here's the best response to pass along:

"Yes, Mr./Ms. X, we are experiencing some delays in our shipping department, and I want to apologize for any inconvenience this may be causing you. The good news is that we still expect to make December 24th arrival dates for all goods ordered before the 15th of December."

Questions, problems, or unusually tough customers? Come see me and we'll figure out a way to make it work.

Developing a Customized Memo? Remember to . . .

- Supply your reader with a direct answer to the question(s) he or she is likely to face from customers.

- Offer help and guidance on dealing with complex calls or abusive callers.

Fulfillment Delay: Memo to Third-Party Fulfillment Service

To:

From:

Date:

Regarding: Shipping delays

Our customers are going nuts! What's up?

Please take a look at the enclosed correspondence and account information. These folks are reporting sixty- to ninety-day delivery cycles . . . which is a far cry from the two weeks we're promising them in our national advertising campaign.

I'd like to hear from you by phone no later than Friday so we can discuss what to do next.

Alternate Version:

We've gotten calls from at least twenty customers complaining about seriously late deliveries on the WidgetMaster 2000. Our television advertising promises delivery within two weeks—but some of our customers aren't receiving the product for two to three *months!*

Please review the enclosed correspondence and account number information. Then call me no later than Friday so we can discuss these problems and figure out what to do about them.

DEVELOPING A CUSTOMIZED MEMO? REMEMBER TO . . .

- Set out the problem you are hearing about from your customers, and consider including their letters or remarks as "supporting evidence."
- Ask for a call back by a certain date.

General Guidelines for Phone Response to Customer Complaints and Queries

To:

From:

Date:

Regarding: Phone demeanor and language

Don't forget: The tone of voice you use during interactions with customers who call us may be the single biggest factor in determining whether or not the call will become difficult.

Show a pleasant, upbeat attitude at the outset of the call and throughout it . . . and take a look at the list of "do" and "don't" words and phrases you'll find in your mailbox. They may help you refine your phone technique—and encounter fewer screamers!

Alternate Version:

Just a reminder—the tone of voice you use with customers and the words you choose during your phone conversations with them have an immense impact on their level of satisfaction with our company.

Please bear in mind that the emotion you project with your voice can help you overcome any obstacle with your customer. So can the words you choose.

Stay away from words like: problem; authorized; unauthorized; unavailable; delay; missed; difficulty; fault.

Emphasize words like: resolve; (your) satisfaction; apologize; sorry; happy; quickly; report; update; handle; complete; thorough; I and me (as opposed to the organization as a whole).

Thanks!

DEVELOPING A CUSTOMIZED MEMO? REMEMBER TO . . .

- Remind employees that attitude and vocal tone have a profound influence on interactions with customers.

- Consider providing a list of "do" and "don't" words (as above) selected specifically for your industry.

General Guidelines: Proper Written Response to Customer Complaints

To:

From:

Date:

Regarding: Written response to customer complaints

Don't wing it!

Odds are that a situation very similar to the problem you're preparing to address in a letter has already been handled at some point over the past sixteen years. Please check the archive response log in the central file cabinet for guidelines on written responses to customer complaints—and come see me in the unlikely event that you can't find a letter that parallels the situation you face. Thanks!

Alternate Version:

Please remember—we have a long history of responding to customer complaints, and the single best way to write an effective letter to a customer who has a problem is to check what we did in the past.

The letters archive is available in the central file cabinet for you to review. If there's a problem we haven't run into yet, a problem that isn't reflected in the archives, please come see me so we can strategize an approach that will fill the gap.

Thanks!

DEVELOPING A CUSTOMIZED MEMO? REMEMBER TO . . .

- If you can, let employees know where to go to gain access to your customer-service letter archives.
- If you can, specify how far back the archive's records extend.

General Memo: Service Levels

To:

From:

Date:

Regarding:

Our customers deserve the best! That's why I want to take two straight days—this coming Monday and Tuesday, August 1 and 2—to get together to talk in detail about how we can give it to them.

That's right. Adjusted schedules (attached) mean that everybody in the department gets one of these days with me in the conference room so we can discuss how best to address the needs of the people who make this business happen . . . the folks who use our widgets.

I look forward to spending the day with you. Check the schedule!

Alternate Version:

Monday and Tuesday, August 1 and 2, are going to be days unlike any other you've spent here.

I want to get your ideas on how we can improve the level of service we offer to the people who keep this joint open—our customers—and I want to offer a few ideas of my own. Check the new schedule: I've turned everything upside down so that everyone gets a full day, either Monday or Tuesday, with me in the conference room.

I look forward to hearing all your brainstorms!

Developing a Customized Memo? Remember to . . .

- Avoid negative or accusatory language (such as "unacceptable" or "poor service").
- Focus on the positive wherever possible.

Handling Requests for Purchase of Customer Lists

To:

From:

Date:

Regarding: XYZ Company request

Selling our customer list to XYZ could well represent a significant income opportunity, as you suggest—but Ms. Jackson needs to review all such requests personally.

I'd ask them to send a cover letter and a brochure to her attention, and then suggest that they check back with you in about a month.

Alternate Version:

Thanks for your recent note about the call you got from XYZ Company concerning the purchase of our customer lists. You're right in suggesting that this may present a new revenue opportunity for the company, but Ms. Jackson has asked to have information on any companies requesting database rights forwarded directly to her.

Why not ask the XYZ representative to send along a request letter and a brochure for her review—and promise a call back within 30 days?

DEVELOPING A CUSTOMIZED MEMO? REMEMBER TO . . .

- Let the employee know who is handling decisions in this area.
- Suggest a possible response to the person or institution requesting information about your customers.

Impending Product Recall

To:

From:

Date:

Regarding: Upcoming product recall

It's official—we will announce a recall of the model 5630 widget tomorrow morning at 10:00. There will be a brief meeting in conference room A at 2:00 this afternoon to review the steps we'll be taking for customers who approach us about 5630s they've purchased. Please be sure to attend.

Alternate Version:

We will be recalling the Model 5630 widget. There's a *mandatory* meeting for all staff members at 2:00 in conference room A concerning tomorrow's formal announcement on this. Be sure you attend! You'll receive important information on how to deal with customers who contact you about returning this product to ABC Corporation.

DEVELOPING A CUSTOMIZED MEMO? REMEMBER TO . . .

- Announce the recall forthrightly and without ambiguity.
- Clearly outline any preparatory steps you want the employee to take.

Implementation of New Toll-Free Customer Contact Line

To:

From:

Date:

Regarding: 1-888-WIDGETS (1-888-943-4377)

It's finally up and running!

Our new toll-free sales and customer service number is 1-888-WIDGETS (1-888-943-4377). Spread the word!

Alternate Version:

1-888-WIDGETS (1-888-943-4377) is our new toll-free contact line for any-body interested in reaching the ABC Corporation's sales and customer service departments.

This number will be featured prominently in all our national advertising, on our World Wide Web site, and in our product packaging. Please be sure to mention it prominently in all your calls with customers!

Developing a Customized Memo? Remember to . . .

- Use the number early on in the memo, preferably in the first sentence or two.
- Give both numeric and alphabetical renderings of the number (if both are being promoted).

Improper Circulation of Toll-Free Number

To:

From:

Date:

Regarding: Personal calls coming in on toll-free line

No kidding, folks! Instructing family and social acquaintances to call you from anywhere on the continent using our 1-888-WIDGETS line for personal calls is a violation of company policy . . . and it is, no kidding, grounds for disciplinary action, including dismissal. (It's also incredibly easy to track.)

Don't use the toll-free line for incoming personal calls!

Thanks.

Alternate Version:

I hate to have to play the Grinch here, but . . .

A review of our recent phone bills and transfer patterns indicates that a significant percentage of our calls on the 1-888-WIDGETS line have been routed, via the reception desk, to staff members who were not on the customer service crew at the time. Many of these calls extend for more than twenty minutes.

It doesn't take a rocket scientist to conclude that some of these unexplained calls are probably personal calls to employees who gave out the toll-free number to friends outside our calling area.

Please don't use the toll-free number for personal calls. It's a violation of company policy, it's really easy to track, and it is, I kid you not, grounds for disciplinary action, including dismissal.

Thanks for your cooperation.

DEVELOPING A CUSTOMIZED MEMO? REMEMBER TO . . .

- Make it clear (if appropriate) that disciplinary action or other unpleasant outcomes may await those who misuse the number.
- Give both numeric and alphabetical renderings of the number (if both are being used in promotional materials).

Initiating a Rush Order

To:

From:

Date:

Regarding: Rush order

The attached order represents a "fix-it" shipment to a long-term customer who received an incorrect shipment some time ago. It's been a long, hairy, and particularly strange trip for this particular customer, and I've authorized overnight shipment on this order as a fence-mending gesture.

Can you make sure it gets out tonight—or come see me before the close of business today so we can talk about other options?

Thanks.

Alternate Version:

I've authorized special overnight shipping on the attached order—we have to find a way to get this important customer back on our good side after an unfortunate series of shipment errors.

Can you please get this out via overnight? If time doesn't permit that, drop by my office so we can discuss other shipment options.

Thanks!

DEVELOPING A CUSTOMIZED MEMO? REMEMBER TO . . .

- Briefly explain why you feel rush status makes sense in this situation.
- Let the other person know that he or she should contact you if there are problems shipping the order expeditiously.

Memo to Customer Service Manager on Proper Training of Temporary Employees

To:

From:

Date:

Regarding: Temps

Bearing in mind some of the problems we've had with temporary employees in customer-service related positions in the past, I want to ask you to spend at least one hour—thirty minutes at the beginning of the first day and thirty minutes at the end of the first day for follow-up— reviewing key points with our temporary personnel who will deal with customers directly.

I've outlined some of the key points I think these folks have to remember on the summary sheet you'll find in your mailbox. Let me know what you think, and get back in touch if you feel there are other issues we need to address with temp workers. Please go over all this material with temporary customer service people.

Thanks!

Alternate Version:

With the rush season upon us, we're going to need to review some rudimentary training procedures for the temps we'll be using over the next month and a half. Please be sure you spend at least one half-hour at the beginning and end of each temp's first day reviewing the following points:

- When in doubt about the availability of a product, *check with a manager.*
- We cannot guarantee December 24th delivery of any product after December 15th.
- Every incoming call must be logged completely and legibly on the call sheets. (This may be the most important step of all!)

I know this stuff is old hat for us—but that's all the more reason to make sure the new people we bring on board have all the basics down.

Thanks for making sure this holiday season is a successful one for us . . . and our customers!

DEVELOPING A CUSTOMIZED MEMO? REMEMBER TO . . .

- Consider requesting a specific amount of time you want the person to spend training the new workers.
- Consider outlining points that will help temps avoid trouble areas that have arisen in the past.
- Thank the employee for his or her help.

Monthly Management Meeting with Customer Service Representatives for Feedback Sessions

To:

From:

Date:

Regarding: This month's meeting on customer issues

This month's meetings between senior ABC Corporation officials and front-line customer service associates will take place on Monday, August 1, at 10:00 am, and Tuesday, August 2, at 3:00 pm. Come and share what you've been hearing from our customers with some very senior people in the company—including president Mark Bigshot.

Alternate Version:

As you know, ABC Corporation has a policy of bringing senior management together with front-line customer service people in order to get the latest information from the people who talk to the folks who actually use our widgets.

This month's meetings are scheduled for Monday, August 1, at 10:00 am, and Tuesday, August 2, at 3:00 pm. Each and every service associate should be able to attend at least one of these meetings. Attendance is not mandatory—but bear in mind that if you miss this month's meetings, you'll miss out on the opportunity to meet with our company's president, Mark Bigshot.

DEVELOPING A CUSTOMIZED MEMO? REMEMBER TO . . .

- Outline when and where the meeting will be taking place.
- If appropriate, highlight senior officials who will be in attendance.
- Keep the tone enthusiastic and upbeat.

Necessity of Rapid Follow-Up on Customer Complaints

To:

From:

Date:

Regarding: Follow-up

Effective January 1, every single incoming customer call to ABC Corporation must receive a follow-up status call (or attempted call) within 24 hours. This process must continue until your supervisor designates the call as "no further action." If you have questions about this policy, feel free to contact me.

Thanks for helping us make ABC Corporation the most customer-responsive company in the industry!

Alternate Version:

Remember—this year's standard for follow-through on an incoming customer call is 24 hours—and not a minute more! The process must continue until the customer's issue is considered resolved by your supervisor.

We are *committed* to responding with updates or solutions to callers to our customer-service line within this time-frame. If you take the call, keep your customer informed as to what's happening—until the problem is designated as "no further action" by your supervisor.

Questions? Problems? Call me or your supervisor, and we'll do everything we can to help.

Many thanks.

DEVELOPING A CUSTOMIZED MEMO? REMEMBER TO . . .

- Make the current guidelines completely clear.
- Let employees know whom they should contact with questions or problems.
- Outline the follow-up standard with energy and enthusiasm.

New Data Management System: General Guidelines for Transition Period

We're going to have significant limitations on the access to our customer data between now and January 1 as we switch over to a new computer system. As a result, we're going to have to put a hold on all refund and warrantee requests that require access to information before May, 19xx.

In your mailbox, you will find some strategies for dealing with the customer service issues we're likely to face over the next (challenging) month or so. Please feel free to drop by my office if you want to discuss the new system, how marvelous it's going to be, or how to look graceful while we're improvising over the next thirty days.

Thanks in advance for your patience. Remember, I'm here to help when things get tricky.

Alternate Version:

A temporary period of profound chaos is about to descend on our department as we transfer all our data from the old Snookero 5000 computer system—complete with its vintage 1974 interface—to the Fasttrack 2000 system that's been especially designed for us by the folks at Hyperware.

For about three weeks, we will only have access to hard copy customer files, material that will not list complete purchase records. Only the past six months of information about the customer will be available, which means that refund requests and other queries that require access to more detailed history will have to wait until January 1 for resolution.

Thank you for bearing with us during the switchover. Please apologize to all affected customers—and see the attached guidelines for dealing with specific problems that may arise during this sure-to-be-fascinating transition period.

DEVELOPING A CUSTOMIZED MEMO? REMEMBER TO . . .

- Get the "downside" news about the transition out quickly and with good humor.
- Let employees know whom they should contact with questions or problems.
- Thank employees in advance for their patience.

New Direct Mail Campaign

To:

From:

Date:

Regarding: Our new direct-mail campaign

When customers start calling in asking about a two-year warranty on the Model 1400 widget, they won't be hallucinating. They'll be responding to our latest mailing piece (check your mailbox for a copy.) I believe this is our sharpest direct-mail entry yet.

Please take a good, long look at this exquisite piece of work from our promotional and design people—I want us all to be able to discuss our department's reaction to this mailing at our monthly meeting with Ms. Bigg.

Alternate Version:

Attached please find a copy of the new mailing that just went out to about 1600 of our best customers. Pretty sharp, huh?

Note the reference to the Model 1400 widget. The warranty on this model has been extended to a full two years, which is something you'll need to know if you field calls from customers who call in as a result of this mailing. There are going to be plenty of them!

Please read the piece in full by the end of this week so we can discuss it at the monthly meeting with Ms. Bigg.

DEVELOPING A CUSTOMIZED MEMO? REMEMBER TO . . .

- Encourage employees to become personally familiar with the latest marketing piece.
- Highlight any customer-service issues the new direct-mail piece will raise.

New Marketing Campaign Requires Extended Phone Shift Schedules

To:

From:

Date:

Regarding: Phone shifts

Everybody (yours truly included) needs to sign up for one night of two-hour call duty during the upcoming month, our biggest month of the year in terms of sales. Head to the sign-up sheet before all the choice slots are taken.

By the way, everyone who signs up (and that has to be everyone) will receive five dollars in scratch-and-win Instant Bucks state lottery cards. So in addition to the overtime pay, you could just walk away from your shift $25,000 richer!

Alternate Version:

The bad news—we're each going to have to find a way to squeeze at least two straight overtime hours per week into the schedule for the next month. Pick a day, any day—as long as someone else hasn't picked it first. The sign-up sheet is posted in the employee lounge.

The good news—at the conclusion of each and every two-hour stint, each associate will receive five dollars' worth of Instant Bucks scratch-and-win state lottery cards. So you never know: you could walk away from your shift $20,000 dollars richer!

Thanks in advance for signing up. Everybody (yours truly included) needs to pick a shift.

DEVELOPING A CUSTOMIZED MEMO? REMEMBER TO . . .

- Strongly consider signing up for a shift yourself.
- Consider using appropriate low-cost incentives (as above).
- Avoid a dictatorial or bureaucratic tone.

New Product Release by Competitor

To:

From:

Date:

Regarding: The New Widgetmaster

As you may have heard, our loyal opposition over at Widgetmaster just released the Widgetmaster 600, a unit that competes directly with our Gizmo 2400. Customers may be asking about the new unit, thanks to a snazzy new nationwide advertising campaign.

FYI: In addition to costing $240 more than our unit and failing to offer a free yearlong service plan as ours does, the Widgetmaster has a significantly lower input-output ratio than the Gizmo 2400. See the enclosed article from *Consumer Reports* (October 3, 19XX).

Alternate Version:

The folks at Widgetmaster are now releasing the Widgetmaster 600 and are accompanying it with a snazzy national media campaign. In case customers who call in mention this, I thought you might appreciate the following points of comparison with the new Widgetmaster product.

- Our Gizmo 2400 has a higher input-output ratio, as verified by *Consumer Reports* in its October 3, 19XX issue (copy attached).
- The Gizmo 2400 costs $240 less than the Widgetmaster 600.
- The Widgetmaster does not come with a free yearlong service contract—the Gizmo 2400 does!

Developing a Customized Memo? Remember to . . .

- Isolate, and briefly describe, the most impressive advantages your product or service holds over the competition.
- Be sure to specify any price or service shortcomings in what the competition has offered.

New Product Introduction

To:

From:

Date:

Regarding: Our new Gizmo 3000 unit

Get ready for the new Gizmo 3000!

This low-priced, high-performance widget, which begins shipping this week, is going to revolutionize the widget industry. I'm enclosing a brochure about the new product, which I'd like you to review carefully as soon as possible. I'd also like you to make a point of passing along any feedback you receive from customers who call us regarding this unit.

Thanks!

Alternate Version:

Ready to help us turn the widget industry upside down?

The new Gizmo 3000 unit, which begins shipping this week, has the highest input-output ratio of any widget in its class. It also features a higher processing speed than any widget available in the United States for under $500—including anything Widgetmaster has to offer.

Enclosed please find a brochure about the Gizmo 3000. Please look it over carefully . . . and be sure to pass along any and all comments from consumers concerning the new unit!

Thanks!

DEVELOPING A CUSTOMIZED MEMO? REMEMBER TO . . .

- Lead the memo with a sentence that conveys excitement and drama appropriate to the event.
- Isolate, and briefly describe, the most impressive advantages your product or service holds over the competition.

Out of Stock on Popular Item

To:

From:

Date:

Regarding: Gizmo 3500 is out of stock

Bad news—but it won't last long.

The Gizmo 3500 is out of stock. We should be receiving another shipment from Virginia around the middle of this month.

Please apologize for the delay and inform customers who call that we'll be back on track soon—no later than the fifteenth. All current in-house orders should be in the customers' hands no later than seven working days from that date.

Alternate Version:

Demand has outstripped supply—for a week or two.

Due to heavy customer response to our new national advertising campaign, our warehouses are currently stocked out of the Gizmo 3500. But you can feel free to tell customers that this situation won't last for long. We'll be back in full swing by the middle of this month.

Please apologize for the delay and tell our customers we truly appreciate their decision to go with ABC Corporation.

DEVELOPING A CUSTOMIZED MEMO? REMEMBER TO . . .

- Let employees know approximately how long the out-of-stock situation is likely to last.
- Offer guidance on exactly what to say to customers whose orders have been delayed.

Prioritizing Incoming Customer Calls

To:

From:

Date:

Regarding: The big twelve

I'm forwarding a list of twelve of ABC's key institutional customers. If you receive a call from anyone representing one of these organizations, please show them how superb our customer service can be.

The businesses on this list represent 64% of ABC Corporation's annual revenue! The better we treat them, the likelier we are to hit our targets this quarter.

Thanks!

Alternate Version:

Every customer matters . . . but when *some* customers call, they matter in a way that is truly extraordinary.

I'm forwarding a list of twelve key organizations who buy from us. Please keep an ear out for references to these groups during your phone contacts. We should, by all means, assume that an incoming customer call is from one of these groups . . . but when we receive undeniable proof that one is, we should make a special effort to go above and beyond the call to satisfy the person who's contacted us.

The organizations on the attached list represent 64% of our gross revenue. Let's be sure we treat them right!

Developing a Customized Memo? Remember to . . .

- Attempt to quantify the importance of the selected customers by highlighting (if appropriate) their dollar value or the portion of the company's revenue they represent.
- Keep the memo's tone enthusiastic and upbeat.

Privacy Considerations Regarding Customer Records

To:

From:

Date:

Regarding: Inquiries concerning customers

Please bear in mind—we do not give out customer names, addresses, phone numbers, or purchase information to unknown parties who contact us.

We do sell customer *lists* under certain situations. If the caller is interested in purchasing a list of 1500 or more customer contact names, please refer him or her to Melanie Enright. Many thanks.

Alternate Version:

"Sorry—we don't give out that kind of information about our customers."

That's what we need to say if people call in asking about individual customers, how to contact them, or what sort of products they buy from us. People who wish to buy customer *lists* should be referred to Melanie Enright.

Thanks a lot!

Developing a Customized Memo? Remember to . . .

- Outline clearly and directly how employees should respond when they are approached for customer information.
- Let the employees know who handles queries for purchases of customer information.

Querying Customers on Key Product Issues

To:

From:

Date:

Regarding: Customer questionnaire on future product features

We need your help in figuring out what the next breakthrough widget will look like!

Please call the thirty people whose names and numbers are featured on the printout you'll find in your mailbox. Get through to as many as you can and ask them the seven questions listed on the enclosed script. Write down the answers in detail.

Your goal: full response sheets from at least ten current customers!

It should take you about three hours. Please drop everything off to me when you're done. Thanks!

Alternate Version:

We're considering a new product launch—and we need your help!

I'm forwarding a list of questions about widget purchase patterns, as well as contact information for thirty current customers. Sometime today, can you call all thirty—and ask as many as you can the questions we've outlined? Your supervisor knows that this assignment is coming your way and will make the time for you. Your goal is to get full responses to each of the questions from at least ten of the thirty people you contact. Please hand the forms back to me when you're done.

Thanks!

Developing a Customized Memo? Remember to . . .

- Briefly describe the resource materials employees will be using to contact people.
- Let employees know who should receive call materials when the job is done.

Relaying Customer Service Information

To:

From:

Date:

Regarding: News from the front

I thought you'd want to hear about this right away.

The people in customer service are reporting unusually high failure rates on the Gizmo 3600 unit. There appears to be some problem with the servo mechanism. I've forwarded verbatim transcripts of some of my discussions with the people in the department.

Do you think it's worth getting engineering to take a look at this?

Alternate Version:

The customer service people may have caught the first evidence of a glitch in the Gizmo 3600.

In your mailbox, you'll find transcripts of some remarks I heard this morning during the weekly meeting. I believe these problems point to a flaw in the servo mechanism.

Do you think it's worth asking the people in engineering to take a look at this?

DEVELOPING A CUSTOMIZED MEMO? REMEMBER TO . . .

- Consider using a stand-alone one-sentence first paragraph that will immediately capture your reader's attention and let him or her know that a possible problem exists.
- Suggest a possible next step.

Reminder: Every Customer Complaint Must Be Treated with Respect

To:

From:

Date:

Regarding: Playing it cool

I realize some customers go off the deep end. But we have to keep our cool—it's in the mission statement!

Seriously, every single customer deserves to be treated with respect, even those who sound like they're hyperventilating. If a particular customer has given you the first signs of a bad day, don't vent back. Come see me so we can talk about what happened!

Alternate Version:

Don't be furious . . . be curious!

Even customers who seem like they're about to have a mental breakdown respond better to calm, persistent, focused nonthreatening questions than to combative talk. Every single customer we have deserves to be treated with respect. Disengage, assume personal responsibility, and then ask appropriate questions. See what happens.

And feel free to stop by my office after those particularly rough calls.

Developing a Customized Memo? Remember to . . .

- Emphasize the importance of staying calm with customers.
- Acknowledge that some customers are difficult to handle.
- Be open to discussion regarding difficult calls.

Reminder: Present Customer is Our Best Prospect for Future Business

To:

From:

Date:

Regarding: Current customers—let's keep 'em!

Our current customer—the man or woman calling in on the phone today—represents our single best prospect for new widget orders.

The more customers we keep happy, the more customers we'll keep. And the more customers we keep, the closer we'll all be to winning that end-of-year bonus!

Alternate Version:

Don't forget—it's a lot easier to keep a customer happy than it is to find a new customer.

The customer who calls in with a question, problem, or suggestion is the life-blood of our organization. He or she doesn't have to come to us for widgets . . . but we have to track down someone else to take his or her place if the relationship ends.

As if that weren't enough, bear this in mind: The fewer customers we lose, the greater our likelihood of meeting this quarter's sales target and earning that quarterly bonus!

Developing a Customized Memo? Remember to . . .

- Emphasize the importance of the customer to the company.
- Mention bonus to be earned as a result of customer satisfaction.

Reminder: Product Development Information is Not for Public Release

To:

From:

Date:

Regarding: Mum's the word

Great meeting on the upcoming WidgetAlert 9000 system! Thanks for all your input—and please remember that the product specifications we discussed on this possible new product are proprietary information. That means nobody gets to hear about it, not even customers, until we set and announce a formal launch date.

Thanks for your cooperation!

Alternate Version:

Thanks for your input on the WidgetAlert 9000 system during our weekly departmental meeting. It was a great session.

Please remember that the product specifications we discussed are still proprietary information, subject to change, and not to be discussed with any individual who is not an ABC Corporation employee. Yes, that includes customers.

Loose lips sink ships! Thanks for keeping this sensitive information embargoed until we determine our final product launch strategy.

DEVELOPING A CUSTOMIZED MEMO? REMEMBER TO . . .

- Acknowledge and applaud the recent productive meeting.
- Stress the proprietary nature of the discussion.
- Emphasize the importance of keeping product information confidential.

Specific Instance of Discourteous Treatment of Client or Customer

To:

From:

Date:

Regarding: Bert Feeney's recent call

Wow! That must have been one tough call.

The discussion you had with Bert Feeney today seemed to me like it could have gone a little better for both of you. Why don't we get together to talk about it today for a few minutes before you head home?

Alternate Version:

I couldn't help overhearing the call you had this morning concerning the warranty on our Gizmo 3200 units. After checking the call reports, I was able to determine that Bert Feeney, the customer who made the call, had made three other calls in an attempt to resolve this problem.

I think you and I should get together to talk about how you handled this account, and figure out some more strategies for handling difficult customers. Can you stop by my office before you leave this afternoon? Thanks.

DEVELOPING A CUSTOMIZED MEMO? REMEMBER TO . . .

- Mention the specific problem that has been observed.
- Note that the problem call could have been handled better.
- Suggest discussing the problem to work out a solution.

Transfer of Employee to Administrative Customer Service Function

To:

From:

Date:

Regarding: Possible new assignment

I was thinking all weekend about the best way to help you make the most positive contribution. Bottom line: I want to help you keep your stress level down to manageable levels.

I've got some ideas on how we can do that, and I think they're pretty exciting. Can you swing by my office at 3:00 today so we can talk about them?

Alternate Version:

After thinking things over long and hard, I've decided that you'll probably be a good deal happier in an administrative setting, rather than a front-line customer service position.

Why don't we get together today to talk about some opportunities you'll be able to take advantage of? I think there are some assignments that will really be up your alley—and leave you feeling less stressed at the end of the day.

Is 3:00 today a good time to talk?

DEVELOPING A CUSTOMIZED MEMO? REMEMBER TO . . .

- Note benefits to the employee of a change in position.
- Express your desire to help the employee make the appropriate change.
- Suggest a time to meet and discuss the situation.

Uniform Response When Answering Phone

To:

From:

Date:

Regarding: Greetings!

We've got a new way of greeting the world!

Our official response when a call is transferred to this department is as follows:

"Thanks for calling ABC—this is (name). How can I help you?"

This is a *mandatory* greeting; we need to use it with every single customer who calls. Please help us keep our service contacts dependable and upbeat. Use the new greeting every time, and smile when you do!

Alternate Version:

The new phone greeting for *every* call that comes into the department is as follows:

"Thanks for calling ABC—this is (name). How can I help you?"

Please be sure to use this greeting in a cheerful, upbeat way with each customer you greet over the phone.

Thanks!

Developing a Customized Memo? Remember to . . .

- Provide the specific wording for the new greeting.
- Note the official greeting is required for all calls.
- Boost a cheerful telephone manner.

Verification of Credit Card Numbers: Guidelines

To:

From:

Date:

Regarding: Credit card numbers

Help!

The accounting department reports a 12% decline rate on our credit card verifications. That's too high! We need to make better use of everyone's time and read back the number and expiration date slowly and carefully to all customers placing credit orders.

Your best bet: pause briefly between each four-number set as you read the numbers back to your customer. Thanks for helping us make the most of your time . . . and the time of the people in accounting, too. If we post another month like that one, they may just make us do all the verification calls ourselves!

Alternate Version:

Please remember—a credit card order is not complete until you've read the card number and expiration date back to the customer slowly and carefully.

When in doubt, pause briefly after each four-number group just to be absolutely sure the customer is reviewing the numbers with you.

Thanks!

Developing a Customized Memo? Remember to . . .

- Note the importance of getting complete credit card information.
- Provide a protocol to follow for credit card orders.
- Emphasize care to be taken in handling credit card numbers.

Voice-Mail Protocol Problems

To:

From:

Date:

Regarding: Transfer of voice-mail messages

We're ticking off customers!

Excessive use of the "call-forwarding" option on our voice-mail system means that customers calling in for a specific rep are being transferred to two, three, or even four voice mailboxes in a row! Please use your "call-forwarding" option only in dire emergencies, and for no more than two one-hour periods per week.

Alternate Version:

Some of our customers are complaining about the excessive use of the "call-forwarding" option on our voice-mail system, and who can blame them? Some of them are dealing with four consecutive voice mailboxes!

Let's keep the use of the "call-forwarding" option to a minimum—and shoot for no more than two one-hour uses per week.

Thanks!

DEVELOPING A CUSTOMIZED MEMO? REMEMBER TO . . .

- Describe the consequences to customers of excessive call-forwarding.
- Suggest a policy to be followed on the use of call-forwarding.

Warning: Inappropriate Response to Customer Query

To:

From:

Date:

Regarding: Your call with Mr. Newman today

Thanks for meeting with me today concerning your call with Mr. Newman.

I know that that call represents an exception to your usually superb interpersonal work with customers, but I have to tell you I was concerned about it. I need to be able to count on you to develop solutions for our incoming callers, and to continue to set an excellent example for the other people in the department. If you feel there's some obstacle to your doing those things that I ought to know about, let me know right away.

Deal?

Alternate Version:

As we discussed during our one-on-one meeting today, I'm very concerned about your responses to our customer Bert Newman today over the phone. I know the language you used with him represents a temporary slip—you're usually excellent on the phone, even with difficult customers—but I really want to make sure it doesn't happen again.

Let's work together to make sure calls like that are a thing of the past! I'm counting on you to continue to set a superb example for others in the office in dealing with tough calls.

DEVELOPING A CUSTOMIZED MEMO? REMEMBER TO . . .

- Summarize the recent meeting.
- Acknowledge employee's normal good track record.
- Offer assistance in dealing with future customer service problems.

Warning to Customer Service Representative: Tardiness

To:

From:

Date:

Regarding: Arrival times

This morning was the fifteenth time over the past sixty days that you arrived for work at least ten minutes after the beginning of your shift.

Our customers are counting on you—and *I'm* counting on you—to take your place at the phone at the proper time and help keep on-hold times to an absolute minimum.

Please find a way to make it in on time for the beginning of your shift. If you don't, you're going to leave me no choice but to post a formal written warning in your personnel file.

Alternate Version:

I need your help.

This morning marked the fifteenth time over the last sixty days that you came in at least ten minutes after the scheduled start time of your shift. Your arrival time has become a real problem, and we have to find a way to work on it together.

This tardiness pattern simply isn't fair, and I know you'll want to work with me to find a way to overcome it. It's not fair to make people on the previous shift (or on your shift) field calls in your place. It's not fair to force customers to wait on hold for longer than they should. And it certainly isn't fair to the organization as a whole for you to collect pay for time when you don't work . . . and set a bad example for other staff members who look up to you (of which there are quite a few).

Please show up for work on time. If you don't, I'll have to issue a formal reprimand, and I don't want to do that.

Developing a Customized Memo? Remember to . . .

- Describe the recurring problem.
- Explain the effect of employee's tardiness on customers and staff.
- Warn of possible consequences if the problem is not corrected.

Wrong Shipments: Authorization for Reshipment

To:

From:

Date:

Regarding: Reshipment

Your caller is absolutely correct; his shipment never went out. It was misshipped to another customer due to a computer error. Please let the people in shipping know that a reshipment to the correct address needs to go out as soon as possible. This memo authorizes the reshipment.

Alternate Version:

You're right; the shipment that went out under our invoice #4345 was mistakenly shipped to another customer, as your caller suspected.

Please let the people in shipping know that the order needs to go out right away to the correct addressee. (This memo, a copy of which is being sent to Operations, authorizes the reshipment.) Then please give the customer a call back to let him know when he can expect delivery.

Thanks!

DEVELOPING A CUSTOMIZED MEMO? REMEMBER TO . . .

- Acknowledge the customer's call about the shipment.
- Explain what happened.
- Provide authorization for reshipment.

Quality Control

This chapter offers memos that cover numerous aspects of quality control, including: clarification of policies and procedures to be followed in matters affecting quality; working with marketing and customer service departments; dealing with clients and vendors; handling existing and potential challenges; soliciting ideas and feedback on a product from employees; and making recommendations for actions to be taken on defective or problematic products.

Addressing Concerns of Marketing Department with Regard to Quality Problems

To:

From:

Date:

Regarding: Quality issues

You're right. The input-output levels on some of the units we shipped last quarter don't live up to the claims you're preparing to make in this quarter's ad copy.

I'm still not sure about how widespread this problem is, or to what degree it has affected our current stock—but I'm working hard to track down the answers. Can I get back in touch with you early next week, so we can review the data together?

Alternate Version:

Thanks for your recent note concerning the unacceptably low input-output ratios on some of our Widgetmaster 6000 units.

There does appear to have been a lapse in production standards here. I understand your concerns, given the emphasis on input-output ratios in the upcoming print advertising campaign.

From all I can gather, the problem appears to be a mechanical one that affects a very small—but certainly noticeable and important—percentage of our shipments this quarter. I am still looking into what happened and how much the problem affects our current inventory. Can I get back to you early next week, when I know more about the scope of the problem?

Developing a Customized Memo? Remember to . . .

- Acknowledge existing quality problems.
- Note that the problem is being investigated.
- Suggest a time frame for follow-up discussion.

Addressing Concerns of Marketing Department with Regard to Revised Production Schedule

To:

From:

Date:

Regarding: Production schedules

We may be able to squeeze a week out of the production dates on the monthly summary, but I really don't think we're going to make delivery any sooner than that. (Even a week is going to be tough to pull off given our current workload!)

I know it's not going to be much fun breaking the news to customers who are expecting delivery at the end of this month. Want some help passing the word along?

Alternate Version:

I had a feeling those new dates were going to capture your attention.

I'm not really sure how much leeway there is to adjust the completion dates, given our current workload. We may be able to juggle schedules somewhat and move things up to the first of the month, but even that looks shaky right now.

Of course, I realize this is going to be less than welcome news to customers who are expecting earlier delivery. If you want help from anyone in this department explaining the hows and whys of the delay, please let me know. I'll be glad to help out in any way I can.

DEVELOPING A CUSTOMIZED MEMO? REMEMBER TO . . .

- Explain why the dates under discussion cannot be met.
- Outline your recent attempts to catch up.
- Offer assistance in dealing with customer concerns.

Client Requires New Specifications

Mel Miller at Acme Equipment has asked for new specifications on the Widget Delivery System I mentioned to you last month. They're pretty complicated.

I've attached a copy of the specs he wants to incorporate. How do you think we should proceed with this?

Alternate Version:

I had a long discussion with Mel Miller over at Acme Equipment today; he's opted for a complete redesign of the Widget Delivery Unit we discussed last month.

The attached sheet outlines the new specifications he wants to incorporate. Can we incorporate these using our standard pricing books? Or should we start from scratch with the people in Production to develop a customized estimate?

Developing a Customized Memo? Remember to . . .

- Name the client and the product requiring the redesign.
- Provide the desired new specifications.
- Ask for suggestions on how to proceed.

Dealing with Unacceptable Quality-Control Procedures on the Part of a Long-Standing Vendor

To:

From:

Date:

Regarding: Quality problems on widget casings

There are significant variations in the thickness of the casings we were just shipped by Friendly Casing. A fairly extensive sample indicates that the casings differ in thickness by as much as 30%.

I really want to get together with the people at Friendly to discuss this. If this problem arose with any other vendor, we would probably switch outfits without a thought. But I think there's still the chance for a good long-term relationship here. Can you set up a meeting between you, me, and the highest-ranking people at Friendly we can get in touch with?

Thanks!

Alternate Version:

The widget casings that Friendly Casing Corporation delivered to us last week have thickness variations of up to 30%.

This figure is significantly above the tolerances mentioned in our specs, and I'll warrant that it's well above industry standards, too. I think you and I need to schedule a meeting with the highest-ranking people we can track down at Friendly Casing to talk about improving the quality level in these shipments.

Our relationship with Friendly is an important one, and it's one that's worth trying to preserve. But we need to talk face-to-face with them about this problem. Can you try to set up a meeting for us?

Thanks!

DEVELOPING A CUSTOMIZED MEMO? REMEMBER TO . . .

- Indicate the vendor and describe the specific product problem.
- Note your desire to maintain a good working relationship with the vendor.
- Request assistance in setting up a meeting to resolve the problem.

Denial of Request for Waiver from Specifications

To:

From:

Date:

Regarding: Your request for a waiver

I know your schedule is tight, but I'm afraid I can't okay the waiver you've requested. The possibility that it would lower the unit's performance level below the necessary 6:1 input-output ratio is just too strong, at least in my estimation.

If you've got other ideas about ways we can make the schedule look better, I'd be happy to talk them over with you.

Alternate Version:

I understand the time sensitivity you outlined in your recent memo, but I'm afraid I can't authorize the waiver you've asked for. The specifications we set out were designed to help our widgets deliver a final input/output ratio of 6:1; if we proceed along the lines you suggest, I think it's quite conceivable that our widget's performance would dip below that level.

If you'd like to discuss other ideas for meeting the deadline, please feel free to drop by my office so we can discuss them.

Developing a Customized Memo? Remember to . . .

- Acknowledge the concerns that led to the waiver request.
- Note any possible effect of a waiver on product quality.
- Suggest a meeting to discuss alternatives.

Design Flaw in Prototype

To:

From:

Date:

Regarding: Design flaw in Widgetron 4000 prototype

I think I may have spotted a design flaw in the Widgetron 4000 unit. Weren't the Greenville baffles meant to be inserted so they spin in a clockwise direction? The current unit features a counterclockwise setup.

Maybe we need to tinker with it some . . . what do you think?

Alternate Version:

I don't know how it slipped past me earlier, but it did. The current prototype for the Widgetron 4000 unit features Greenville baffles that are meant to circulate in a counterclockwise direction. I checked the plans—these baffles are supposed to circulate clockwise.

Can you please retool the prototype ASAP? Thanks!

DEVELOPING A CUSTOMIZED MEMO? REMEMBER TO . . .

- Describe the particular design flaw.
- Suggest a re-design to correct the flaw.

Encouraging All Employees to Develop Familiarity with Product

To:

From:

Date:

Regarding: Check it out!

The Widgetron 2000 is now up and running. Stop by the employee lounge and try it out!

I'm eager to hear what you have to say—positive or negative—about this new product, which begins shipping on January 1. Feel free to use the special forms you'll find near the sample units to provide feedback . . . on an anonymous basis if you wish.

Alternate Version:

Come try out the Widgetron 2000!

This unit, which is due to ship on January 1, is now available for inspection and use. Please swing by the employee lounge; there you'll find a half-dozen of the new units. Try them out and let us know what you like (or don't like) about this new product. You can make comments—anonymously if you wish—by using the special forms you'll find nearby.

I think this is a pretty exciting widget. I bet you will, too.

DEVELOPING A CUSTOMIZED MEMO? REMEMBER TO . . .

- Note when the product will begin shipping.
- Indicate where the employee may go to inspect the product.
- Request employee feedback.

Encouraging Customer Service Department to Relay Complaints Quickly to Quality Control People

To:

From:

Date:

Regarding: Keep engineering and quality control people posted

Is there something you're not telling me?

Seriously, if there's a pattern of complaints from customers that indicates a problem in shipping, design, or manufacturing, I want to hear about it as soon as possible. You can always relay the specifics of consumer complaints to me—in writing, and on a confidential basis, if you wish.

Thanks for helping me isolate problems early on—and reduce your workload!

Alternate Version:

No one likes to be the bearer of bad news, but . . . we want to hear bad news from you sooner, rather than later!

If there are consumer complaints you think we ought to hear about—complaints that might, for instance, indicate a pattern in shipping, manufacture, or design that needs to be addressed immediately—please don't put off the job of letting the appropriate people know. The details of any and all consumer complaints can *always* be relayed confidentially, in writing, to me.

Help us solve the little problems *before* they become big problems.

DEVELOPING A CUSTOMIZED MEMO? REMEMBER TO . . .

- Emphasize the importance of addressing recurring customer complaints.

- Note that problems may be addressed confidentially.
- Mention the benefits of timely attention to customer service problems.

Encouraging Operations Department to Be on Lookout for Quality Problems Before Shipment

To:

From:

Date:

Regarding: Shipping protocol: Quality control

I'm out to lower our return and reshipment levels dramatically. A few simple steps can help us do it.

Before you ship a lot, please unbox one unit and run the self-diagnostic test (i.e., depress the red button on the back of the unit). If the unit performs properly and displays the green "on" signal, we'll assume the lot is good to ship. If it doesn't, please set the lot aside and let me know about the diagnostic problem.

Thanks!

Alternate Version:

I know you're busy with the holiday rush, but . . .

We can cut down significantly on reshipments if we make a quick "sample check" of one widget per 2000 units shipped. All this requires is that someone in your department (I'd recommend the shop foreman) unbox a unit at random from the lot that's been selected and run a self-diagnostic test by pressing the small red button on the back of the widget. If everything checks out—and the process takes about forty-five seconds—the lot goes out. If there's a problem, just put the lot aside and get someone in engineering to review it.

This is a simple step that can cut down on returns by up to 30%!

DEVELOPING A CUSTOMIZED MEMO? REMEMBER TO. . .

- Emphasize the benefits of quality control.

- Make recommendations for spotting problems.
- Provide a solution for handling problems.

Encouraging Subordinates to "Stop the Line"

To:

From:

Date:

Regarding: Hold everything!

We're shooting for a 99.99% error-free rate this quarter on randomly select-ed lots of widgets. Help us hit that mark! If you see a problem, stop the pro-duction line and tell your supervisor.

Alternate Version:

Remember: If you spot a problem on the production line, you are autho-rized to stop the line! Any employee who keeps a defective widget from going out the door gets a pat on the back—not a lecture about schedules. That's a promise.

DEVELOPING A CUSTOMIZED MEMO? REMEMBER TO. . .

- Reassure the employee that it's all right to stop the line.
- State the importance of stopping the line when necessary.

Encouraging Subordinates to Pass Along Ideas for Better Quality Control

To:

From:

Date:

Regarding: Your ideas for quality control

If you've got an idea about how we can lower our error rates on our wid-gets, please come and tell me about it. We need everyone's help if we're going to hit this quarter's error-free targets.

Thanks!

Alternate Version:

Have you got a brainstorm about how we can lower our error rate this quarter, or otherwise improve the quality of the widgets we ship? I want to hear about it!

Please feel free to drop me a line or e-mail me with any ideas you have on quality improvement. Speak up—because the sooner you do, the closer we'll be to hitting our quality targets this quarter.

DEVELOPING A CUSTOMIZED MEMO? REMEMBER TO. . .

- Make clear that new ideas are welcome.
- Emphasize that ideas will help to meet goals.
- Convey a feeling of togetherness.

Explaining Employee Error to Superior

To:

From:

Date:

Regarding: Analysis of assembly problem

As you requested, I've figured out why the sizing was off on our prototype for the X-2000 unit. Sheila Banyon made a spreadsheet error that was not detected by the design team.

I've spoken to Sheila about the importance of attention to detail. I don't think we'll have this problem again.

Alternate Version:

Well, I figured out what caused the sizing problem. A minor spreadsheet error on Sheila's part in Estimating slipped past us. I've spoken to her about the importance of double-checking her work before she turns it in.

Developing a Customized Memo? Remember to. . .

- Explain the cause of the problem clearly and concisely.
- Avoid assigning too much blame.
- State how the problem has been solved.

Explanation of New Quality Standards to Front-line Customer Service People

To:

From:

Date:

Regarding: New ways to work

We're taking a new approach to responding to customer complaints on minor variations on input-output rate. If a customer reports a variation of above one percent, please offer to service the unit—whether or not it is still under warranty.

Thanks!

Alternate Version:

As you may recall from the recent remarks of the president of the firm, we're implementing some important new quality standards here at ABC.

Among these is the fluctuation of the input-output rate. In the past, if customers reported a fluctuation below 6% on their widgets, our customary response was to inform them that such variations were "within industry standards." *This response is no longer adequate!*

Please inform customers that they may return widgets for service that display variance readings of *above one percent*.

Thanks!

DEVELOPING A CUSTOMIZED MEMO? REMEMBER TO. . .

- State up front that new standards are being implemented.

- Clearly explain the new policy.
- Provide a statement to be given to the customer.

External Packaging and Related Items: Proofreading Checklist

To:

From:

Date:

Regarding: Proofreading of packaging and ad copy

I'm forwarding a detailed checklist that will help us minimize—or even, Lord willing, eliminate—errors in our packaging materials and ad copy. Please review it carefully, and follow it before submitting any copy for production. Questions? Feel free to contact me.

Alternate Version:

Here's a list of important elements to check for on all advertising and packaging materials. Please review the list carefully before *anything* is sent to the printer.

- Is the name of the company spelled and formatted correctly? (ABC Corporation)
- Has the document been spellchecked?
- Have all relevant product code numbers and prices been checked against the most recent master list (available from Brian in operations)?
- Have at least three people read and initialed galley copies, marking all errors?
- Have spelling questions been resolved by the Burnhardt's International Dictionary, Third Revised Edition? (There's a copy in my office.)
- Have usage questions been resolved by the Atlanta Manual of Style? (Ditto.)
- Has the final version of the document been reviewed by either Ellen, Steve, or Dave?

Thanks for helping us minimize errors in packaging and advertising materials.

DEVELOPING A CUSTOMIZED MEMO? REMEMBER TO. . .

- Provide a precise and bulleted checklist.
- Explain why the checklist is necessary.
- Stress the importance of reviewing and following the list.

General Memo: Quality Problems on Recent Project

To:

From:

Date:

Regarding: Assembly on recent lot of Widgets

The work we did on Lot #3412 of the WidgetMaster 3000 units was not up to our usual high standards.

I'd like to hold a meeting in my office today at 2:00 for all the members of the Group A assembly team to discuss why the assembly of the retro housing on these units was off by as much as it was—and what we can do to keep problems like this from happening again.

Alternate Version:

We had some problems with Lot #3412 of the Widgetmaster 3000, but I know we can figure them out and prevent this from happening again.

Let's get together in my office at 2:00 today to discuss what happened and how we can keep it from happening in the future.

DEVELOPING A CUSTOMIZED MEMO? REMEMBER TO. . .

- Mention the specific problem that generated the memo.
- Provide positive reassurance that the problem can be solved.
- State the purpose and goal of the meeting.

Handling Persistent Quality-Control Problems in a Single Department

To:

From:

Date:

Regarding: Strategies for High Achievement

I think you and your people are capable of great things, but there seem to be some obstacles in the way. I'm concerned about the error rate our random samples are uncovering.

Why don't we get together in my office today at 2:00 to discuss the ways I can help you get your folks back on the right track?

Alternate Version:

You and the people in your department are superstars-in-waiting. I want to go over today's random-sample checks with you in person so we can talk about the obstacles that may be standing in the way—and the steps you and I can take together to get performance levels in your area up where they should be.

Let's talk at 2:00 in my office. I'm looking forward to talking about this!

DEVELOPING A CUSTOMIZED MEMO? REMEMBER TO. . .

- Accentuate the positive aspects of the department.
- Express but don't overstate your concerns.
- Offer your help by way of a meeting.

Importance of Consulting Checklists Before Passing Work On

To:

From:

Date:

Regarding: Checklists

Don't forget: The job isn't finished until at least two people have signed off on the appropriate checklist!

Please don't submit lots for shipment until the relevant checklist has been reviewed thoroughly—and initialed—by two people in your department.

Thanks a lot!

Alternate Version:

Just a reminder—no lot should proceed to shipment until it's been reviewed by at least two people for compliance to the appropriate quality checklist. Please initial the checklist and file it before you send the lots on to the next step.

Thanks for helping us keep customer complaints and reshipments to an absolute minimum.

DEVELOPING A CUSTOMIZED MEMO? REMEMBER TO. . .

- Emphasize the importance of checklists.
- Re-state the procedure to be followed.
- Thank the employee for adhering to the procedure.

Managers: Importance of Spot-Checking Checklist Compliance

To:

From:

Date:

Regarding: Spot checks

Thanks for going over the importance of keeping up with the checklist system with your people.

Over the next week, I'd like to take a look at how this initiative is working out in actual practice. Please (quietly) pull every twentieth lot and check the units against the checklists that were—or weren't—filed. After we've got thirty or so to look at, please get back to me and let me know what the results look like.

Alternate Version:

I know we've gone over the whole checklist thing again and again with your people, and I don't think there's much to be gained by holding another meeting about that. I would like to suggest, though, that we institute a spot-check program under which, say, every twentieth lot of widgets has its checklist (quietly) pulled from the file and double-checked against the unit.

Let's try this for a week. Why not get back to me at that time to let me know what results you come up with?

DEVELOPING A CUSTOMIZED MEMO? REMEMBER TO. . .

- Acknowledge that this issue has been discussed previously.
- Suggest an unobtrusive way in which spot-checks can be performed.
- Offer to review the results in a week's time.

Multiple Review of Product Prototypes Is Essential

To:

From:

Date:

Regarding: Review of the Widgetron 3400

Now that we have the prototype of this unit up and running, please remember: We need everyone's feedback to make the product launch a success.

All group managers should review the prototype closely and supply written comments and suggestions by October 1. Thanks!

Alternate Version:

Now's the time!

Get your licks in on the Widgetron 3400 prototype and let us know what needs to be changed. All group managers should review the prototype closely and supply written comments and suggestions by the first of October. Thanks a lot!

> DEVELOPING A CUSTOMIZED MEMO? REMEMBER TO. . .
>
> • Encourage feedback from the employees.
> • Ensure that group managers review the prototype.
> • Provide a due date for written comments.

Planning Random Quality Tests Throughout the Production Process

To:

From:

Date:

Regarding: Quality tests

I'd like to institute a random quality-test program that will give us some feedback on how our recent efforts at quality improvement are (or aren't) paying off.

What would you think of a series of quietly conducted tests, to be performed on lots chosen at random, scheduled for the first, seventh, and nineteenth of this month?

Alternate Version:

Let's find out whether or not our quality program is producing the results we want.

I'd like to institute a series of tests of randomly selected lots on irregularly scheduled dates. Let's shoot for the first, seventh, and nineteenth of this month.

- Explain the purpose of the quality tests.
- Suggest dates for random testing.

Possible Product Defect: Plans for Action

To:

From:

Date:

Regarding: Baffle problems

We should have a meeting to discuss something disturbing I've found on the Model 1000 widget. The baffles may have some problems.

I suggest we get together at your earliest convenience to discuss:

- The specifics of the problem I've located.
- The degree to which the rest of the inventory may be subject to this problem.
- The steps we should take from here.

Alternate Version:

Something important has come up on the Model 1000 widget. We should discuss it as soon as possible.

The first chance you get, can you please let me know what a good time for a meeting might be?

DEVELOPING A CUSTOMIZED MEMO? REMEMBER TO. . .

- Mention that a problem has been detected.
- Stress the need for immediate action.
- Suggest a meeting to discuss the problem.

Proposing New Specifications

To:

From:

Date:

Regarding: New specs on the Widgetron instruction manual

Based on the feedback I'm getting from the people in Customer Service, I think we should increase the type size on the instruction manual that goes out with all our Widgetron units.

I'd propose a type size of 14 points rather than 10, with perhaps a 15% increase in total page length. I'd also increase the overall size of the volume from 6" × 9" to 7" × 10".

The revised cost estimates are attached. What do you think?

Alternate Version:

Approximately 30% of the customers who call our toll-free line are complaining about the difficulty of reading our instruction manual with the Widgetron line.

I'd like to suggest that we up the point size to 14 points and revise the overall size of the book from 6" × 9" to 7" × 10". The appropriate cost estimates are enclosed. What do you think?

DEVELOPING A CUSTOMIZED MEMO? REMEMBER TO. . .

- Highlight the customer service aspect of the situation.
- Make specific suggestions for new specifications.
- Provide cost estimates.

Recommending a Product Recall

To:

From:

Date:

Regarding: Possible recall of Widgetron 6400

Based on the design review we've just gotten, I think we should consider a recall of the Widgetron Model 6400 unit.

The casing assembly on the units that have already been shipped could cause us some real problems if they're left unrepaired. I realize that this type of decision is never an easy one to make, but I believe it's the best option available to us.

Alternate Version:

Given the specifics of the recent design review (enclosed), I'm going to recommend that we recall the recent shipment of Widgetron Model 6400 units. I realize that a product recall isn't anyone's idea of a step forward, but it appears to be the best option available to us, given the existing problems on the casing assembly.

Developing a Customized Memo? Remember to. . .

- State the reason for the recall recommendation.
- Describe the existing problem.
- Emphasize the necessity of the decision.

Refusing to Move Forward with Project Until Key Questions Are Resolved

To:

From:

Date:

Regarding: Smedley project

For a variety of reasons—including the design of interface software, internal power issues, and an extremely aggressive schedule I'm not sure we can make—I want to put a hold on the Smedley project.

When you get the chance, why not stop in to my office so we can talk about where we should go from here on this project.

Alternate Version:

After a good deal of thought, I've decided to put the Smedley project on hold until we resolve the following outstanding issues:

- There's no realistic schedule for the development of the interface with the customer's existing widget software. How do we plan to address this?
- As it stands, we have no backup plans in the event of an internal power problem in the widgets we're proposing to deliver. When will we?
- The people at Smedley want finished product by January 1, and I think that's unrealistic. Before we make any further commitments, I think we should talk to them about schedules.

DEVELOPING A CUSTOMIZED MEMO? REMEMBER TO. . .

- Emphasize that thought has been given to the decision.
- List the reasons why the project is being put on hold.
- Suggest further discussion of the situation.

Requesting Additional Funds to Address Recent Quality Concerns

To:

From:

Date:

Regarding: Your recent notes on product quality

The bad news: To hit the quality marks we talked about earlier this week during our discussions about the widget interface, we're going to have to exceed our budget allocation by about $1400.

The good news: If we take this step now, we'll probably avoid lots of later problems from customers, problems that could cost us tens of thousands of dollars.

What do you think?

Alternate Version:

I think we can address the quality problems we discussed at our most recent meeting—with a (modest!) upward revision in our budget allocation.

If I can get authorization from you to exceed my redesign figure by $1400, we can get a complete overhaul from the people at Botelho Associates, who have done superb work for us in the past.

When we consider the cost of not redesigning the interface—which could conceivably run into the tens of thousands of dollars if there are problems on the customer's end—this seems like it's the best option.

What do you think?

DEVELOPING A CUSTOMIZED MEMO? REMEMBER TO. . .

- Mention the previous discussion on the subject.
- Provide the cost of overhauling the project.
- Emphasize the overall benefits of doing the redesign.

Requesting Extension of Deadline to Address Recent Quality Concerns

To:

From:

Date:

Regarding: Request for change in schedule

I'm very concerned about the design of the input/output baffles on the McWidget unit. I don't think they'll hold up to heavy use by consumers as designed, and the tests I've done indicate that this could be a serious problem.

I want to propose a two-week extension, with a new completion date of October 16th, so we can address this problem. What do you think?

Alternate Version:

In order to complete the McWidget project at the highest possible quality level . . . it's going to take us an additional two weeks beyond what's listed on the schedule.

I'm very concerned about the possible end-user problems that we may encounter if we don't redesign the input/output baffles on the units before moving forward. This could cause serious problems if the units are subjected to any heavy use by customers.

Is a schedule revision to October 16th all right with you?

DEVELOPING A CUSTOMIZED MEMO? REMEMBER TO. . .

- State the cause of your concern about the project.
- Stress the possible consequences of not addressing the problem.
- Suggest an alternate date for completion.

Requesting Help in Eliciting Consumer Feedback

To:

From:

Date:

Regarding: Additional time for consumer input

I'm not certain the new marketing plan is ready yet. I think more interview time with potential consumers is essential.

Can I authorize eight hours of Alma's time to review some key points that still need resolution?

Alternate Version:

The main concerns and motivations of the consumers we're targeting still seem to me to need review. Is it all right with you if I put Alma on the phones with potential consumers for eight hours to resolve some outstanding questions that will help us target the marketing plan further?

DEVELOPING A CUSTOMIZED MEMO? REMEMBER TO. . .

- Clearly state the necessity for further review of consumer feedback.
- Identify the individual and time frame needed for the task.

Requiring Overtime from Employees to Address Recent Quality Concerns

To:

From:

Date:

Regarding: Baffle adjustments

Orders from on high department: It looks like we've got to review and over-haul the baffle assemblies on the Widgetron units over the next three weeks, and I need your help.

Everyone should sign up for at least one two-hour overtime slot during this period to help pitch in on this challenge. The sign-up sheet is in the employ-ee lounge.

Thanks in advance for helping us deliver the finest quality to our customers.

Alternate Version:

We've got a challenge to meet. Ms. Bellingham has instructed me to over-see a top-to-bottom review and overhaul of the baffle assemblies on our Widgetron units, which may be improperly machined.

I need everyone on staff to sign on for at least two hours of overtime over the next three weeks to help us deal with this problem. The shift sign-up sheet is posted in the employee lounge area. We'll throw a big party after the units ship, but right now we need to come together and address this problem.

Thanks in advance for your help.

DEVELOPING A CUSTOMIZED MEMO? REMEMBER TO. . .

- Note that the order has come from upper management.
- Stress that all employees must work some overtime.
- Thank the employees for their help.

Requesting Private Meeting to Address Quality Concerns

To:

From:

Date:

Regarding: Request for private meeting

I've spotted something unusual in the baffle housing assembly on the Widgetron 5600 unit, and I'm a little bit concerned. Have you got a free moment to talk about it with me? I think it could be important.

Alternate Version:

This could be important.

There's something in the baffle housing assembly on the Widgetron 5600 unit that looks troublesome to me. When you get the chance, can we go over it together?

Thanks.

Developing a Customized Memo? Remember to. . .

- Mention the specific problem to be discussed.
- Express your concern about it.
- Ask for a personal meeting to discuss the issue you've raised.

Spot-Checking for Quality in Problem Department

To:

From:

Date:

Regarding: Continuous overview

I think we've gotten the message across in the Widget Review department, but I want to be sure.

Over the next week or so, would you please quietly spot-check their work on a daily basis and let me know how things look?

Alternate Version:

Well, I think we've made our point. Just to be sure, though—and in the name of making meetings like the one we just went through unnecessary—would you quietly spot-check the output in the Widget Review department at least once a day over the next week and let me know how things look?

> DEVELOPING A CUSTOMIZED MEMO? REMEMBER TO. . .
>
> - Note that the problem has been addressed.
> - Suggest spot-checks to ensure that the problem has been solved.
> - Propose a time frame for the spot-checks to be performed.

Chapter 11

Internal Efficiency

Setting standards in the workplace is essential for maintaining corporate efficiency. While some workers may balk at being "reined in," most recognize that new efficiency-based instructions and guidelines serve an important purpose. In this chapter, you'll find memos focusing on the many ways in which company efficiency can be improved. These memos cover topics ranging from general policy and procedure to specific personnel-related issues. The subjects include: use and abuse of e-mail and fax systems; protocols for filing, telephone etiquette, dress codes, office decoration, recycling, and expense reimbursement; guidelines and procedures for the use and servicing of company equipment and vehicles, as well as for ordering office supplies, obtaining proper authorizations, and so on; announcements of meetings on a variety of efficiency-related topics; reviews of company policies; and addressing efficiency challenges directly with team members.

Abuse of Company Charge and Expense Accounts: Strategies for Review by Accounting Department

To:

From:

Date:

Regarding: Problems in Expense Accounts

I think we need to institute a more thorough review of our expense account practices. I've got a good idea that Anthony and Hollis have been padding their accounts, and I'm willing to bet they're not the only ones.

I'd like you to ask them for *original* receipts on all the items that appear on their most recent reports. You need to develop a new policy paper on this that sets clear upper limits for the most common monthly expense categories.

Please get back to me soon with recommendations on what you think we should do about Anthony and Hollis.

Alternate Version:

The expense reports submitted by Anthony and Hollis this month seem ludicrously padded. I'd like you to ask them for original paperwork on all the items they've specified, and then get back to me with a recommendation on what you think we should do next.

Could you also set up a new set of upper-limit guidelines on the most common monthly expense report categories for me to review? Thanks.

DEVELOPING A CUSTOMIZED MEMO? REMEMBER TO . . .

- Note where irregularities have been spotted.
- Provide suggestions for the action to be taken.
- Request recommendations for further action.

Announcing the New E-Mail Network

To:

From:

Date:

Regarding: The new e-mail system

We're online!

The company e-mail system is up and running. We'll be having a brief meeting that will help you become familiar with the new functions tomorrow at 10:00 am in my office.

See you there!

Alternate Version:

Get all the facts about the new e-mail system!

We'll be having a short company meeting in my office to unveil and explain the new system at 10:00 tomorrow morning. See you then.

Developing a Customized Memo? Remember to . . .

- Announce that the new system is in place.
- Emphasize the brevity of the meeting to explain the new system.
- Provide a time and place for the meeting.

Attendance Problems: Company Meetings

To:

From:

Date:

Regarding: Company meetings

Just a reminder: The Monday morning meetings are *mandatory* . . . so please attend, and please be prompt.

We're going to talk about some exciting new initiatives the company will be pursuing in the coming year during next Monday's meeting. I look forward to seeing you there.

Alternate Version:

The company meetings are for everyone . . . and we miss you when you're not there to contribute.

The Monday morning meetings are *mandatory*. Please attend, and please make every effort to be in the conference room by 9:00.

Thanks!

DEVELOPING A CUSTOMIZED MEMO? REMEMBER TO . . .

- Stress that meetings are mandatory.
- Encourage timely attendance.

Breaks that Run Beyond Allotted Time

To:

From:

Date:

Regarding: Coffee breaks

I need your help. Please remind the people in your department that coffee breaks are not to extend beyond ten minutes, twice a day.

Thanks for helping us to keep things humming!

Alternate Version:

I like a good cup of coffee as much as the next person, but . . .

The coffee breaks some people are taking are extending to as long as thirty or forty minutes. Please help us all out and remind your people that the twice-daily coffee breaks are meant to extend to a maximum of ten minutes each.

Thanks!

DEVELOPING A CUSTOMIZED MEMO? REMEMBER TO . . .

- State the policy regarding coffee breaks.
- Request the manager's help to keep employees in line with the policy.

Car Pooling Problems: Tardiness

To:

From:

Date:

Regarding: Car pools

It's a great idea, but it needs a little fine-tuning.

Seriously, most of the people who are using the new car-pooling program are reporting no problems. But a good percentage of the people in the program are arriving up to thirty minutes late.

Can you take a look at the schedules and see what can be done to tighten them up?

Alternate Version:

We need to streamline the car-pool arrangement. Some people are showing up thirty to forty minutes after the scheduled start of the work day.

Can you take a look at the current program and get back to me with any ideas you have?

DEVELOPING A CUSTOMIZED MEMO? REMEMBER TO . . .

- Highlight the specific problem with car pools.
- Request an examination of the problem and possible solutions.

Change of Service Agreements on Company Computers

To:

From:

Date:

Regarding: Service contracts

As it stands, we have what might be called a bare-bones service agreement on the six Comdell computers in your department with Zerum Corporation. I'd like to consider expanding this service. Could you take a look at the enclosed service agreement details and let me know which you think is best for us?

Alternate Version:

Last week's hardware problem was a bit of a nightmare. I'd like to consider upgrading our service contracts.

Could you take a look at the attached service agreements and get back to me with your thoughts on which one you think would be best for us?

Developing a Customized Memo? Remember to . . .

- Indicate a reason for considering a service upgrade.
- Provide service agreements to be examined.
- Request a recommendation regarding the best way to go.

Company Dress: Casual Day Guidelines

To:

From:

Date:

Regarding: Casual dress day

As you probably know, Wednesday is dress-down day here at ABC Corporation. It's a day when we can use a little more creativity in selecting personal attire . . . but it's *not* "anything goes" day.

Please remember: Clothing with holes, shorts, tee-shirts, and clothing with questionable or suggestive slogans are all off limits. So is pierced jewelry that goes anywhere other than an earlobe. Other than that . . . have fun!

Alternate Version:

Let's have fun on dress-down day . . . but please remember that some types of clothing aren't appropriate for workday wear, no matter what day it is.

Tee-shirts, articles of clothing with unpatched holes, and articles of clothing that bear suggestive or potentially offensive language are off limits, even on Wednesday. So is any form of body-pierced jewelry other than earrings in earlobes.

Thanks for helping to make ABC Corporation the kind of environment that keeps customers and other important visitors impressed!

DEVELOPING A CUSTOMIZED MEMO? REMEMBER TO . . .

- Acknowledge the fun aspects of a casual dress day.
- List the prohibitions.
- Be encouraging, not discouraging.

Company Dress: General Guidelines

To:

From:

Date:

Regarding: Dress code

It's no big deal, but . . .

Jeans are not part of the approved company dress code, except on Wednesday, our dress-down day. I know how easy it is to forget something like this, and I've done it a time or two myself. But from here on out, please limit jeans to Wednesdays.

Thanks—and keep up the good work!

Alternate Version:

You probably just forgot about the dress code we talked about during orientation, but . . .

The only time blue jeans are considered appropriate workplace attire is on Wednesday, our dress-down day. Next time around, save the jeans for that day, okay?

Thanks—and don't worry, this happens all the time with new employees.

DEVELOPING A CUSTOMIZED MEMO? REMEMBER TO . . .

- Remind the employee of the company policy regarding dress codes.
- Provide reassurance that first-time offenses are not serious.

Computer and Copier Servicing Procedures

To:

From:

Date:

Regarding: Copier service

"The copier's on the blink!"

Well, it happens. Actually, de-jamming it is pretty easy—come see me or Helen if you need a demonstration. If there's a more serious problem, something involving a diagnostic code flashing on and off, please let Helen know immediately. If she can't fix it, she'll contact a service person who can.

Alternate Version:

When the copier's on the fritz (and it sometimes is), the problem is usually that there's a paper jam. These are pretty easy to resolve after you've seen someone else fix the problem once. If your document jams and you need a demonstration, please come see me or Helen.

More complicated (and rarer) problems may involve flashing numbers in the diagnostic-code window. When this happens, please let Helen know immediately. If she can't fix it, she'll get in touch with someone who can.

DEVELOPING A CUSTOMIZED MEMO? REMEMBER TO . . .

- Provide a possible solution to what may be wrong with the copier.
- Note whom to see for more serious problems.

Control of Confidential Company Information

To:

From:

Date:

Regarding: The Davis report

I know we went over this with everyone at the meeting, but . . .

Please remember that the Davis report contains confidential product information that should not be shared with anyone outside of the executive committee.

Thanks!

Alternate Version:

Just a reminder: The Davis report you were given at the recent executive committee meeting contains confidential company information. Please don't share it with anyone who's not on the committee.

DEVELOPING A CUSTOMIZED MEMO? REMEMBER TO . . .

- Note that information in the report is confidential.
- Stress that the information is not to be shared with unauthorized personnel.

Display of Photographs, Posters, Etc., in Work Area

To:

From:

Date:

Regarding: Posters in cubicles

"Can we put up pictures in the cubicles?"

The answer is yes and no. *Yes* if the picture is in good taste and free of offensive images or language, and if it is smaller than eight and a half inches by eleven inches. *No* if the picture features offensive slogans or imagery, or if it's larger than eight and a half inches by eleven inches.

Thanks!

Alternate Version:

What's the policy on pictures in personal cubicles? They're fine if they're small (eight and a half by eleven or smaller) and in good taste (i.e., no offensive language or imagery).

Pictures of the family are a great idea. Put 'em up . . . we all want to see their smiling faces!

DEVELOPING A CUSTOMIZED MEMO? REMEMBER TO . . .

- Set the exact parameters for what is allowable in cubicles.
- Clearly describe any taboo decorations.

Disposition of Files: When to Destroy

To:

From:

Date:

Regarding: Archived files

New policy alert! The warehouse people are now *only* accepting files for archive storage if they are clearly marked with a "feel free to destroy" date.

They won't destroy any archived files already in storage without such markings. They will refuse new archive requests if you don't identify a time within the next five years at which the files can be disposed of.

If the files can never be disposed, guess what? They belong in your area!

Feel free to contact me if you have questions about this.

Alternate Version:

Effective immediately, the good people in the warehouse can *only* accept files for archive storage if they're marked with a clear "destroy by" date that falls sometime within five years of the date of submission.

If your files can't be destroyed within that time period, they need to stay with you.

Questions? Feel free to give me a call.

DEVELOPING A CUSTOMIZED MEMO? REMEMBER TO . . .

- Provide instructions for how files should be marked.
- Indicate what will happen to unmarked files.
- Note whom to contact for questions about the policy.

Duration of Authorized Lunch Period

To:

From:

Date:

Regarding: Lunch breaks

I need your help!

Some of the people in your department are taking lunch breaks that last from 90 to 120 minutes. If we can't convince them to keep within the allotted one-hour limit, we're going to hear about it.

Can you please issue a few discreet reminders to the right people? Thanks.

Alternate Version:

I don't know whether you've noticed this, but . . .

Some of the lunch hours your people are taking are extending well beyond the sixty-minute mark. Can you please remind the appropriate people of the importance of getting back to work by 1:00? Otherwise we're likely to get some nasty looks from the people upstairs.

> DEVELOPING A CUSTOMIZED MEMO? REMEMBER TO . . .
>
> • Briefly describe the problem.
> • Note the company policy on lunch breaks.
> • Suggest how the department manager should handle the problem.

Employee Time: Non-Work-Related Reading Materials During Office Hours

To:

From:

Date:

Regarding: Non-work-related magazines

The last four or five times I've been through your department, I've noticed Barbara leafing through *House and Garden* or some such magazine. She always puts the magazine away when I start talking, but I can't help wondering how much time she's spending on this type of activity every day.

If you haven't already talked to her about keeping personal reading on personal time, would you mind doing so?

Alternate Version:

Unless it's part of some project you've assigned to her (which it may be), *House and Garden* magazine appears to be taking up an inordinate amount of Barbara's time. The last four or five times I've been through your department, she's been studying it intently. What's up?

You may have already talked to her about keeping personal reading on personal time, in which case please disregard this memo. If you haven't, would you mind meeting with her briefly (and tactfully) about this?

DEVELOPING A CUSTOMIZED MEMO? REMEMBER TO . . .

- Acknowledge that the supervisor may already be aware of the problem.
- Describe what has been observed.
- Suggest the action to be taken.

Entry to Building During Nonstandard Hours

To:

From:

Date:

Regarding: Off-hours entry

From time to time, it's necessary to do work on site outside of standard business hours. Any employee wishing to discuss how to gain access to the building during evenings or weekends can do so by contacting me directly. In some cases, a manager must be present while you are doing your work.

Alternate Version:

If you've got plans to work on-site during evening, weekend, or holiday hours, please come and see me first. Access to the building is restricted during this time . . . and a manager may have to be on-site while you work.

DEVELOPING A CUSTOMIZED MEMO? REMEMBER TO . . .

- State whom is to be contacted regarding off-hours entry to the building.
- Note any restrictions for off-hours entry.

Excessive Personal Telephone Calls

To:

From:

Date:

Regarding: Incoming calls

Something's wrong here.

Yesterday you spent well over an hour on non-work-related telephone conversations. Is there a problem you want to discuss? Extraordinary circumstances at home sometimes mean we have no choice but to take time out from work. If you're facing one of those unpredictable situations, please let me know. If you're not, please help us all out by keeping personal calls to an absolute minimum during working hours.

Alternate Version:

Is something wrong?

You spent a great deal of time on personal calls yesterday. If there's a family emergency or other dire event that needs your attention, I'd certainly understand. If there's not . . . please help me set a good example for others in the department and save long personal calls for non-work hours.

Thanks.

DEVELOPING A CUSTOMIZED MEMO? REMEMBER TO . . .

- Inform the employee of the problem that has been observed.
- Express understanding/concern in case there is a personal problem.
- Note that personal calls are not appropriate during work hours.

Improper Use of E-Mail System

To:

From:

Date:

Regarding: Internet use of e-mail system

Sorry, folks, but . . .

Our liability insurance requires that only authorized users be permitted to use the company e-mail system to post messages on the Internet. If you are allowing someone else to use your account to review and post to Internet boards, you are in direct violation of company policy and subject to disciplinary action.

Alternate Version:

"Them's the rules" department: For liability reasons, our attorneys have advised that only authorized users be permitted to access the Internet with the company online system. If you let someone else use your account, you're subjecting the company to unacceptable legal risk . . . and courting disciplinary action!

Please keep your password to yourself.

DEVELOPING A CUSTOMIZED MEMO? REMEMBER TO . . .

- Clearly outline the policy regarding authorized users.
- Emphasize that violation of the policy could bring disciplinary action.

Incoming Fax Message: Routing Protocol

To:

From:

Date:

Regarding: Incoming fax messages

Please don't distribute incoming faxes!

We've had some problems with truncated or misplaced messages in the past. Unless the message is for you, please leave it in the "Faxes In" box. If the message is for you, please review it carefully for completeness before you leave the fax area. If there's something missing, you'll want to ask about it immediately . . . not tomorrow morning, when someone may have inadvertently walked off with your material.

By the same token, you should also check your fax closely to make sure you're not walking off with someone else's message!

Alternate Version:

Please: When in doubt, leave the fax where it is!

If an incoming fax is addressed to you, by all means snag it from the clutches of the "Faxes In" box. (Check for completeness before you leave.) If the fax isn't addressed to you, please leave it in its entirety in the "Faxes In" Box.

Please check your message twice to make sure you're not walking off with someone else's transmission!

DEVELOPING A CUSTOMIZED MEMO? REMEMBER TO . . .

- Urge employees to be certain of retrieving only their own faxes.
- Suggest that faxes be checked thoroughly for completeness.
- Stress that faxes not their own should be left in the in-box.

Incoming Telephone Call Protocol

To:

From:

Date:

Regarding: Incoming calls

How not to tick off incoming callers, volume 14, chapter 6 . . .

If a call is misrouted to you, please don't route the call back to the switchboard. (The caller will have to wait at least one, and perhaps as many as two minutes to get back to the receptionist.) Either check your directory and patch the person through directly to the correct number, or politely ask the caller to call back and ask the receptionist for help.

Thanks!

Alternate Version:

Due to a system problem, incoming calls that are mistakenly sent to the wrong extension must wait for an extended period before they're picked up again at the front desk. That's why we ask that, if you receive a call that's meant for someone else, you either . . .

   a) check your directory and connect the caller to the right extension, or . . .

   b) politely ask the caller to call the main number again.

Obviously, the more often we pick option A, the happier our callers will be.

We're working on the switching problem. As soon as it's corrected, we'll let everyone know. Thanks for your help.

Developing a Customized Memo? Remember to . . .

- Explain the possible consequences of misrouted phone calls.
- Provide the correct protocol to be followed.
- Emphasize the importance of keeping callers happy.

Instituting Monthly Team Output Reports

To:

From:

Date:

Regarding: Team reports

I think we should institute a system whereby each department head files monthly reports on the status of current projects. I've enclosed a sample form that will help us keep track of projects on a monthly basis. If you've got suggestions or revisions, please let me know by the close of business on Friday.

Alternate Version:

Starting next month, I want all department heads to summarize the status of current projects by means of regularly submitted reports. A progress form (attached) will help us keep track of what's happening.

What do you think of the approach I've taken with the enclosed form? Please get back to me with proposed revisions or additions by the close of business on Friday.

DEVELOPING A CUSTOMIZED MEMO? REMEMBER TO . . .

- Outline the new system to be instituted.
- Provide a sample form.
- Ask for suggestions on the new system.

Missed Deadline

To:

From:

Date:

Regarding: Schedule on the MalWorks Project

The deadline on the above project has come and gone. Can I get a written summary from you outlining what still remains to be done on this—and how long you think it's going to take?

Once you've established what still has to be completed, I'd like to meet with you in person to talk about the project as a whole.

Alternate Version:

The due date for the above project was yesterday.

I think you should take the time you need today to put together a detailed written summary of what still remains to be done on this job. Once you've done this, I'd like to meet with you in person tomorrow to talk about the best ways to proceed. Please let me know when we can get together.

Developing a Customized Memo? Remember to . . .

- Note that the deadline has been passed.
- Request a written status report.
- Suggest a follow-up meeting to discuss the project.

New Equipment and Software: Training Session

To:

From:

Date:

Regarding: New computer training

The new Whizbang 6.0 software that's been installed on your computer is faster and more powerful than anything you've worked with before. To help everyone in the department get the most from this program, we've scheduled a *mandatory* two-hour training session in Conference Room A for this coming Monday, August first.

See you there!

Alternate Version:

You've probably already noticed that the new Whizbang 6.0 software has some very exciting features. In order to help you get the most from this new tool, we've scheduled a special two-hour training session for all department members.

The training, which is *mandatory,* will take place in Conference Room A at 10:00 this coming Monday, August 1st.

See you there.

DEVELOPING A CUSTOMIZED MEMO? REMEMBER TO . . .

- Mention the benefits of the computer enhancements.
- Provide date, time and place for the training session.
- Stress that the session is mandatory.

Obtaining Authorization Before Engaging Temporary Employees

To:

From:

Date:

Regarding: Temporary employees

Hold everything!

Yes, the mailing project you're working on is a perfect candidate for temporary help. No, we can't just pick up the phone and ask them to come in tomorrow morning.

All requests for temporary help have to be cleared by Human Resources; there's a form I need to fill out before we can get authorization. Let's meet later today so you can tell me the specifics of what you're trying to accomplish.

Alternate Version:

I think you're absolutely right that the mailing project would benefit from temporary help. We'll need to get authorization from Human Resources before we can proceed with this, though, and there's some paperwork I need to attack before they can give us authorization.

Stop by my office later today so we can talk about what needs to happen on this project.

Developing a Customized Memo? Remember to . . .

- Acknowledge that temporary help is a good idea.
- Note that authorization is necessary to hire temporary help.
- Suggest a meeting to discuss the issue.

Obtaining Authorization Before Undertaking Joint Department Project

To:

From:

Date:

Regarding: Joint project with the people in accounting

I think you've hit on a great idea with the account-review project, and you're quite right—it's only fair that the folks in Accounting pitch in. Before we start in on this, though, we're going to need to clear the project with Wayne.

Let me talk things over with him before we get too wrapped up in the planning. Please check with me tomorrow so we can talk about the status on this.

Alternate Version:

You're right!

It's a great idea for a project, one that has the potential to make life easier for us and for the people in Accounting. Since we're talking about a joint time undertaking, though, I should discuss this with Wayne before we spend too much time in the planning phase.

Can you hold off for now and check in with me tomorrow on this?

- Applaud the idea and note its benefits.
- State whom must be consulted before proceeding.
- Request a delay until the project can be discussed further.

Obtaining Multiple Bids Before Assigning Purchase Order

To:

From:

Date:

Regarding: Purchase order #42525

Technically, the purchase order you issued for widget assembly cleaners should have gone through a bidding process involving at least three vendors. I can let this pass this time, but next time around, please check with me on purchases over $100. Some of these purchases have special requirements.

Thanks!

Alternate Version:

If I don't miss my bet, the above purchase order went out without a multiple bid request. We've set a policy this year to obtain at least three bids on products in this category for purchases over $100.

This one is no particular big deal, but you'll help us keep costs down if you track down bids from at least three potential vendors on future purchases.

Thanks a lot!

Developing a Customized Memo? Remember to . . .

- Mention that an error was detected.
- Restate the company policy on bidding.
- Request future compliance with the policy.

Office E-Mail Guidelines

To:

From:

Date:

Regarding: Use of e-mail

We're trying to keep e-mail traffic to manageable levels . . . because some people are getting deluged with completely overwhelming amounts of mail.

Please help out! Only use the "CC:" function to circulate mail to specific individuals within the organization who need to see your mail. Please don't use the "CC:" function to circulate mail to everyone in the company!

Thanks for helping us keep this exciting technology user-friendly for everyone.

DEVELOPING A CUSTOMIZED MEMO? REMEMBER TO . . .

- Stress the importance of managing e-mail traffic.
- Provide specific guideline(s) to be followed.
- Offer thanks for employee cooperation.

Office Supplies: Procedure for Acquisition

To:

From:

Date:

Regarding: Office Supplies

Out of supplies? Come see me!

We probably have what you need in the supply cabinet, in which case all you have to do is sign your name next to what you're taking. If what you need isn't in the supply cabinet, let me know, and I'll tell you whether we've got the budget for it.

Alternate Version:

"How do we get supplies we need?"

Well, it's actually pretty easy. It's not as easy as running down to the OfficeMart and presenting a company check for what you need, but almost.

Please check the supply cabinet first. If it's got what you need, all you need to do is sign your name and exactly what you've requisitioned on the sign-out sheet. Please don't hoard—otherwise our "take what you need" policy may collapse!

If you don't find what you need in the cabinet, please come to see me so we can discuss what you need. If it's in the budget, I'll try to find a way to track it down for you.

Developing a Customized Memo? Remember to . . .

- Outline procedure to be followed for taking supplies.
- Note what to do when supplies are lacking.
- Provide a contact for supplies issues.

Organization of Files: Upcoming Meeting

To:

From:

Date:

Regarding: File organization

A short meeting on filing systems—including advice on how to customize your system so other people can make sense of it when they have to—is scheduled for tomorrow at 4:30 in the main conference room.

Please attend!

Alternate Version:

I'd like to hold a brief meeting tomorrow at 4:30 pm in the main conference room to talk about filing systems. Some customization to individual needs for personal files is essential, of course, but I think we need to talk about a few basic techniques that will help everyone access important information when the need arises.

I look forward to seeing you there!

Developing a Customized Memo? Remember to . . .

- Explain the purpose of the meeting.
- Note when and where the meeting will take place.
- Encourage attendance.

Promptness for Company Meetings

To:

From:

Date:

Regarding: Meeting times

The last three staff meetings have had to be delayed for significant periods (once for nearly thirty minutes) because people scheduled to attend were missing or late.

Help us keep the show running smoothly. If the meeting is scheduled for 10:00 am, please be there at 10:00 am—or even (gasp!) a minute or two beforehand.

Thanks for your cooperation.

Alternate Version:

Help!

We need to make getting to meetings at (or before) the scheduled start time more of a priority. The last three staff meetings we've held have been delayed for significant periods . . . once as long as half an hour . . . because we were missing people.

If a dire emergency forces you to be late to a staff meeting—and that should happen rarely—please let me know about the problem as soon as you can.

Thanks.

Developing a Customized Memo? Remember to . . .

- Note existing problems due to late arrivals.
- Clearly state the need and desirability for promptness.

Proper Disbursement of Petty Cash Funds

To:

From:

Date:

Regarding: Petty cash

Careful!

Petty cash withdrawals are only to be made by authorized personnel—department managers or one permanently designated person within the manager's department. Please help use this fund responsibly. Don't permit unauthorized people to use the petty cash fund.

Alternate Version:

The petty cash fund is for the use of department managers or one permanently designated member of the manager's department. "Rolling" use of the fund by multiple members of the same department is not allowed! Please follow these guidelines . . . and insure responsible use of this fund. Thanks.

Developing a Customized Memo? Remember to . . .

- Outline the company policy regarding petty cash.
- Stress fiscal responsibility.

Recycling Procedures

To:

From:

Date:

Regarding: Recycling

We're recycling standard white paper in the bin next to the copier. If you should happen to make extra copies of something . . . or if you're just looking for something a little more constructive to do with that early original draft you'd otherwise discard . . . please bring it to the bin.

Alternate Version:

We're recycling!

Please bring standard white paper that you would otherwise throw away to the bin next to the photocopier on the first floor. We'll help keep the earth green . . . and our company in the black.

Developing a Customized Memo? Remember to . . .

- Emphasize what specifically is being recycled.
- Indicate where the recycling bin is located.

Reimbursement of Business-Related Expenses

To:

From:

Date:

Regarding: Expenses

Now it's time to answer that burning question . . . "When is my expense check going to be issued?"

If you turn in an expense report by the first Monday of the month, it will always be turned around by the end of the month. If, however, your expense report is filed later than the first Monday of the month, it may have to wait until the next month.

So . . . file early! (But not often.)

Alternate Version:

Why do expense checks sometimes take so long?

Because our accounting work is arranged on a monthly cycle. If you turn in an expense report by the first Monday of the month, you can rest assured that you'll see your check by the end of that month. If you wait until after the first Monday of the month, however, there's a good chance it will wait until the next month's cycle.

DEVELOPING A CUSTOMIZED MEMO? REMEMBER TO . . .

- Acknowledge employee concern about expense check turnaround.
- State exactly when expense reports are to be filed.
- Note the consequences of late filing.

Reporting Equipment Failures Promptly

To:

From:

Date:

Regarding: Equipment failures

Help us help you! If you've got a problem with a piece of equipment, let us know. Most of the equipment and computers we use here are under service contract. The sooner we hear about the problem, the sooner you're likely to be up and running with your own equipment again.

Alternate Version:

Is there a problem with your equipment? Let us know . . . sooner, rather than later! Most of our machinery and hardware is covered by service contracts that will allow you to be up and running with your familiar equipment in next to no time.

DEVELOPING A CUSTOMIZED MEMO? REMEMBER TO . . .

- Stress timely reporting of equipment failures.
- Note the existence of service contracts for speedy attention to problems.

Review of Company Policy on Eating Snacks or Lunch in Work Areas

To:

From:

Date:

Regarding: Eating snacks or lunch at work stations

If you work in or near the Widget Assembly Department, tiny food particles in your area can cause big product quality problems.

That's why we've established a policy limiting snacks and lunch items to the employee lounge only. Please observe it—our customers deserve the very highest-quality products.

Alternate Version:

Please, please, please don't eat in or near the Widget Assembly area!

The policy on eating only in the employee lounge isn't there to make your life difficult—it's there to keep our products going out the door at the highest possible quality level. Even microscopic food particles can have catastrophic effects on our widget performance.

Thanks!

DEVELOPING A CUSTOMIZED MEMO? REMEMBER TO . . .

- Note the effect of food particles on product quality.
- Provide the company policy on eating locations.

Standardizing Software on Company Computers

To:

From:

Date:

Regarding: Software

Please remember—as of January 1, the *only* word processing, spreadsheet, and database software that should be on your computer is the integrated Whizbang 6.0 package. If you've got other packages installed, please *delete them*. We're aiming for 100% compatibility on all records and documents!

Alternate Version:

Don't forget: After January 1, the only word processing, database, and spreadsheet software that should show up on your system is the Whizbang 6.0 system. Thanks for helping us keep all our documents and projects 100% compatible with one another!

DEVELOPING A CUSTOMIZED MEMO? REMEMBER TO . . .

- State the deadline for transition to the new software.
- Mention the name of the new software.
- Stress the desire for 100% compatibility.

Telephone Systems: Problems with Forwarding

To:

From:

Date:

Regarding: Phone etiquette

Please help us keep customers, investors, and other outside callers happy. Instead of simply transferring a person who has been routed to you incorrectly, say something along the following lines: "You need Mark Smith—Hold on, and I'll connect you, but if we get cut off, you can reach him by asking for extension 636."

Alternate Version:

It's no fun being transferred to limbo!

Instead of transferring a call with a brisk "Hold on," why not give the caller a little more information? Please say something like this: "You need Cheryl Green—let me connect you. If we get cut off, she's at extension 454."

Thanks for helping us keep incoming callers happy.

DEVELOPING A CUSTOMIZED MEMO? REMEMBER TO . . .

- Note the importance of keeping callers happy.
- Suggest a protocol for transferring calls.

Travel

To:

From:

Date:

Regarding: Travel

All of our travel bookings and reservation work is now being coordinated through DSW Travel of Centerburg. Our contact there is Sherry Wilson; you can reach her at 617/555-1212.

Alternate Version:

We've got a new travel agent! All our bookings and hotel arrangements are now being handled through DSW Travel in Centerburg. If you have a trip to arrange, please call Sherry Wilson at DSW. Her number is 617/555-1212.

DEVELOPING A CUSTOMIZED MEMO? REMEMBER TO . . .

- State the name of the new travel agency.
- Provide a contact name and phone number.

Unauthorized Use of Personal Stereos at Work

To:

From:

Date:

Regarding: Personal stereos

Music hath charms, but . . .

Company policy and our insurance guidelines prohibit the use of personal stereos on the job. Please help us keep the workplace atmosphere professional (and safe!)—leave personal stereos at home.

Alternate Version:

Everybody likes great music, but personal stereos are, alas, off limits during office hours.

Please leave personal stereo units at home—or save them for authorized weekend hours when you're working on-site with a supervisor's permission.

DEVELOPING A CUSTOMIZED MEMO? REMEMBER TO . . .

- Sympathize with the employee's desire to have music in the workplace.
- Emphasize company policy on the use of personal stereos.

Use of Company Computers for Non-Work Activities

To:

From:

Date:

Regarding: Computer use

This should probably go without saying, but the use of company computer hardware for unauthorized activities (such as Internet access, personal projects, or adventure games) is off-limits.

It's only fair, folks: When you're using company property, you should be working on company projects. Thanks.

Alternate Version:

You probably don't need me to tell you this, but just for the record . . .

The only acceptable use of ABC Corporation computers is work related to ABC Corporation projects. Please save Internet connections, personal projects, or adventure games for home time.

Thanks!

DEVELOPING A CUSTOMIZED MEMO? REMEMBER TO . . .

- Acknowledge that the employee may already be aware of the policy.
- Note prohibitions on personal use of company computers.

Use of Company Online Information Resource

To:

From:

Date:

Regarding: FactNet service

We're now hooked up to FactNet, one of the country's most respected on-line data services.

Only department managers have access to the service, but if you have a project that would benefit from knowing, say, the average monthly charge purchase amounts of men in Indianapolis over the age of 55, talk to your manager. We've got the world at our fingertips.

Alternate Version:

Need facts? Ask your manager about FactNet.

This online information service, to which we have recently subscribed, provides us with a truly breathtaking amount of information—all just a few keystrokes away. If you're working on a project and need background data, check to see whether your manager may be able to arrange a FactNet download for you.

DEVELOPING A CUSTOMIZED MEMO? REMEMBER TO . . .

- Announce the existence of the online information resource.
- Note who has access to the service.
- Indicate how the service might be utilized.

Van Pool: Tank Refill Etiquette

To:

From:

Date:

Reminder: Company van

If you use the company van, please remember to fill up the tank on the ABC charge card if the tank is half-full or lower.
Thanks!

Alternate Version:

Everyone who uses the company van knows how dispiriting it can be to begin a trip to pick up a coworker . . . only to notice that the tank is nearly empty.

If the tank is half-full or lower, the driver is responsible for filling the van up on the ABC charge account before returning to work. Thanks for minimizing everyone's down time by keeping the tank full.

DEVELOPING A CUSTOMIZED MEMO? REMEMBER TO . . .

- Remind employees to fill the tank when using the van.
- Note at what point the tank should be filled.

Virus Prevention

To:

From:

Date:

Regarding: Viruses!

No, we're not talking about the flu, but a particularly nasty computer bug that we may or may not have been exposed to.

Mark in Operations has virus-check software that everyone who works on a computer should run immediately.

Better safe than sorry, right?

Alternate Version:

Virus alert!

There's a nasty computer bug running around, and we may or may not have been exposed to it. If you value your data (and don't we all?) you should see Mark immediately for a copy of the software that will help you detect and combat this virus on your system.

Do it now!

DEVELOPING A CUSTOMIZED MEMO? REMEMBER TO . . .

- Alert employees to the computer virus.
- Indicate who to see for virus-check software.

Voice Mail Message Problems

To:

From:

Date:

Regarding: Voice mail

Help us send the most competent, positive message possible to customers and other incoming callers. Keep your voice-mail greeting brief and to the point! Please avoid humorous messages or background music—these may send the wrong impression.

Your home answering machine is the place for creative messages. Please keep your greetings on the ABC voice mail system subdued, competent, and professional.

Alternate Version:

Keep it simple, straightforward, and businesslike!

Those are the guidelines to follow when setting up personal messages on the ABC voice mail system. Jokes, background music, or cryptic literary references? Save them for your home machine, please!

Thanks for helping us project a professional image to our clients, customers, and all incoming callers.

DEVELOPING A CUSTOMIZED MEMO? REMEMBER TO . . .

- Emphasize the importance of professionalism in voice mail greetings.
- Provide guidelines for recording messages.
- Indicate what is not allowed or desirable in greetings.

Working through Lunch Hour

To:

From:

Date:

Regarding: Lunch hour work periods

Puzzle resolved!

The folks in Human Resources have informed me that the policy on lunchtime work is as follows. Any salaried ABC employee who wishes to work through lunch hour is certainly free to do so . . . but such tough-to-track time is not eligible for comp credit.

One less gray area to worry about, I guess. . . .

Alternate Version:

Well, we've finally resolved it. Any salaried employee who decides, of her own volition, to work straight through a lunch hour does so without earning comp time credit. If you need to work at your desk between 12:00 and 1:00, feel free to do so . . . but know that the people in Human Resources have decided it's just too tricky to track and verify these hours.

It may not be the answer people were hoping for, but it is an answer, and at least we now know what guidelines to follow.

DEVELOPING A CUSTOMIZED MEMO? REMEMBER TO . . .

- Note that the employee issue has been examined.
- Explain the policy clearly.
- Mention the reason(s) for the policy.

Implementing New Policies and Initiatives

Change is inevitable. All companies must grow and adapt to the changing times if they are to succeed. Even so, this process of change can sometimes create confusion among employees if they are not well informed concerning what is about to happen. In this chapter, you will find a variety of memos designed to help you make pertinent announcements and keep change-related problems to a minimum. Areas covered include: discussions of the types of change about to occur; explanations of different kinds of potentially challenging or disorienting policies; introductions to new personnel or creative teams in a reorganization or restructuring; and motivation of employees to welcome new corporate initiatives.

Announcement of Price Increase

To:

From:

Date:

Regarding: Prices on the Widgetron 1600

Make a note of it . . .

Effective January 30, the price on the above unit will be $195.00, not $180.00. Please notify customers that the 15% quantity discount on orders above 30 units will still apply.

Alternate Version:

As a result of increased costs related to the recent run-up in the international polydoubleflex materials market, the price on the Widgetron 1600 unit will be revised to 195.00, rather than the current 180.00, effective January 30. Please inform customers that the standard quantity discounts will still apply.

DEVELOPING A CUSTOMIZED MEMO? REMEMBER TO . . .

- Indicate the item that is affected by the price increase.
- State what the increase will be and the effective date.
- Provide any pertinent information to be passed on to the customer.

Announcing a Meeting for the Unveiling of a New Mission Statement

To:

From:

Date:

Regarding: Important meeting!

An all-company meeting is scheduled for this coming Tuesday, January 16th, at 2:00 pm in conference room A. Don't miss it—we'll be discussing ABC Corporation's new mission statement!

Alternate statement:

Where do we go from here?

You'll learn the answer at the all-company meeting scheduled for this Tuesday, January 16th, at 2:00 pm, in Conference Room A. We'll be going over the ABC Corporation's new mission statement.

It's going to be an exciting meeting—see you there!

DEVELOPING A CUSTOMIZED MEMO? REMEMBER TO . . .

- State the purpose of the meeting.
- Provide the date, time and location of the meeting.
- Stress the meeting's company-wide importance.

Announcing a Merger

To:

From:

Date:

Regarding: Great news!

Yes, it's true!

At a press conference today, Doug Becker and Len Freeberg will announce the merger of ABC Corporation and International Widget. This is a move that significantly improves the competitive position of both companies.

The next few months promise to be exciting and eventful. We all have questions about the specifics of the upcoming merger. You have my word that I'll keep you advised with updates from the front.

Alternate Version:

The wait is over, and now it's official. ABC Corporation will be joining forces with International Widget in a merger that will combine the unique strengths of these two industry giants. We all have questions about the merger, of course; a news conference tomorrow morning will fill everyone in on the most important details.

This is a time of unparalleled opportunity in the widget industry, and the union between ABC and International Widget means that we will be positioned for long-term success. I know you have questions and concerns about this. Your patience during what promises to be an exciting and rewarding transition period is much appreciated.

DEVELOPING A CUSTOMIZED MEMO? REMEMBER TO . . .

- Note the benefits of the merger.
- Mention the press conference for official information.
- Acknowledge and allay employee questions and concerns.

Announcing a New Advertising Campaign

To:

From:

Date:

Regarding: New advertising campaign

We're unveiling an exciting new advertising campaign this year. The theme is, "Widgets that work as hard as you do."

Our customers will be asking about the details of this campaign, which debuts on January 1. To find out more about it, please feel free to stop by my office.

Alternate Version:

"Widgets that work as hard as you do!"

That's the theme of the new ABC Corporation advertising campaign. Stop by my office to find out more about the campaign—which will be storming through national print and media outlets in an impossible-to-ignore way on January 1.

DEVELOPING A CUSTOMIZED MEMO? REMEMBER TO . . .

- Provide the new advertising theme up front.

- Indicate when the new campaign will begin.
- Note whom to see for information.

Announcing a New Community Outreach Program

To:

From:

Date:

Regarding: WRITE WAY program

WRITE WAY is an ABC-sponsored outreach program that helps adults in the Smalltown area improve their literacy skills. If you'd like to help out, please contact Margaret Bestway as soon as possible.

Alternate Version:

As part of our ongoing efforts to give something back to the community within which we operate, ABC is unveiling its exciting new WRITE WAY program, an adult literacy effort that helps adult residents of the Smalltown area develop their reading and writing skills. If you would like to volunteer to help out as part of this program, please see Margaret Bestway by the end of this week.

DEVELOPING A CUSTOMIZED MEMO? REMEMBER TO . . .

- Explain the program and its benefits.
- Provide a contact name for volunteers.

Announcing a New Department or Work Group

To:

From:

Date:

Regarding: The new team!

The long-awaited Special Sales Department becomes a reality today. Mel Lane, our new Director of Special Sales, is setting up office space next to

Conference Room A. Drop by and say hi to him—and to the members of his team!

Alternate Version:

Effective immediately, our Special Sales Department is up and running! Mel Lane is heading up the department, and he is assisted by the very able Bert Harrison (a recent transfer from the Accounting Department) and our newest employee, Dolores Perez.

Mel is currently setting up shop in the work area next to Conference Room A. Drop by and say hello!

DEVELOPING A CUSTOMIZED MEMO? REMEMBER TO . . .

- Announce the name of the new department.
- Note the department head's name and location.
- Encourage support for the new team.

Announcing a New Incentive Program

To:

From:

Date:

Regarding: Our new bonus plan

The new bonus program is simplicity itself.

If we hit $3,000,000 in sales this fiscal year, everyone gets a $5,000 bonus. All full-time employees who stay with the company for the entire year are eligible.

So let's do it—the new fiscal year is just around the corner. Ready . . . set . . . go!

Alternate Version:

This one's pretty simple—if we hit $3,000,000 in sales this year, everyone gets a $5000 bonus. Hard to beat, eh?

No confusing formulas. No small print. No elaborate preconditions. If you're a full-time employee of ABC as of January 1, and you put in a full year on that basis, you're eligible.

I don't know about you, but I'm sure motivated. Let's make it happen!

DEVELOPING A CUSTOMIZED MEMO? REMEMBER TO . . .

- Define the sales target and bonus goal.
- Note who is eligible for the program.
- Motivate the employee to achieve goals.

Announcing a New Management Team

To:

From:

Date:

Regarding: Welcome to Vera Ferrone and Dan McKee

Vera and Dan start work today as our Senior Marketing VP and Senior Design Consultant, respectively. They bring a combined 38 years of experience to ABC Corporation, and we're very lucky indeed to have them on board. Let's wish them all the best as they take on their new responsibilities.

Alternate Version:

As our new Senior Marketing VP and Senior Design Consultant, Vera and Dan bring a combined total of 38 years of experience in the widget industry to ABC. We wish them all the best as they undertake their new responsibilities with ABC.

DEVELOPING A CUSTOMIZED MEMO? REMEMBER TO . . .

- Provide the names of the new team members in the subject line of the memo.
- Mention the team members' titles and experience.
- Encourage employees to wish the new team well.

Announcing a New Product Line

To:

From:

Date:

Regarding: New Coleman 6100 product release

It's our biggest new product release in years!

The new Coleman 6100 line of personal widget management software represents a breakthrough for ABC and for the widget industry as a whole. To learn more about this exciting new line of products, take a look at the enclosed brochure—or stop by my office for a demonstration.

Alternate Version:

The Coleman 6100s are here!

This breakthrough line of personal widget management software represents a significant leap forward for our company . . . and the industry as a whole. Take a look at the color brochure available in the Marketing department to get the whole story on this exciting new line . . . or drop by my office to take a look at a demonstration model.

DEVELOPING A CUSTOMIZED MEMO? REMEMBER TO . . .

- Note the name of the new product.
- Indicate the product's importance/value.
- State how further information about the product may be obtained.

Announcing a New Service

To:

From:

Date:

Regarding: WidgetClean service

Effective February 1, we will be offering our WidgetClean service on a full-time basis. This service allows widget users the opportunity to take advantage of customized cleaning and upkeep of their widgets . . . no matter what brand or system they use.

For more information on this exciting new service, check the bulletin board in the employee lounge!

Alternate Version:

WidgetClean is available nationally on February 1 of this year!

Effective on that date, ABC offers full-scale widget cleaning and retooling services to widget users of all kinds—regardless of make, system, or brand. It's an exciting new service . . . one we should all become familiar with. To find out more, see me in person—or check out the display in the employee lounge.

DEVELOPING A CUSTOMIZED MEMO? REMEMBER TO . . .

- Describe the new service and its benefits.
- Note the start date of the new service.
- Indicate how further information may be obtained.

Announcing Mandatory Open-Door Policy for Selected Senior Managers

To:

From:

Date:

Regarding: Open door policy

We talked about it . . . now we're going to do it.

Effective immediately, all senior managers (including—you guessed it—me) are *required* to keep open schedules on Mondays and Fridays from one pm to three pm. During this time, any and all employees may drop by to ask questions, suggest new ideas, and report on problems.

In other words-we're here for you. Take advantage of us!

Alternate Version:

The doors are open—no kidding!

Effective immediately, all senior management (including yours truly) will be keeping open office hours between the hours of one and three pm on Mondays and Fridays. Drop in and tell us what's on your mind!

DEVELOPING A CUSTOMIZED MEMO? REMEMBER TO . . .

- Note when the new policy takes effect.
- Provide specific hours for the open-door policy.
- Encourage employees to take advantage of the policy.

Announcing the Acquisition of a New Company

To:

From:

Date:

Regarding: Acquisition of WidgetWorks

Great news! WidgetWorks has agreed to be purchased by ABC Corporation. This acquisition, which will take effect on September 1 of this year, significantly improves our competitive position in the widget industry.

For more information on the WidgetWorks acquisition, please see Ellen Greer in Public Relations.

Alternate Version:

Great news!

We've just purchased WidgetWorks, one of the most exciting and dynamic manufacturers of small widgets in the industry. For more information on this exciting development, check out the press conference in the main conference room this afternoon at 4:45 pm . . . or see Ellen Greer in Public Relations.

DEVELOPING A CUSTOMIZED MEMO? REMEMBER TO . . .

- Convey corporate excitement about the acquisition.
- Explain the acquisition's significance.
- Note how and where to acquire further information.

Canceling Popular Group Activity

To:

From:

Date:

Regarding: Morning coffee klatsch

Tight budgets have forced us to scale back on every possible expense . . . and one of those, unfortunately, is our Monday-morning company-sponsored coffee klatsch.

Suppose we continue to get together Monday at 8:00 . . . but bring our own home-baked goodies? Let's try it and see what happens.

Alternate Version:

Due to budgetary restrictions—restrictions nobody is thrilled about, but everyone, alas, has to live with—the morning coffee and Danish sessions between 8:00 and 9:00 will be phased out. December 30 will be the last date we enjoy company-sponsored goodies . . . but there's no rule saying we can't bring our own home-baked yummies during the same time period.

I'll volunteer for the first day of the employee-sponsored coffee klatch. Any requests for Monday, the third of January?

DEVELOPING A CUSTOMIZED MEMO? REMEMBER TO . . .

- Explain why the change in policy is necessary.
- Note the date that the new policy takes effect.
- Consider suggesting an alternate (no-budget) idea.

Change in Annual Salary Review Process

To:

From:

Date:

Regarding: Changes in salary review process

A new—and, we believe, fairer—way of conducting salary reviews is in place this year. Managers will get together and work as a group to determine the level of performance of each of the company's employees under review.

Questions? Come see me or Sheila.

Alternate Version:

In past years, we've evaluated people's salaries by means of a single rating from a superior. This year, the evaluations will not take place in a statistical vacuum—each manager will propose a numerical value to his or her subordinate, and will then be called on to support that rating during an extensive series of meetings with other managers.

The bottom line: The raises will be fairer, because what *one* manager considers to be "excellent" performance will come closer to matching up with what all the *other* managers consider to be "excellent" performance.

If you have questions about the new review process, feel free to talk to Sheila or to me about the new system.

DEVELOPING A CUSTOMIZED MEMO? REMEMBER TO . . .

- Describe the new procedure for reviewing salaries.
- Emphasize the benefits of the change.
- Note whom to see for questions about the new system.

Change in Company Grievance Procedure

To:

From:

Date:

Regarding: Grievances

A brief word on a change in procedure: Grievances are now being handled through the Human Resources office. If you would like information on filing a grievance, please see Diane Dibell in that office for details.

Alternate Version:

Given ombudsman Tom Berreson's transfer to the Finance Department, it seems like a good time to update our grievance procedures. After a good deal of thought, we've decided to handle all grievances through the Human Resources office. Jane Kennedy or Mildred Cole can handle any questions you have on this new procedure.

DEVELOPING A CUSTOMIZED MEMO? REMEMBER TO . . .

- State which office will now be handling grievances.
- Provide specific contact(s) for questions.

Change in Policy

To:

From:

Date:

Regarding: Widget use at home

Well, we tried it, but it didn't work out as well as we'd hoped.

Effective immediately, all employees who wish to try out ABC widgets must do so on-site. The practice of loaning out widgets for home use will no longer be in place.

Alternate Version:

Starting immediately, ABC employees who want to test widget units on a personal basis to gain greater familiarity with the company's products must do so on-site. No further at-home loaners will be issued.

> DEVELOPING A CUSTOMIZED MEMO? REMEMBER TO . . .
> - Clearly outline the change in policy.
> - Note effective date of the new policy.

Change in Product/Service Focus

To:

From:

Date:

Regarding: New market

Widgets—they're not just for engineers anymore!

Our new WidgetMaster line incorporates a number of exciting new features designed to help us crack the home-use market. Please see the attached brochure—or talk to me or Nancy McKenzie—for more details.

Alternate Version:

We've discovered an exciting new market for our widgets!

Previously, engineers at Fortune 500 firms constituted 90% of our market base. With the new line of WidgetMaster 760 units, we're incorporating a host of features that will make it easier for home users to take advantage of our widget technology.

For more information on the new line and the customers we're trying to reach, please feel free to see me or Nancy McKenzie.

> DEVELOPING A CUSTOMIZED MEMO? REMEMBER TO . . .
> - Note in what way(s) the market base has expanded.

- Mention the product line.
- Provide contact name(s) for further information.

Changing the Company Name

To:

From:

Date:

Regarding: New company name

It's official!

As of January 1, the company will be changing its name to ABC Widget Technologies, to further emphasize our intense focus on the widget market.

A major advertising campaign will blare the news to the outside world . . . but please inform clients, customers, and outside callers of the change during your contacts with them!

Alternate Version:

Effective January 1, our new name is ABC Widget Technologies.

Over the next 30 days, a major promotional effort will get the word out about the name change. You can help out by telling clients, customers, and members of the media with whom you come in contact about the name change.

DEVELOPING A CUSTOMIZED MEMO? REMEMBER TO . . .

- State the new name of the company and effective date of the change.
- Mention any promotional campaign.
- Note the importance of informing customers of the change.

Contest: Who Can Come Up With the Best New Product Idea?

To:

From:

Date:

Regarding: Contest!

Five hundred dollars!

That's what's at stake in our new contest. Everyone who enters is eligible to win the cash first prize—or three months of unlimited online service from InternetAccess, the second prize.

So—what do you have to do? Simple. Help us come up with a new product for the next fiscal year. The two best ideas win big.

Please get your ideas in to me by no later than 5:00 on Thursday, the 31st of this month.

Alternate Version:

Do you have a great product idea? It could be worth $500 to you.

That's the first prize in our new contest. The second prize is three months of unlimited online service from InternetAccess.

So—put on your thinking cap and come up with our next breakthrough product. Please submit entries to me no later than 5:00 on Thursday, the 31st of this month.

Developing a Customized Memo? Remember to . . .

- Mention the contest prizes early in the memo.
- Describe the purpose of the contest.
- Provide a deadline date and time for contest entries.

Creativity Meeting

To:

From:

Date:

Regarding: Let's brainstorm!

An exciting meeting about some new creativity techniques will take place in Conference Room A at 11:00 tomorrow morning. Everyone is welcome— but attendance from members of the Editorial and Graphics departments is mandatory.

See you there!

Alternate Version:

This is going to be fun.

Tomorrow at 11:00 am in Conference Room A, we'll be having a one-hour meeting on some exciting creativity techniques. The gathering is meant for the members of the Editorial and Graphics departments, but everyone is welcome.

See you there!

Developing a Customized Memo? Remember to . . .

- Explain the nature of the meeting and for whom it is mandatory.
- Provide a time and place for the meeting.
- Encourage participation from all departments.

Discontinuing an Incentive Program

To:

From:

Date:

Regarding: Changes in incentive program

I learned today from the people in Headquarters that we are phasing out the Unit Production Incentive Program, effective January 1. As of that date, no further payouts will be taking place under this program.

A number of parallel programs are being considered for the new year, but the timing is far from certain as to when these will be implemented. I'll keep you posted on new developments on this score.

Alternate Version:

It's true: The Unit Production Incentive Program is being discontinued as of January 1.

On that date, payouts under this program will stop. There may or may not be a replacement program on our horizon . . . I'll let everyone know when word comes down from headquarters on this.

> ### DEVELOPING A CUSTOMIZED MEMO? REMEMBER TO . . .
>
> - Note the date that the incentive program is being discontinued.
> - Mention the possibility of new programs.
> - Promise to keep employees informed.

Encouraging Adherence to an Unpopular Policy

To:

From:

Date:

Regarding: Parking spaces

No one is crazy about this, but . . . we really, truly, can't park in the lot on the far side of the building until after 8:30 am.

This lot belongs to our neighbors, Comexcon Corporation. They've been kind enough to lease the space to us during off-hours, but they need the parking for their own night shift employees.

If you use the lot at a time you're not supposed to, you may well get towed!

Alternate Version:

It's tempting, I know. All the same:

Don't park in the lot at the far side of the building until after 8:30 AM!

This lot belongs to our neighbors, Comexcon, who've been nice enough to lease us the spaces for use after their own employees have concluded the graveyard shift. If you use the lot at the wrong time, you may well get towed!

Developing a Customized Memo? Remember to . . .

- Strongly emphasize the parameters of the policy.
- Explain the importance of adhering to the policy.
- Note the consequences if the policy is ignored.

Encouraging Participation in New E-Mail Suggestion Box Program

To:

From:

Date:

Regarding: Electronic suggestion box

Now that we're all online together, there's an exciting new program you may want to take advantage of: the Electronic Suggestion Box!

By posting a message to greatideas@abc.com, you can let us know about your latest brainstorm . . . or your latest headache. If you want to send an anonymous suggestion, just use the terminal set up in the employee lounge specifically for this program.

We look forward to hearing from you!

Alternate Version:

Got a great idea? Eager to shine a light on a current problem? Zap us at greatideas@abc.com, the company's Electronic Suggestion Box.

If you use the terminal in the employee lounge, your suggestion will be completely anonymous.

Tell us what's on your mind!

DEVELOPING A CUSTOMIZED MEMO? REMEMBER TO . . .

- Encourage use of the Suggestion Box for both suggestions and complaints.
- Provide the exact e-mail address for messages.
- Note anonymity of the system for employee comfort.

Expense Reports to be Filed Monthly, Not Quarterly

To:

From:

Date:

Regarding: Expense reports

Because of the quarterly bottlenecks in the accounting department, we're now moving to a *monthly* system of expense reimbursement. Please help us avoid traffic tie-ups. Turn in your expense reports no later than the fifth of each month.

Alternate Version:

Change in plans department: We can make things faster and easier for the people in the Accounting Department . . . and get checks turned around more quickly . . . by turning in expense reports on a monthly, rather than quarterly basis. Starting now, monthly reports will be required of all employees with expense accounts.

Thanks for filing your expense reports no later than the fifth of each month . . . and helping us make this process run more smoothly for everyone!

DEVELOPING A CUSTOMIZED MEMO? REMEMBER TO . . .

- Explain the reason(s) for the change.
- Note new deadline for filing expense reports.

Explaining Change in Company Ownership

To:

From:

Date:

Regarding: Our new owners

"What's going to change when Bigcorp takes over our company?"

Actually, not very much. Bigcorp, as most of us already know, is the world's leading specialty widget corporation. They've been in business since 19XX, and their recent purchase of ABC Corporation was a friendly acquisition. We've received every assurance that Bigcorp is interested in maintaining continuity and goodwill among current employees.

I'll keep you posted on specifics about the transition period as ABC takes its place among the Bigcorp family of companies.

Alternate Version:

Yes, we've joined the Bigcorp family of companies . . . but you may not notice it all that much.

Since acquiring ABC Corporation, Bigcorp has sent senior executives to meet with some of our key people. The message we've received is a simple one: They may have minor changes to make, but they won't be turning the place upside down, and no major personnel moves are anticipated in the near future.

Over the next few weeks, as the transition takes place, I'll keep you posted on new developments that will help all of us operate more efficiently with the people at Bigcorp.

DEVELOPING A CUSTOMIZED MEMO? REMEMBER TO . . .

- Acknowledge employee concerns about the change in ownership.
- Clearly indicate how the change will or will not affect employees.
- Assure employees that they will be kept posted on developments.

Identifying Responsibilities of Newly Organized Team

To:

From:

Date:

Regarding: New team responsibilities

The members new graphics team will assume following responsibilities . . .

Ellen will develop new overall concepts.

Vera will develop new copy.

Gene will oversee the execution of computer graphics.

Myra will provide administrative support, and report directly to Ellen.

Questions? See me!

Alternate Version:

Who does what?

The new graphics team reports to Ellen (who's in charge of concept and overall approach). The team breaks down along the following lines:

Vera will develop new copy.

Gene will oversee the execution of computer graphics.

Myra will provide administrative support, and report directly to Ellen.

Questions? Feel free to ask Ellen or me.

Developing a Customized Memo? Remember to . . .

- Clearly describe who will be administering what areas.
- Provide contact name(s) for questions.

New Employee Recognition Program to Be Implemented

To:

From:

Date:

Regarding: Employee of the Month

Is there a superstar in your department?

Starting immediately, ABC Corporation will be highlighting an Employee of the Month. Selected employees win their choice of a cash bonus or additional comp time. Managers who wish to forward nominations should speak to myself or Annie Vestrich by the end of this week.

Alternate Version:

Show off your superstar!

Starting immediately, ABC Corporation is instituting an Employee of the Month program. The individual selected will be awarded either a cash bonus—or additional comp time.

Who's your superstar? If you'd like to nominate someone in your department, please see me or Annie Vestrich no later than the end of this week.

DEVELOPING A CUSTOMIZED MEMO? REMEMBER TO . . .

- Note start date of the new employee recognition program.
- Indicate what the prize will be.
- Provide contact name and deadline for nominations.

Outlining New Policy on Use of Company Facilities

To:

From:

Date:

Regarding: Weekend work

If you've got work to do on a pressing project, and are used to being able to drop in on the weekend to access files on your computer, read this!

Effective immediately, only work *approved ahead of time for a specific time period* will be allowed on-site during the weekend. If you don't set up the time and agenda with your supervisor ahead of time, your computer won't turn on . . . and the security guard won't let you in!

Save yourself a headache—check in with your manager first when scheduling weekend work.

Alternate Version:

Working this weekend? Check with your manager first!

New security policies requires us to *preschedule* all weekend work. You'll need to get clearance from your supervisor to set up a time slot when you'll be working on a specific project . . . otherwise the security guard won't let you in the building!

DEVELOPING A CUSTOMIZED MEMO? REMEMBER TO . . .

- Alert employee to the change in policy.
- Clearly describe new security procedures.
- Stress the importance of prescheduling weekend work time.

Policy on Official Signature Authority

To:

From:

Date:

Regarding: Use of signature

"Who can sign Paul's name on letters?"

Well, Paul can, of course. Others include Frank McCarthy, George Miller, and Vera DeLeon. Everyone else . . . don't use Paul's name on the signature line!

Thanks for helping us keep everything straight.

Alternate Version:

If you're not authorized to sign letters for Paul—don't sign letters for Paul!

Remember . . . only Frank McCarthy, George Miller, and Vera DeLeon are authorized to use Paul's signature software while he is away, or to sign his name to letters for him. If you're not one of these people, you cannot compose a letter and send it out under Paul's signature!

Thanks in advance for your cooperation.

DEVELOPING A CUSTOMIZED MEMO? REMEMBER TO . . .

- Name the person whose signature authorization is in question.
- Detail those employees who are authorized to sign for the person.
- Emphasize who does not have signature authorization.

Recruiting "Secret Customer" Volunteer

To:

From:

Date:

Regarding: "Secret customer" project

This month, I'd like to get some first-hand feedback on how much information retailers are supplying about our widgets. Would you be willing to "play the part" of a customer . . . and visit half a dozen retail locations this weekend to let me know what the people at the customer service desks are saying about our products, our guarantee, and our service plan?

Alternate Version:

Feel like taking part in an espionage project?

This doesn't have anything to do with secret agents, but it does have plenty to do with learning what retailers are telling our customers. I'd like you to pretend to be a consumer in the market for a new home widget system.

Let's ask half-a-dozen retailers about our products, our warranty, and our service plans . . . and see what they have to say.

Developing a Customized Memo? Remember to . . .

- Explain the purpose of the espionage project.
- Request the employee's assistance in carrying out the plan.
- Outline what is to be done.

Reorganization on the Horizon

To:

From:

Date:

Regarding: Organizational changes

Changes in the way we work are on the way.

In order to become a more efficient, competitive organization, we'll be taking some important new steps over the next few weeks that will help us serve our customers better. New internal structures are going to help us do that.

I've scheduled a meeting for 9:00 am on Thursday, January 14, to discuss some of the new initiatives and organizational shifts we'll be undertaking. I hope to see everyone there.

Alternate Version:

In order to become more competitive, ABC Corporation is going to be reassigning some duties and establishing some new internal partnerships. I'll be talking about the changes on the horizon in an all-company meeting scheduled for Thursday, January 14 at 9:00 am.

The next few weeks will demand flexibility and discipline from all of us . . . but I am firmly convinced that they will also leave ABC in a better position to satisfy its customers. I look forward to talking to each of you about our new ways of working.

DEVELOPING A CUSTOMIZED MEMO? REMEMBER TO . . .

- Mention the reasons for the organizational changes.
- Give some idea of what changes are in store.
- Provide day and time for meeting to discuss changes.

Team Assigned Task of Developing New Profit Center— Please Assist

To:

From:

Date:

Regarding: Fred Casey's New Work Group

Fred Casey is heading up a brand-new workgroup that's focused on developing a new small-circulation magazine on widget use.

I thought that, given your background in the magazine industry, you might be the perfect person to review his plans and strategies. Have you got an hour or so to talk over the new project with him?

Alternate Version:

Fred Casey is working on a very exciting new project—a magazine aimed at the institutional market that will help readers make sense of their widget use. You've got all kinds of experience in the magazine field . . . perhaps you could spare him an hour or two this week?

DEVELOPING A CUSTOMIZED MEMO? REMEMBER TO . . .

- Name who is heading up the new work group.
- Explain the work group's purpose.
- Mention the employee's expertise when requesting assistance.

Chapter *13*

Workplace Safety

No one can dispute that safety standards in the workplace are essential, but employees often remain uninformed about important company policies in this area. Clear explanations of procedures and firm enforcement of regulations are necessary to the well-being of both the company and its employees. This chapter will offer memos focused on critical safety issues such as smoking policies, fire drills, use of emergency exits, alarm systems, and corporate safety standards. It will also offer you some tools for handling violations of the standards.

Addressing Recent Smoking Incidents in Hazardous Areas

To:

From:

Date:

Regarding: Workplace safety in hazardous areas

If you smoke in the warehouse, you take your life into your hands . . . and the lives of others, as well.

Please help us avoid a catastrophic accident. Observe all posted "No Smoking" signs, especially those in hazardous areas, such as the warehouse, where flammable materials are constantly being handled.

Alternate Version:

It's not "political correctness"—it's life and limb.

"No smoking" signs are posted in the warehouse area for a very good reason: There are plenty of flammable materials passing through that area. The no-smoking policy must be observed in this area. Those who violate this rule will be subject to immediate termination.

Please help us keep ABC a safe place to work—observe all posted "No Smoking" signs.

DEVELOPING A CUSTOMIZED MEMO? REMEMBER TO . . .

- Stress life or death consequences up front.
- Explain the importance of the "No Smoking" signs.
- Request employee cooperation in observing the signs.

Addressing Subordinate Who Is Lax in Meeting Workplace Safety Standards

To:

From:

Date:

Regarding: Steel-toed boots

Yesterday was the third straight day you reported to work without the steel-toed boots purchased for you by ABC Corporation.

Your job as warehouse assistant *requires* the use of steel-toed boots at all times. These boots are not additional "precautions," but rather essential pieces of safety equipment. If you can't find the boots we bought for you, let me know, and we'll find some way to get replacements for you.

Please don't report to work tomorrow without your steel-toed boots!

Thanks for helping ABC keep your workplace safe.

Alternate Version:

I need your help.

If you show up for work one more day without the steel-toed boots we bought for you, or a pair of replacement boots just as strong, I'm under instructions to send you home without pay for the day. Please remember to wear your safety boots when you report to work tomorrow, and every day you report to the warehouse thereafter.

If the boots are lost, let me know, so we can work something out . . . but whatever you do, help us help you keep your workplace safe. Wear the safety equipment we provide!

Developing a Customized Memo? Remember to . . .

- Note that the employee has not been adhering to safety standards.
- Emphasize the importance of the safety procedures.
- Instruct the employee to adhere to the proper procedures.

Authorized Personnel Only to Operate Heavy Equipment

To:

From:

Date:

Regarding: Use of forklift

Please remember . . . the only people who are authorized to use the fork-lift are the foremen who are on duty in the warehouse. If you're not on the list, please don't drive this vehicle!

Thanks for helping us follow our insurance guidelines . . . and keep ABC Corporation a safe place to work.

Alternate Version:

Sorry! "Just this once" isn't a good enough reason.

Only the warehouse foreman on duty is authorized to use the forklift! Our insurance policy *requires* that we limit use of this vehicle to people with at least four years of heavy equipment experience. Please help us keep ABC a safe place to work. Don't use the forklift if you're not authorized to do so.

DEVELOPING A CUSTOMIZED MEMO? REMEMBER TO . . .

- Emphasize who is and is not authorized to operate heavy equipment.
- Mention insurance requirements.

Emergency Exits to Be Left Accessible and Unlocked at All Times

To:

From:

Date:

Regarding: Emergency exits

No kidding. No exceptions. No doubt about it. All emergency exits must remain unlocked and accessible at all times.

If you need to talk about this, drop by any time. Thanks in advance for helping us keep ABC a safe place to work.

Alternate Version:

It should go without saying, but . . .

Emergency exits should never be locked, no matter what reasons arise to tempt someone to do so.

Please make sure all the emergency exits are easy to get to, clearly marked, and unlocked at all times. Questions? Objections? Problems with the alarm system? Feel free to give me a call and we'll talk.

DEVELOPING A CUSTOMIZED MEMO? REMEMBER TO . . .

- Clearly state the need to keep emergency exits unlocked and accessible.
- Be open to discussion about the policy.

Fire Drill

To:

From:

Date:

Regarding: Fire preparedness

Do you have any objections to my calling a fire drill today—just to keep everyone attuned to the importance of fire safety?

Please let me know. I think today would be a good day to do something like this.

Alternate Version:

Considering the importance of keeping everyone aware of exit procedures during fire and emergency situations, I thought today might be a good day for a fire drill.

What do you think?

DEVELOPING A CUSTOMIZED MEMO? REMEMBER TO . . .

- Note your reason for requesting a fire drill.
- Suggest when a drill might take place.

Importance of Keeping Work Areas Clean and Well Organized

To:

From:

Date:

Regarding: Work station cleanliness

If you were out sick, and someone else had to make sense of your work station in order to find an important piece of paper or computer file, would that person be able to?

Just on the off chance the answer was "no," I thought we all might take the period from 4:30 to 5:00 pm tomorrow to spruce up individual cubicles. I've selected some special high-energy music that will make the task fun.

Let's rock and roll tomorrow afternoon—and keep ABC looking sharp and well organized!

Alternate Version:

Wouldn't you hate to lose something important—or delay your work trying to find it—because something was misfiled in your work area? Half an hour could make a big difference in whether your cubicle is user-friendly or not.

Let's take the time between 4:30 and 5:00 pm tomorrow afternoon to mount an all-department cleanup campaign. Rock tunes will be provided . . . and our floor will look so sharp when we're done that Felix Unger himself would be proud.

DEVELOPING A CUSTOMIZED MEMO? REMEMBER TO. . .

- Give a scenario that stresses the importance of keeping work areas organized.

- Suggest a time for a joint clean-up campaign.
- Provide an incentive for employee cooperation.

Importance of Obtaining Help In Driving if Necessary After Overtime Shifts

To:

From:

Date:

Regarding: Late hours—need a ride home?

If you're working late . . . really late . . . please don't try to drive home your-self if you're exhausted.

We appreciate any employee's willingness to put in hours on-site on tough projects. But if it's the middle of the night (after 11:00 pm), and you're not up for driving, please consider calling a cab; you can submit the receipt as part of your expense report. You can do the same thing the next morning to get back to work.

Alternate Version:

It's after 11:00 at night. You've been working late on an important project. You're exhausted. Ask yourself: Should you really be driving home?

If the answer is "no," please call a cab to get home, and again in the morn-ing to get back to work, and then submit your expenses to Alan in account-ing. We want you to make it home in one piece!

DEVELOPING A CUSTOMIZED MEMO? REMEMBER TO . . .

- Note importance of not driving when overtired.
- Suggest an alternative to driving late at night.
- Offer to reimburse cab expenses.

Importance of Using Supplied Safety Equipment at All Times

To:

From:

Date:

Regarding: Safety equipment

Your vision is precious to you. It's precious to us, too. Please don't take chances with it!

Use your safety goggles *at all times* when engaged in widget assembly work.

Alternate Version:

If you're assembling widgets without wearing safety goggles—even for a moment—you're taking a risk you shouldn't take. Is your vision worth that chance?

Don't do work on the shop floor without using the appropriate safety equipment!

DEVELOPING A CUSTOMIZED MEMO? REMEMBER TO. . .

- Note possible consequences of not using safety equipment.
- Stress importance of using appropriate safety equipment.

Installation of New Alarm System

To:

From:

Date:

Regarding: New alarm system

If you're used to coming in to work early or leaving late . . . please read this carefully!

Our workplace has been equipped with a new security system that uses motion detection to set off an alarm system that notifies both our security company and the local police. If you come in early or stay late, you'll need to know how to punch in a personal code that will disable the system when you enter or turn it on when you leave. Please see Ellen Revere for more details.

Alternate Version:

"Say . . . what's that loud beeping sound?"

It's probably our new alarm system notifying the local police that there's a burglar on the premises. It's not really a burglar, of course. It's you, inadvertently setting off the motion detector nobody told you how to disable.

For information on avoiding needless run-ins with the law when you come in to work early or stay late, see Ellen Revere.

DEVELOPING A CUSTOMIZED MEMO? REMEMBER TO . . .

- Describe how the new alarm system works.
- Note necessity of employee familiarity with the system.
- Provide contact name for further information.

Notice of Violation of Company Safety Standards

To:

From:

Date:

Regarding: Too close for comfort!

Four boxes of widgets were opened and left strewn on the floor in the warehouse last week. That's a real safety problem—even if the widgets were only left out for a day!

ABC Corporation has a tough set of safety standards; those standards are rigorously enforced. A copy of our standards is available on request from my office. Please read the standards—and help us make them a reality.

Alternate Version:

Widgets can't be left spread around the warehouse floor. Period.

Please help us maintain the minimum safety standards that will benefit every ABC employee. Read and follow the warehouse safety guidelines— including section four, which focuses on keeping floor space clear of debris. The guidelines are posted on the wall near the main entrance to the warehouse.

DEVELOPING A CUSTOMIZED MEMO? REMEMBER TO. . .

- Note any observed violation of safety standards.
- Stress the importance of maintaining standards.
- State where employee guidelines for safety standards may be obtained.

Notifying Superior that Possible Unsafe Condition Exists

To:

From:

Date:

Regarding: Possible problem in shop

I think we may have a safety problem in the shop—at least half of the employees on the line are not using safety goggles when assembling units. What do you think we should do? I suggest a meeting tomorrow morning to review safety procedures.

Alternate Version:

People on the assembly line aren't wearing safety goggles.

At least half of the workers I monitored today are treating the goggles as "optional" equipment. Should we call a meeting to go over safety procedures?

DEVELOPING A CUSTOMIZED MEMO? REMEMBER TO. . .

- Mention the specific safety violation that has been observed.
- Suggest a meeting to discuss the problem.

Reminder: Violating Company Smoking Policy Means a More Dangerous Workplace

To:

From:

Date:

Regarding: Smoking outside of designated areas

Warning! Cigarette smoking in the wrong places can be hazardous to your health . . . and your job.

If you smoke in unauthorized areas—restrooms, for instance—you're subject to immediate disciplinary action, up to and including dismissal.

Why do we take smoking so seriously? Because it's dangerous to the smoker, to those around him or her, and to the facility! The chance of fire or other mishap increases dramatically when people smoke in unauthorized areas. So don't do it!

Alternate Version:

Fire hazards exist when people smoke in unauthorized areas—not to mention the potential health risks associated with second-hand smoke.

If you must smoke, do so only in authorized areas, and never in the restroom or warehouse. Thanks.

DEVELOPING A CUSTOMIZED MEMO? REMEMBER TO . . .

- Note the fire hazards created by smoking in unauthorized areas.
- Mention health risks.
- State company policy on authorized areas for smoking.

Reminding Manager that Visitors Must Not Be Allowed into High-risk Areas of Facility

To:

From:

Date:

Regarding: Upcoming visitors from Eyes Front

I'm very much looking forward to meeting your friends from Eyes Front, Incorporated. Please remember, though, when you show them around the company, that our insurance guidelines prohibit any visitors in the shop floor area.

Thanks—and let me know when your guests arrive!

Alternate Version:

The upcoming visit from the people at Eyes Front is very exciting indeed . . . but please remember to follow our insurance guidelines as you show them around the place. According to our policy, outsiders are not permitted to enter the shop-floor area.

I look forward to meeting our visitors.

DEVELOPING A CUSTOMIZED MEMO? REMEMBER TO . . .

- Acknowledge visitors' anticipated arrival.
- Note area(s) where visitors are not allowed.
- Mention insurance considerations.

Renovation Scheduled

To:

From:

Date:

Regarding: Renovation work

It's finally happening!

Our reception area is being renovated this week and next. For your own safety and the safety of all visitors to ABC Corporation during that time, the main entrance to the building will be closed. Please enter the building via the side entryway—our new temporary reception area—while the workers are upgrading our main entry.

Alternate Version:

Work has finally begun on renovating the reception area!

While the work is going on, the front entryway will not be accessible. Please enter the building via the temporary reception area now set up at the side entrance of the building.

DEVELOPING A CUSTOMIZED MEMO? REMEMBER TO . . .

- Specify which area is being renovated.
- Indicate changes to area access while construction is ongoing.

Requesting Private Meeting to Address Safety Issues

To:

From:

Date:

Regarding: Can we talk?

There are some important safety issues I think we should go over in a face-to-face meeting. Have you got a minute or two to discuss them?

I look forward to getting together with you soon.

Alternate Version:

Something's come up, and I need to talk about it with you as soon as possible. When can we get together to discuss some safety issues I've been looking at?

DEVELOPING A CUSTOMIZED MEMO? REMEMBER TO . . .

- Mention that there are safety issues to be discussed.
- Request a meeting to discuss issues.

Suggesting New Workplace Safety Awareness Campaign

To:

From:

Date:

Regarding: Awareness of safety issues

You can't be too careful . . .

That's why I think we should consider making workplace safety the focus of a major series of meetings this month with everyone in the department. Can we get together to discuss this idea?

Alternate Version:

What would you think of setting up a series of meetings, announcements, and memos to highlight specific areas of workplace safety?

I'd like to hear what ideas you have on making this topic the focus of attention this month for everyone in the department. Can we get together this afternoon in my office at 2:00 to discuss this?

DEVELOPING A CUSTOMIZED MEMO? REMEMBER TO . . .

- Emphasize the desirability of regular meetings to discuss safety issues.
- Suggest a meeting to discuss the idea.

Chapter *14*

Internal Scheduling, Management Information Gathering, Training, and Other Operational Issues

This chapter offers memos that help you deal with a variety of issues that may arise in day-to-day operations. Included are memos that address situations such as: changes in company policies and procedures; announcements about training sessions, performance reviews, conferences, and schedules; requests for information on a product or problem; confidentiality and security issues; and exploring the reasons for delays and/or the need for additional staff.

Announcing a Meeting

To:

From:

Date:

Regarding: Meeting to discuss budgets

We'll be having our annual budget review meeting next Tuesday, the 5th, at 9:00 am in Conference Room B. Please bring any information you need to support your budget request.

See you there!

Alternate Version:

The annual budget meeting is coming up soon!

The meeting to review annual budgets will be held on Tuesday, November 5th at 9:00 am in conference room B. Please bring six copies of next year's budget and all supporting documentation. We look forward to seeing you.

DEVELOPING A CUSTOMIZED MEMO? REMEMBER TO . . .

- Announce the purpose of the meeting up front.
- Provide a date, time and place for the meeting.
- Indicate what materials may be required.

Announcing Mandatory Training Session

To:

From:

Date:

Regarding: Mandatory Dentitup 2000 training session

A training sesssion for all managers will take place on Tuesday, June 6th at 10:00 am in the Executive Conference Room. This two-hour session will introduce you to the new Dentitup widget deconstruction system.

Everyone at the manager pay grade is required to attend! See you there.

Alternate Version:

All managers are required to attend a training session that will introduce the new Dentitup 2000 widget deconstruction system.

As you know, we have a lot of work to do in the widget deconstruction area over the next two months. It is critical that we obtain maximum output from everyone on this score, and that we understand how widget assembly and disassembly issues ultimately affect everyone's performance. The Dentitup training session will take place on Tuesday, June 6th at 10:00 am in the Executive Conference Room.

DEVELOPING A CUSTOMIZED MEMO? REMEMBER TO . . .

- State the purpose of the training session.
- Provide a date, time and place for the meeting.
- Note that attendance is mandatory.

Announcing Schedule of Performance Reviews

To:

From:

Date:

Regarding: Performance Reviews

Please see my secretary as soon as possible to schedule time next week for your annual review. This meeting will last approximately ninety minutes. Thanks—and I look forward to talking to you!

Alternate Version:

Our annual round of performance reviews has been scheduled to begin next week. We will spend approximately ninety minutes in each review discussing your job performance over the past twelve months. Please see my secretary before Friday to schedule your specific time. I look forward to seeing you.

- Note when the reviews will be taking place.
- Indicate how long the review will last.
- Note whom to contact to schedule an appointment for review.

Announcing Voluntary Training Session

To:

From:

Date:

Regarding: Upcoming training in spreadsheet software

There will be four training sessions next week to provide instruction in the new spreadsheet program.

Interested? Please call me at extension 2542 for details and registration.

Alternate Version:

Training in our new spreadsheet software will be available next week.

Many of you told us that you needed training in the new spreadsheet program in order to use it effectively. We've listened to your requests and will be providing four two-hour training sessions next week. They are scheduled from 8:00 am to 10:00 am and 2:00 pm to 4:00 pm on both Tuesday and Wednesday. Please try to sign up for one of these sessions as soon as you can, so we will know how many to expect in attendance. You can reserve a slot by calling me at extension 2542.

DEVELOPING A CUSTOMIZED MEMO? REMEMBER TO . . .

- State the purpose of the training sessions.
- Indicate when training sessions will take place.
- Provide contact information for registration.

Announcing Yearly Conference or Retreat

To:

From:

Date:

Regarding: Annual company retreat

The annual company retreat will be held the second weekend in February (Friday evening through Sunday morning) at the Meadows Lodge. All managers are required to attend this meeting; please contact Joyce in Employee Relations for further details on registration.

Alternate Version:

Our annual company retreat will be held the second weekend in February.

I look forward to joining all of you at our company retreat, to be held from February 11th to the 13th at the Meadows Lodge. We will be reviewing last year's performance . . . and describing this year's strategies. An agenda and directions to the lodge can be obtained from Employee Relations.

This is a required event for departmental managers.

DEVELOPING A CUSTOMIZED MEMO? REMEMBER TO . . .

- Indicate when the retreat will take place.
- If desired, note the purpose of the retreat.
- Make it clear who must attend.
- Provide contact information for obtaining details.

Assigning Deadline on New Project

To:

From:

Date:

Regarding: Client satisfaction report

It is imperative that we complete our review of the Acco-Light client satisfaction summary by September 30th. Marketing needs this data in order to prepare the company's marketing strategy for next year. Can we meet soon to discuss the best ways to make this deadline?

Alternate Version:

The Acco-Light review is an extremely important project.

Our marketing department must have this data to input into next year's overall marketing strategy. All data from the client satisfaction project must be finalized by September 30th. I realize that a great deal of work on all of our parts will be required to make this happen, but I'm confident that we can achieve the necessary results in the time frame given if we all work together.

Let's meet soon so we can discuss the best strategies for making this project happen.

DEVELOPING A CUSTOMIZED MEMO? REMEMBER TO . . .

- Emphasize the importance of the project.
- Explain marketing department needs.
- Provide a deadline for project completion.

Change in Daily Schedule

To:

From:

Date:

Regarding: Daily schedule change

We have decided to move to an 8:00-4:00 work schedule in order to accommodate the needs we discussed at our recent all-company meeting. These hours are effective this coming Monday, July 3.

Please see your immediate supervisor as soon as possible for further details about this schedule.

Alternate Version:

Based on input from an employee task force, the company has decided to allow workers to engage in a flexible work schedule. Instead of all employees working from 9:00 to 5:00, there will now be the options of working from 7:00 to 3:00 and 11:00 to 7:00. While we cannot guarantee availability of all schedules to everyone, we will try to provide your preference.

Developing a Customized Memo? Remember to . . .

- Announce the nature of the change.
- Provide details, or indicate whom to see for details.

Change in Break Schedule

To:

From:

Date:

Regarding: New schedule for morning break

A minor change to report in the scheduling of morning breaks . . .

Beginning June 1st, all employees whose last name begins with N to Z will take their breaks at 10:30 am. Everyone else will continue their current schedule.

Alternate Version:

Starting on June 1st we will be implementing a new schedule for morning breaks.

All employees whose last name starts with the letters A to M will continue to take their break at 10:00 am; employees whose last name begins with N-Z will take their break at 10:30 am.

Thank you in advance for your cooperation!

DEVELOPING A CUSTOMIZED MEMO? REMEMBER TO . . .

- Note when the schedule change will take effect.
- Clearly explain what the new schedule will be.

Change in Late Arrival Policy

To:

From:

Date:

Regarding: New policy for late arrivals

While there may be valid reasons for an occasional late arrival, lateness hurts us all and needs to be minimized. We hope to see an immediate improvement in this trend. Starting on March 1st any employees arriving more than five minutes late will be required report to their supervisor before signing in.

Alternate Version:

I know the traffic can be rough, but . . .

We really need to start estimating commute times more efficiently. Our customers are depending on us all to arrive on time, ready to contribute.

Starting March 1, all late arrivals (i.e., team members arriving at 9:05 or later) will be required to check in with their supervisor before beginning work. Thanks in advance for your help.

DEVELOPING A CUSTOMIZED MEMO? REMEMBER TO . . .

- Mention existing tardiness problems.
- Emphasize the need for improvement.
- Provide the new policy and its effective date.

Change in Interview Policy

To:

From:

Date:

Regarding: Interviewing

Two heads are better than one department: I'd like to develop a strategy whereby we use two senior managers, rather than one, to interview all managerial applicants. No new hire at this level would be made without the recommendations of both the managers who oversaw the interview process.

I'd like to get started on this immediately.

Alternate Version:

Effective immediately, I'd like all interviews for open managerial positions to be conducted by two senior officials with the company, with both people meeting together at the conclusion of the interview process to formulate a single recommendation on the hiring decision.

Questions? Please see me.

Thanks!

DEVELOPING A CUSTOMIZED MEMO? REMEMBER TO . . .

- Describe the new procedure to be followed.
- Mention when the new method is to be used in evaluating new hires.

Change in Company Dress Code

To:

From:

Date:

Regarding: Casual dress on Fridays

Beginning June 3, all workers will be allowed to wear casual clothing on Fridays. Please remember that customers often visit the building, so neatness (and a judicious philosophy in attire selection) will still be expected.

If you have questions about what to wear, please feel free to see me. I think we all know, though, what is and isn't appropriate workplace attire. Let's make this experiment work!

Alternate Version:

Beginning June 3, casual dress will be allowed on Fridays.

Based on employee requests, management has decided to allow all workers to dress in business casual clothing on Fridays. Please bear in mind, however, that "business casual" does not include dungarees, shorts, halter tops, T-shirts, or sneakers, and that neatness makes a big difference in any work environment.

Thanks for helping us foster a committed, professional atmosphere.

DEVELOPING A CUSTOMIZED MEMO? REMEMBER TO . . .

- State when the change in the dress code will take effect.
- Stress the importance of neatness and professionalism on dress-down day.

Confidential Correspondence Issues

To:

From:

Date:

Regarding: Confidentiality Issue

Any mail sent internally with confidential information should be marked 'CONFIDENTIAL' in bold letters on the front of the envelope. Of course, opening mail that has been marked "confidential" is a breach of trust with potentially serious implications.

For a detailed review on transmitting confidential work-related messages to team members, please see me.

Alternate Version:

A friendly reminder: Confidential mail should not be opened by persons other than the recipient. Improper circulation of confidential company materials will not be permitted.

Opening company correspondence clearly marked as 'CONFIDENTIAL' is a serious ethical lapse that may result in disciplinary action. Please don't do it.

If you'd like more information on the best ways to manage confidential mail traffic, please drop by my office.

DEVELOPING A CUSTOMIZED MEMO? REMEMBER TO . . .

- Emphasize that confidential mail is to be opened only by the addressee.
- Make it clear that breaches of the confidential mail policy may result in disciplinary measures.

Confidentiality in E-Mail Correspondence

To:

From:

Date:

Regarding: E-Mail confidentiality

Lately, there have been a couple of lapses in the handling of confidential company information, especially when transmitted via e-mail.

Let me remind you that unauthorized use and circulation of confidential information could be damaging to our company. I urge you to review the company rules governing confidential transmissions via electronic mail.

Thanks!

Alternate Version:

A growing concern has arisen over the transmission of confidential company information via e-mail. E-mail is, of course, very easily retransmitted. From now on any company information considered confidential must state in the heading "XYZ Company Confidential, Receipt of this information subjects recipient to XYZ rules governing use of confidential information."

And, as always, please remember to double-check the address of the person to whom you're sending your message!

Many thanks.

DEVELOPING A CUSTOMIZED MEMO? REMEMBER TO . . .

- Note concerns about the confidentiality of e-mail transmissions.
- Mention the consequences of breaching confidentiality.
- Stress use of proper procedures to maintain e-mail confidentiality.

Data Security

To:

From:

Date:

Regarding: Data security

We've had some lapses in our data security procedures recently which could have led to important information going to our competitors. Please review the Management Information Services guidelines for data security and ensure that you and your staff are in compliance.

Alternate Version:

If you're entrusted with confidential information, you've got a responsibility to *keep* it confidential.

As you know, our company's confidential data is highly sought after by our competitors. Their access to this data could undermine our business and our competitive advantage. We must all be more careful with the transmission and storage of data, making sure we have passwords for all of our systems and that diskettes are locked away nightly.

I'm certain that we can work together to improve this situation.

DEVELOPING A CUSTOMIZED MEMO? REMEMBER TO . . .

- Note any lapses in data security procedures.
- Stress the consequences of such lapses.
- Ensure that data security guidelines are reviewed.

Dealing With Subordinate Who Fails to Attend Training

To:

From:

Date:

Regarding: Missed training session

We had an excellent turnout at our departmental training session last week; unfortunately, you were one of the few department members unable to attend. Please stop by and see me so I can give you some of the extra materials.

Alternate Version:

I noticed that you were unable to attend the department training session held last Tuesday, and that you did not notify anyone of your intended absence.

It is extremely important for everyone in the department to be versed in the latest procedures; these training sessions are held to help you do your job more easily and effectively. Please stop by and see me so I can provide you with some of the information from the training period.

DEVELOPING A CUSTOMIZED MEMO? REMEMBER TO . . .

- Mention the employee's absence from the meeting.
- Ensure that the employee will get necessary information.

Holiday/Vacation Schedule Changes

To:

From:

Date:

Regarding: Christmas week schedule change

Only a Grinch would want you to overlook this . . .

Our schedule over the Christmas week has been changed. Since so many people take vacation during this week, we will be closed from Wednesday through Friday. We will be open for business as usual on Monday and Tuesday.

Alternate Version:

Don we now our holiday schedule . . .

We're changing our Christmas week schedule such that we will only be open on Monday and Tuesday. The building will be closed the remainder of the week.

Have a happy holiday!

DEVELOPING A CUSTOMIZED MEMO? REMEMBER TO . . .

- Announce when the change in the schedule will take place.
- State what the schedule will be.

Importance of Filling Out and Submitting Time Sheets

To:

From:

Date:

Regarding: Time Sheets

It is very important that we submit completed time sheets promptly.

Time sheets are necessary in order to ensure that you are paid the correct amount for the time worked. Additionally, government regulations require that we maintain these records on a timely and accurate basis. Please help us help you. Turn your completed weekly time sheets in to Carol no later than Monday at 3:00 pm.

Alternate Version:

If Carol doesn't have your complete and accurate weekly time sheet by Monday at 3:00 pm, she can't process your check, and you won't receive it by the following Friday!

Please help her help you get the correct pay amount. Turn in your time sheets on schedule.

Developing a Customized Memo? Remember to . . .

- Emphasize the importance of prompt submission of time sheets.
- Tell employees when, and with whom, time sheets must be filed.

Parking Policy: Visitor Spaces

To:

From:

Date:

Regarding: Employee Parking

Many of our guests have expressed concern that there is a lack of sufficient visitor parking. After investigating the situation, I've found that many employees are using visitor parking spots for their personal vehicles. Please help me reverse this problem. Obey the posted signs and do not park in visitor spaces.

Alternate Version:

I've noticed that many of our employees are parking in the visitor section of the parking lot. Not only is this unfair to other employees who do park across the street, but it also forces our guests to walk a longer distance. Yesterday, representatives of a long-courted prospect company had to carry a box of samples a considerable distance before a meeting with me!

Please help us show our visitors the courtesy they deserve. Abide by the company's parking rules.

Developing a Customized Memo? Remember to . . .

- Mention the effect of parking violations on visitors.
- Emphasize the importance of following company parking rules.

Peak Workload Period Approaching; Schedule and Related Points to Bear in Mind

To:

From:

Date:

Regarding: Peak period

From now through the end of November, we will be working two shifts for six days per week in order to meet demand for the Christmas season. As we approach this peak period please keep the following points in mind:

- Quality is more critical now than ever.
- The fact we are working hard is a good sign; it means the company is doing well.
- Work hard—but never at the expense of safety.

Thanks in advance for all your help.

Alternate Version:

We are approaching the Christmas season, which is our peak work period.

During this period our factory will be on a two-shift schedule from Monday through Saturday. Please contact your immediate supervisor for your individual schedule for the next four weeks.

Additionally, there are some important points I would like you to keep in mind during this time.

- Quality is more critical now than ever.
- The fact we are working hard is a good sign; it means the company is doing well.
- Work hard—but never at the expense of safety.

Many thanks!

DEVELOPING A CUSTOMIZED MEMO? REMEMBER TO . . .

- Note when the peak period takes place.
- Indicate what the schedule will be during the peak period.
- Stress important points to remember during peak work periods.

Reason for Delay in Order Fulfillment

To:

From:

Date:

Regarding: Delayed shipments

Because of a faulty component, our manufacturing plant was shut down for four days, causing us to miss our delivery schedules. (See the technical summary I've forwarded.) Would you please have your people review this with each of our customers—and assure them that we are back on line and will be caught up within 10 days?

Many thanks.

Alternate Version:

Shipment of several recent orders was delayed because of an accident in manufacturing which caused us to shut down the plant for three days. This accident was caused by a faulty component in the machinery and could not have been avoided.

Please tell your people to advise our customers of our deep regrets at being unable to fulfill their orders in a timely manner and assure them that we are doing everything possible to prevent this from happening again.

Thanks for your help.

DEVELOPING A CUSTOMIZED MEMO? REMEMBER TO . . .

- Explain the cause of the manufacturing shutdown.
- Acknowledge the consequences to delayed order fulfillment.

Request For Additional Permanent Staff

To:

From:

Date:

Regarding: Personnel

You are probably aware that my department is processing twice the output that we were doing at the same time last year, and that we are doing it without any personnel increases. While we have been able to dramatically improve our efficiency to this point, we need additional people if we are going to maintain the same rate of growth in the coming year.

Is there a good time for us to get together to discuss this?

Alternate Version:

I need to speak with you about the requirement for additional staff in my department. I believe we've done a great job reengineering our processes and becoming more efficient, but we've reached the point where additional head count is required.

I hope we can get together to talk about this as soon as possible.

DEVELOPING A CUSTOMIZED MEMO? REMEMBER TO . . .

- Mention any relevant improvements in department efficiency.
- Emphasize the need to increase personnel to maintain efficiency.
- Request a meeting to discuss the staffing requirements.

Request for Employee to Complete Self-Review

To:

From:

Date:

Regarding: Individual review

Your review is scheduled for next Friday. Please complete the self-assessment provided to you last week as soon as possible. Once I've had a chance to review it we can schedule some time for your annual performance appraisal.

I look forward to talking to you soon.

Alternate Version:

You are scheduled for your annual review on Friday, October 6th. Prior to that meeting, I need your help; you need to complete your own self-assessment, based on the outline provided to you last week.

This will provide us both an excellent starting point to discuss your performance over the last year.

DEVELOPING A CUSTOMIZED MEMO? REMEMBER TO . . .

- Emphasize the importance of completing the self-appraisal.
- Note that it is needed prior to when the performance review takes place.

Request for Short-Term Workers

To:

From:

Date:

Regarding: Temporary workers

I've taken a good, long look at the production schedule, and I've concluded that we need twelve temporary workers to help us through our peak period, starting next month. It's very important that they start ASAP so they can become familiar with our processes before the peak season actually begins.

Does this expense make as much sense to you as it does to me?

Alternate Version:

I think we are going to need additional workers for the peak season.

Our peak season will be starting in two months and forecasts show that demand for our products will increase significantly over last year. In order to meet this demand, I estimate that we will need 12 temporary workers for three months; they should start within the next four weeks in order to come up to speed on our processes.

What do you think of this approach?

DEVELOPING A CUSTOMIZED MEMO? REMEMBER TO . . .

- State the need for additional workers clearly and directly, preferably at the beginning of the memo.
- Note how many additional workers will be needed.
- Outline the reason(s) you feel the workers are needed.

Requesting Help in an Informal Market Research Effort

To:

From:

Date:

Regarding: Request for market research assistance

I don't have a lot of time, or a budget, per se, but I'm still dedicated to finding out how to crack the Boston market.

I'm working on a new project and need some market research assistance as soon as possible. Please contact me today to discuss the details.

Alternate Version:

I need your help with some market research. I've been working on a new cereal package design and need some information on the Boston health food market. Please let me know if you will be able to provide assistance. I won't need more than a couple of hours of your time—I just want to make some calls and see how health food store owners react to the ideas I'm considering.

Talk to you soon.

DEVELOPING A CUSTOMIZED MEMO? REMEMBER TO . . .

- Mention or describe the particular project.
- Indicate what sort of assistance is desired.

Requesting Input on a New Product Name

To:

From:

Date:

Regarding: Suggestions for name of new exercise product

What's in a name? Well, when it comes to launching a new product, just about everything. And we still do not have a workable name for our newest exercise product.

Please help! If you have any suggestions on this score, please contact Juan Hernandez in Marketing.

Alternate Version:

We need a name for our newest exercise product.

Development has been completed on the new thigh stretcher; however, we still do not have a name for it. Please provide three suggestions by Friday to Juan Hernandez in Marketing. The person whose selection is used will receive a night on the town.

DEVELOPING A CUSTOMIZED MEMO? REMEMBER TO . . .

- Mention the product that needs a name.
- Indicate to whom suggestions should be submitted.

Requesting Input on a Problem

To:

From:

Date:

Regarding: Need to solve subcontractor problem

We are still having problems with our major subcontractor.

For the last six months our subcontractor deliveries from XYZ have been late, causing us to miss our delivery schedules. We have a long-term contract with the vendor.

Please give some thought as to how we can best address this issue. I'd appreciate your thoughts by Friday.

Alternate Version:

We really need to come up with a solution to the XYZ delivery problem that's been plaguing us for the last few months. They can't seem to ship anything to us on time, but we're committed, contractually, to working with them. Can you help us find a resolution?

I'd be eager to hear your thoughts in this area. If you need some background, the files are in Jack Smith's office.

Developing a Customized Memo? Remember to . . .

- Indicate the nature of the problem and how long it has existed.
- Request assistance in resolving the problem.

Requesting Information from Management Information Services

To:

From:

Date:

Regarding: Sales Reports

Red alert!

We need a copy of the last six monthly sales reports for an upcoming meeting with the president. Can you please send it today?

Alternate Version:

We need copies of our sales reports for the past six months.

We'll be having a meeting with the president soon. As usual, he will want to see copies of the sales reports for the last six months. Could you please send us that information today? If there's a problem following through on this, I'd appreciate it if you would get in touch with me.

Thanks a lot.

DEVELOPING A CUSTOMIZED MEMO? REMEMBER TO . . .

- Specify what information is needed.
- Mention what the information is needed for.

Requesting Change in Management Information Services Procedure

To:

From:

Date:

Regarding: Procedural change

I've gotten the word from the president's office: From now on we need to receive inventory reports weekly. Can that start next month?

Let me know if you think there's going to be a problem with this. Otherwise I'll assume we can work on this schedule.

Alternate Version:

We need weekly inventory reports starting next month, according to Mr. Wells.

Because of a change in our tracking methods, we will need you to produce our sales report on a weekly basis instead of once a month. I assume this is no problem?

Please confirm with me, by Friday, your receipt of this message. If, for some reason, you believe that you'll have a problem meeting this schedule, then let's get together as soon as possible to discuss the alternatives.

Developing a Customized Memo? Remember to . . .

- State the desired change to be instituted.
- Suggest a time frame to institute the change.

Rescheduling a Meeting

To:

From:

Date:

Regarding: Budget meeting rescheduled

The monthly departmental budget meeting will need to be rescheduled to Thursday, June 10th at 10:00 am in my office. Several members of the department will be traveling next week. In order to allow everyone to attend, we've rescheduled the budget meeting for the following week.

Please let me know if this new date poses a problem for any of you. Thanks!

Alternate Version:

Several people will be out of the office next week, so it looks like we need to reschedule the budget meeting to June 10th at 10:00 am in my office. Thanks for shifting this in your schedule; I look forward to seeing you at the meeting.

Developing a Customized Memo? Remember to . . .

- Note why the meeting needs to be rescheduled.

- Provide the new date for the meeting.
- Express appreciation for employee's flexibility.

Review of Purchasing Procedures

To:

From:

Date:

Regarding: Purchasing procedures

We have been losing many volume discounts we are entitled to on supplies because we've ordered directly from vendors on an individual basis (often, without any purchase order!).

Help us make sure the company makes its dollars work as hard as possible. Please go through Purchasing for all of your orders. Thanks!

Alternate Version:

In order to secure the best prices from vendors, it is critical that we follow the company procedures for procurement. The most important rule is that all supply requests must go through our purchasing department. (A valid purchase order must *always* be issued for departmental purchases.)

We have numerous discount contracts with vendors, and we can only be sure we're getting the very best prices by forwarding orders through purchasing.

Questions on a particular order? See Vera Miles.

Thank you, in advance, for your cooperation.

Developing a Customized Memo? Remember to . . .

- Note the adverse consequences of purchasing directly from vendors.
- Emphasize the need to use the purchasing department for orders and following established procedures.
- Stress the financial benefits of following company policy on purchasing.

Sharing Computer Time

To:

From:

Date:

Regarding: Computer Time

Until we are able to have additional terminals delivered (which should not be long), please use a sign-up sheet to reserve time on the system— and please spend no more than one hour at the terminal if others are waiting.

Friendly reminder: Terminals are usually free after 6:00 in the evening and on the weekends.

Thanks for your help and understanding during this (temporary) crunch period.

Alternate Version:

Good news, bad news department: So many of you have responded to the training sessions and are using the system that we are experiencing difficulty ensuring that everyone gets his or her fair share of terminal time.

The company does plan to secure additional terminals but until then please use the signup sheet posted in my office. Be considerate of the needs others when using the system, and don't try to skip ahead on the list.

Thanks for your cooperation.

DEVELOPING A CUSTOMIZED MEMO? REMEMBER TO . . .

- Mention the problems experienced in sharing computer terminals.
- Acknowledge the need for extra terminals.
- Request the patience and cooperation of employees in waiting their turns.

Summarizing Results of Training Session for Superior

To:

From:

Date:

Regarding: Spreadsheet training session

The advanced spreadsheet training session held last Thursday was very valuable to me. I appreciate your selecting me to participate.

We learned a number of new skills such as:

- PC problem determination
- exporting and importing information between the mainframe and the PC
- creating our own calculations

All of these new proficiencies will help me to perform my job better. Thanks for supporting my growth in the business.

Alternate Version:

Thanks for sending me to the spreadsheet training session last week; I really got a lot out of it. We learned several new ways to manage data, including transferring information from the mainframe and creating our own calculations.

Please consider me for any future advanced training. I really believe this will help me with my job.

DEVELOPING A CUSTOMIZED MEMO? REMEMBER TO . . .

- Acknowledge the value of the training session.
- Summarize the skills that were learned.
- Thank the supervisor for the benefits gained from the session.

Of Particular Interest to Managers Supervising Off-Site Workers

It is occasionally necessary to employ workers who are situated out of the office. Whether they are out on the road as sales reps or working out of their own homes, off-site employees still require supervision and monitoring. This chapter will address many of the issues that distinguish this unique aspect of management, particularly those that affect home workers.

Abuse of Comp Time Policy by Home Worker

To:

From:

Date:

Regarding: Excessive comp time

Your use of comp time far exceeds that of other department members. I need you to make more of an effort to manage your time better, and to bring your average day into conformity with the hours you worked while you were here in the office.

If there's a problem on this score, I'd like to be able to count on you to review it with me, either in person or by phone.

Thanks!

Alternate Version:

We've got a problem.

The amount of compensatory time you have logged over the past three months is significantly out of line with that of other members of this department. While we try to be flexible with employees who work at home, we do expect you to manage your time as you would if working at the office. If you have a particular reason for this excessive comp time please call me today; otherwise, I expect your hours (standard and comp time) to reflect the average fluctuations you posted while working here in the office. If this is a problem, let's meet to talk it over in detail.

Thanks for helping me out with this.

DEVELOPING A CUSTOMIZED MEMO? REMEMBER TO . . .

- Note the problems incurred by taking excessive comp time.
- Request the worker to make appropriate schedule adjustments.
- Be open to discussing the situation.

Accelerated Deadline on Home Worker's Project

To:

From:

Date:

Regarding: New deadline on market analysis software

We have to move up the delivery date for the market analysis software. Marketing group members saw the prototype and are anxious to get their hands on it. They believe it has the potential to increase revenues by 19% next quarter. I need you to complete this project by May 30th, so that we have a full thirty days for testing. You are authorized to work as many hours as necessary in order to meet the schedule; please provide me with a weekly status update from now until project completion.

Alternate Version:

Marketing saw the prototype and loved it. In fact they want it operational by the beginning of next quarter. We're going to have to test it for thirty days, so that means we'll need your part complete by May 30th. All of senior management is on board so let's make this one a priority. Don't hesitate to get me involved if anything impedes your progress.

Developing a Customized Memo? Remember to . . .

- Note the reason(s) for moving up the deadline.
- Stress the need for product testing.
- Provide a new date for project completion.

Change in Scheduled Meeting Time; Home Worker Must Confirm Availability ASAP

To:

From:

Date:

Regarding: Department meeting changed to Monday

Because of some scheduling conflicts we need to move Thursday's meeting to this Monday. I really apologize for the late notice, but it couldn't be helped. Can you please call me today and confirm your attendance? Thanks.

Alternate Version:

We need to hold the department meeting on Monday next week instead of Thursday. Several department members will be attending a seminar on Thursday, and Monday is the only other day that fits into everyone's calendar. We really need you to be present, as your work on the Peterson project touches on what everyone else is doing.

Please contact me ASAP to confirm that you will be able to attend.

Developing a Customized Memo? Remember to . . .

- Clearly indicate the change of date.
- Explain why the date needed to be changed.
- Ask for confirmation of the employee's attendance.

Change in Weekly Home Work Schedule

To:

From:

Date:

Regarding: Weekly schedule

Many of our people are coming in earlier these days, and are in dire need of phone help from you early in the morning. (Isn't it great to be irreplaceable?)

Can you modify your schedule to start and end your work two hours earlier than you're now doing? Please give me a call so that we can discuss the options.

Alternate Version:

The first chance you get, I'd like to talk to you about modifying your schedule in order to better accommodate the needs of the business.

I realize that you normally start working at 9:00 am and finish your day at 5:00 pm. Many of our on-site team members, however, are now coming in at 7:00 am, and need to have someone they can call for assistance with their computer applications.

I'd like to find a way for you to be available, at your home office, from 7:00 am until 3:00 pm from now on. Can you contact me immediately so we can discuss this?

Developing a Customized Memo? Remember to . . .

- Provide reason(s) for the schedule modification.
- Describe the specific desired modification in the schedule.
- Be open to discussion about the change.

Dealing with Persistently Unavailable Home Worker

To:

From:

Date:

Regarding: Keeping in touch

Despite the policy we established when you began working at home, I haven't been able to get in touch with you during the pre-established times we agreed to leave open (weekdays, between one and five). I either get a busy signal or your voice mail.

Can you call me as soon as possible so we can work this out?

Alternate Version:

We've got to talk.

When you and I first discussed your request to work from home, we agreed that you'd be available to take calls from coworkers (and me) on weekday afternoons between one and five. I tried contacting you during this period three times this week, and could not reach you. I had similar problems last week.

I need to talk to you as soon as possible to discuss this problem. Please call me as soon as you get this memo.

Thanks.

Developing a Customized Memo? Remember to . . .

- Appeal to any appropriate past agreements you've made with this employee.
- Make it clear that you need to discuss a way to change the situation.

Emergency Main Office Meeting Requires Home Worker's Attendance

To:

From:

Date:

Regarding: Upcoming meeting

Mark this one on your calendar!

I know this visit to headquarters will not be on your standard schedule, but you're going to need to make an exception for this Thursday, October 1, at 1:00 pm. An all-division meeting is scheduled for the main conference room, and the president of the company will be in attendance.

Please get back to me as soon as possible to confirm that you'll be able to make this emergency on-site meeting.

Alternate Version:

There's been a problem in production. The president wants to talk to everyone about it . . . and that means everyone.

I need you to alter your home-work schedule so you can make the emergency meeting that has been scheduled for this coming Thursday, October 1, at 1:00 pm in the main conference room. Please get back to me as soon as possible.

> Developing a Customized Memo? Remember to . . .
>
> - Give the details about the meeting: When and where will it take place?
> - Consider requesting a confirming message in return from the home worker.

Home Worker Fails to Acknowledge Receipt of Mailed Materials

To:

From:

Date:

Regarding: Did you get my package?

I mailed a copy of the Peterson proposal to you via priority mail earlier this week—did you receive it?

Please let me know one way or the other. This is a vitally important piece of work, and if it hasn't landed on your desk yet, I should arrange an overnight delivery of a copy.

Talk to you soon.

Alternate Version:

We spoke about the Peterson project last week, and I sent it to you via priority mail on Monday. I was expecting a call one way or the other on this by the end of business yesterday.

Can you let me know what the status of this is ASAP? And one more thing—I know you're busy, but if you can keep me posted on your receipt of these kinds of packages, it will make my job a lot easier on this end.

Thanks—talk to you soon!

Developing a Customized Memo? Remember to . . .

- Describe what you sent and when you sent it.
- Ask, in no uncertain terms, for a call or return message from the home worker.

Necessity of Participating in Scheduled Conference Call

To:

From:

Date:

Regarding: Conference call with home office

An important conference call is scheduled for this coming October 1 at 2:00 pm. The home office wants to review any outstanding problems on the McCarter project.

I need you to clear a spot in your schedule to be available for this call, which should take about an hour. Please get back in touch with me soon to confirm on this.

Alternate Version:

This coming Thursday, October 1, the home office wants to review the hurdles we're still facing on the McCarter project.

This is an important call—I'd like you to review the files closely and clear an hour in your schedule so we can go over all the relevant details. The call is scheduled for 2:00. Please get back to me as soon as you can to confirm your availability.

Thanks!

- Mention when the conference call is scheduled to take place.
- Estimate how long the call is likely to last.
- Request a message back confirming that the home worker will be able to take part.

Notifying Home Worker of Upcoming Training Seminar

To:

From:

Date:

Regarding: Training seminar

There's going to be a software training session on-site next week. It's going to help people become more familiar with the Change-a-tron software. Are you interested in attending?

The session will last about two hours—it's scheduled to take place on July 8 at 10:00 am, in conference room A. If you get back to me by Friday, I can reserve a slot for you. Is this worth a trip to the home office for you?

Alternate Version:

Do you think you'd benefit from a software training seminar meant to help get the most out of the Change-a-tron program?

A training seminar is scheduled for this coming Monday, July 8, at 10:00 am, in conference room A. The session lasts two hours. If you're interested in attending, please let me know, and I'll set aside a slot for you. If you don't think you need to take advantage of this program, disregard this message.

Hope all is going well. Talk to you soon.

DEVELOPING A CUSTOMIZED MEMO? REMEMBER TO . . .

- Briefly outline what the training will cover.
- Let the employee know when and where the training session will be taking place.

Warning: Status as Home Worker Will Be Revoked if Performance Does Not Improve

To:

From:

Date:

Regarding: Re-evaluation of your status as a home worker

I'm concerned.

There seems to be some very real evidence that your work-at-home status isn't helping you hit your goals. I'd like to have a face-to-face meeting to discuss how we can make this situation work for you. I'm willing to give this situation a fair chance—but I need, in turn, a commitment from you to make some changes and to deliver on some specific productivity commitments.

Let's get together in my office on Thursday, October 2, at 10:00 am.

Alternate Version:

Over the past few weeks, I've seen some troubling signs that the "work-at-home" experiment just isn't working out for you. I'm concerned about this trend, and I want to help you work out a solution.

I'd like you to meet with me in my office this coming Thursday, October 2, at 10:00 am. I have some targets I want your input on. Once we've discussed your goals for the next thirty days, I want your commitment that you're either going to find a way to make them happen—or accept my decision that you must work on-site for the foreseeable future.

I look forward to reviewing these important issues with you.

Developing a Customized Memo? Remember to . . .

- Make it clear that you want the employee to work with you and to commit to specific quantifiable goals.
- Consider scheduling a face-to-face meeting, preferably away from the employee's home office, to add a measure of realism to the situation.
- Consider setting a "review period"—and allowing the employee the chance to deliver on commitments in order to retain home-worker status.

A Brief Guide to Style and Usage

You know what you want to say, but you don't quite know how to say it. Here are a few tips that will help you write a crisp, correct, professional-looking memo that gets the point across quickly and is easy to read.

Five Basic Rules for Writing a 60-Second Memo

1. Be brief!

The wordier you are, the less likely you are to hold your reader's attention. Remember that details of whatever your memo covers can be discussed verbally or followed up in a later memo. Your main concern is to state your immediate purpose in writing as concisely as possible. Don't over-elaborate.

2. Get to the point at the beginning.

It is important that your reader know up front what your memo is about. Make sure your opening sentences back up the subject line of your memo. Then expand as necessary.

3. Keep it (relatively) formal.

Always remember that you are writing a business memo, not a note to a friend. Depending on the subject matter of the memo, it may be all right to use a "light touch." Still, you should never inject clearly personal material, or use inappropriate or overbearing humor that others may misinterpret.

4. Be consistent.

Formatting should not vary from one paragraph to the next. Be consistent in your use of tabs, indenting, highlighting text, and punctuation. Also take care that spellings, especially of proper names, are the same throughout the memo.

5. Proofread before you send.

Check for punctuation, grammar, and spelling; make sure you haven't accidentally omitted any words; ensure that paragraphs are lined up; and look your memo over for general neatness and consistent formatting. Many word processing programs now feature easy-to-use spelling and grammar checks; these should be considered a supplement to, and not a replacement for, careful review and proofreading.

Thirteen Specific Rules of Form and Style

1. Avoid the passive voice—Use the active voice!

Who is doing what? The active voice in writing conveys more strength than the passive voice. It helps reinforce vigor and directness in your message.

Wrong (passive):
At the meeting on Friday, Brenda Jones will be honored by us.

Right (active):
We will honor Brenda Jones at Friday's meeting.

2. Avoid relying too heavily on contractions.

Most business documents, long or short, will look better if they keep contractions to a minimum. Consider spelling things out. Ask yourself: Does it sound better to use "it is" for "it's," "they are" for "they're," "I am" for "I'm," and so on? As a general rule, incorporating non-contracted forms when you can do so will formalize and strengthen your sentence structure.

3. Complete your thought.

Do not use incomplete or run-on sentences. Most grammatically correct sentences will have a subject and a verb, especially in business writing. Use proper form and punctuation to define and complete your thought; separate it from other thoughts.

Wrong:
Happy to introduce our new Customer Service Manager, Brenda Jones. Starting on Monday! Brenda will be located in Room 702, you know, it is next to Phil Johnson's office. A big welcome for Brenda.

Right:
I am pleased to introduce our new Customer Service Manager, Brenda Jones. Brenda will begin work on Monday, April 1. She will be located in Room 702, right next to Phil Johnson's office. Please make her feel welcome.

Always start a new paragraph whenever you have completed a string of related thoughts and are about to start a new string. Never lump everything together in one paragraph.

4. Be clear about your subject.

Watch those pronouns! Things can get very confusing for your reader if you talk about two or more subjects in your memo without making clear which is which. Pronouns must agree with their subject.

> *Example:*
> Brenda told Mike to give Donna Henry a report on the project specs. She would then follow up with him after he had met with her about it.

In the second sentence, the words "she" and "her" clearly refer to someone, but it's hard to say whether that someone is Brenda, Donna, or a combination of the two. Although your reader may guess correctly, you can avoid confusion by inserting the proper name in place of one or both of the pronouns in this sentence, or rewording it. Here's how a corrected version might look:

> Brenda told Mike to give Donna Henry a report on the project specs. Brenda would then follow up with him after he had met with Donna.

Be careful, too, that your subject does not hook up with an inappropriate verb:

> *Wrong:*
> Walking into my office yesterday morning, the misplaced wastebasket caused me to stumble and fall.

> *Right:*
> Walking into my office yesterday, I stumbled and fell over the misplaced wastebasket.

5. Use italic and bold for emphasis.

It is better not to use capital letters to emphasize a point. To make something important stand out from your memo, bold the relevant words. To stress the importance of a statement, put it into italic. Be careful, however, not to overuse italic or bolding, or else your memo will begin to look too busy (or even strident).

6. Beware of redundancy.

Repetition can make a memo uninteresting. Unless it is necessary for emphasis, avoid repeating what has already been said, as well as any redundancy. You may say office staff or office workers, but why office staff workers? And reconsider a formulation such as, "A new and innovative product." Use either "new" or "innovative," but not both. A rule of thumb: Say it once and get on with the rest of the message.

7. Avoid unnecessary or pretentious words.

Brevity is a virtue, and one way to make your memo virtuous is to omit words that contribute nothing new. You should also think twice before using a fancy-sounding word when a short and simple one would do the job just as well.

"The question as to whether" = "Whether"

"Owing to the fact that" = "Since" or "Because"

"This most unique feature" = "This unique feature" (Something is either unique or it isn't!)

"She asserted that" = "She stated that"

8. Capitalize names and titles.

Make sure that proper names, company names, and appropriate titles and designations are capitalized.

Example:

Ms. Dana Plovnick, President of the Widget Manufacturing Company, will visit the Customer Service department at 3:00 today.

9. Watch those plural nouns . . . and beware of misplaced apostrophes.

This is one of the most common mistakes in either formal or informal writing. An "s" at the end of a noun makes that word plural. An apostrophe-s, on the other hand, denotes possession or a contraction. Always be aware of the difference. Watch out for the potentially tricky forms "its" and "it's." The latter is always a contraction (for "it is"), while the former indicates possession.

Wrong:

Its Tuesday, the day she does spot-check's. I think the widget department is going to have it's problems.

Right:

It's Tuesday, the day she does spot-checks. I think the widget department is going to have its problems.

10. Use proper punctuation.

If you don't already know when and how to use commas, periods, colons, semi-colons, hyphens, dashes, slashes, apostrophes, parentheses, exclamation points, question marks, and quotation marks, track down a style manual and review the appropriate chapters closely! In particular, beware the excessive use of commas. Although the placement of commas is an inexact science, the easiest and most reliable rule of thumb is to read your sentence aloud and insert a comma only where there would be a natural pause.

Example:

Please make sure the emergency exits are easy to reach, clearly marked, and unlocked at all times.

Placing a comma after the word "unlocked" above would be an error.

11. Use parentheses and quotation marks correctly.

In a sentence containing a parenthetical expression, place the punctuation outside of the parentheses (like this). (The exception to this is when the expression is wholly contained within the parentheses, as this sentence is.) Conversely, punctuation is generally placed inside quotation marks.

Example:

The themes "Service," "Quality," and "Dependability" will form the heart of the president's upcoming address (scheduled for July 16).

12. Write out numbers.

When writing any number from one to ninety-nine, spell it out rather than putting it into numerical form. This does not include dates, addresses, or very long numbers, although whole numbers such as one hundred and one thousand should generally be spelled out. If several numbers are included in one sentence, be consistent in choosing the numeric or the spelled-out form. The same holds true for rankings (i. e., 1st or first, 10th or tenth, etc).

Examples:

On August 15, 1999, we will celebrate our fifth anniversary in business with thirty executives, seventy sales reps, and five hundred of our best customers at the Berkeley Hotel, 25 Main Street.

The Acme Company celebrated its fifth year in business on August 15, 1999. In attendance were 35 executives, 72 sales reps, and 495 of the company's best customers.

13. Stick to one tense.

It is bad form to mix your tenses within a single sentence.

Wrong:

If you wanted help, you should ask me.

Right:

If you wanted help, you should have asked me.

Index